D1616149

Self-Consciousness

Self-Consciousness

Sebastian Rödl

Harvard University Press

Cambridge, Massachusetts, and London, England | 2007

ISBN-13: 978-0-674-02494-6
ISBN-10: 0-674-02494-X

The Cataloging-in-Publication Data is available from the Library of
Congress.

Contents

Preface

The topic of this book is self-consciousness. Its chapters treat of action, of belief, of reason and freedom as a material reality, of receptive knowledge, and of the concept of the second person. Of course, each of these topics deserves its own book. And yet these books, whether they acknowledge it or not, will all be books on self-consciousness, for self-consciousness is the principle of their subject matter.

Self-consciousness is the nature of a subject that manifests itself in her thinking thoughts whose linguistic expression requires the use of the first person pronoun, "I". Our theme, then, is a manner of thinking of an object, or a form of reference. Our inquiry into this form of reference is guided by a principle we find in the work of Gareth Evans, which says that forms of reference are to be understood through corresponding forms of predication. This should not be surprising. As aspects of thinking a predicative thought, referring to an object and predicating a concept of it bear a unity, which suggests that formal distinctions in the one are linked to formal distinctions in the other. Since, fundamentally, reference is to something *real*, the relevant forms of predication are forms of *knowledge*, forms of knowing how things stand with the object. An inquiry into self-consciousness, then, is an inquiry into a form of knowledge, which is knowledge of oneself as oneself.

A first person thought is of the subject thinking it; Descartes' "I know that I am a thinker" is contained in any first person thought. There is nothing Cartesian in this. On the contrary, a theory of self-consciousness that does not reveal a subject of first person thought to know herself as a thinker is on that account inadequate. This suggests that the first person thoughts we must investigate first are those that predicate concepts of thought. The form of knowledge associated with first person reference will be, in the primary instance, a form of knowing acts of thinking. We shall distinguish two kinds of thinking: practical and theoretical thinking, i.e., action and belief. After an introductory chapter that explains why self-consciousness is to be understood as a form of predication, or knowledge, we describe in Chapter 2 the way in which I know that I am doing something when my knowing it is an act of self-consciousness, and in Chapter 3 the way in which I know that I believe something when, again, I know it in such a way as to know that *I* believe it.

It does not so happen that action and belief fall within the purview of self-consciousness. Belief and action are such as to be known by their subject in a first person way; acts of thought are essentially self-conscious. Therefore, a theory of self-consciousness is a theory of action, belief, and knowledge. If we are led into the territory of action theory, philosophy of mind, and epistemology, then this reflects the nature of our topic. It is a central thought of the German Idealist tradition that the philosophical study of action and knowledge must be pursued as part of an inquiry of self-consciousness. It would not be inept to read this book as an attempt to comprehend this tradition.

Contemporary philosophy has lost this central thought of German Idealism. There are authors who, rightly, are impressed by the fact that she who is doing something intentionally knows that she is doing it, and, so it seems, not from observing that she is doing it, but in virtue of being the one who is doing it. But these scholars do not reflect on the fact that the subject would express this knowledge with the first person pronoun. It is true that they call the relevant knowledge self-knowledge, but this signifies no more than that its subject is its object. On the other hand, authors who are studying the use of "I" have noticed that it is essential to the manner in which a subject represents herself in first person thought that such thoughts are fit to figure immediately in the explanation of her intentional actions. But these authors do not inquire into the nature of intentional action and the form of its explanation. As the inquiries into the concept of intentional action and into the logical character of first person thought have but one topic, they must be made one if they are to yield comprehension. And what here is true of the philosophy of action equally holds true of the philosophy of mind.

First person reference is to be understood in terms of ways of knowing, which are ways of knowing an object as oneself. Our principle claim will be that first person knowledge of action and belief is not *receptive*; one does not know an object first personally by being affected by it. Rather, first person knowledge of acts of thought is *spontaneous*. In contrast to receptive knowledge, which is of an independent object, spontaneous knowledge is identical with its object: my knowing first personally that I am doing such-and-such is the same reality as my doing it, and my knowing first personally that I believe that such-and-such is the case is the same reality as my believing it.

While the source of receptive knowledge is sensory affection, spontaneous knowledge springs from thinking: I know what I am doing, in the first person way, from ascertaining *what to do,* and I know what I believe, in the first person way, from ascertaining *what to believe.* It has been said that speaking of reasons is ambiguous, as reasons may be explanatory or justificatory. Explanatory reasons explain why someone did what she did, while justificatory reasons speak in favor of doing something and represent it as good to do. Or again, explanatory reasons explain why someone believes what she believes, while justificatory reasons speak in favor of believing it and represent it as being, or as likely to be, true. If this distinction is valid, then thought about what to do and what to believe cannot be a source of knowledge of what one is doing and what one believes. However, while people often do things on account of considerations that do not justify doing it, this does not disprove that, in fact, there is only one concept of a reason: the concept of a cause that explains an act in such a way as to reveal it to conform to a rational order, or else a cause such that it is no accident that its effect conforms to a rational order in virtue of having this cause. If this is right, then the word "reason" signifies a form of explanation: explaining an act in this way is revealing it to be just, that is, in conformity with a rational order, which thus is internal to the act explained. We shall find that this form of explanation is the source of self-consciousness. It is in virtue of the unity of explaining why one is doing something and showing it to be good, and of explaining why one believes something and revealing it to be true, that action and belief are known in a first person way. This is the nexus of self-consciousness and reason.

Philosophy of action and mind is badly served by ignoring its principle: self-consciousness. So is epistemology. When Kant expounds the questions that articulate the interest of reason, among them "What can I know?", he uses the first person pronoun. "I" must be used here not because one would ask a different question asking "What can he know?", but because knowledge is essentially self-conscious. The primary deployment of the concept of knowledge, the one without which there would be no other, is in first person thought, "I know . . ." We shall trace the conceptual impasses of contemporary epistemology to the fact that it does not conceive of itself as part of a theory of self-consciousness.

In recent times, the special relation I bear to my own actions and beliefs has attracted renewed attention, as the first person point of view seemed a bulwark against empiricism and psychologism in the philosophy of thought and action. In this defensive effort, some authors appear to grant that empiricism and psychologism correctly describe the manner in which a self-conscious subject is apprehended from a third person point of view. But thought of oneself cannot bear a distinct form from thought of someone else. Thought of another self-conscious subject must be a guise of the same form of thought of which first person thought is the other guise. In line with the above tendency, the opposition of first person and third person standpoint is often represented as an opposition of the practical, deliberative, and normative on the one hand and the theoretical, explanatory, and descriptive on the other hand: the first person view is the view of an agent, who seeks to justify acts of which she regards herself as the author, while the third person view is that of an observer, who seeks to explain what happens as the result of psychic forces. It is one of the principal aims of this book to show that this opposition is unsound. Of course, one may take different stances toward a self-conscious subject. But as Hegel says in a similar context, the first question to ask is which stance is true, and whether one is the truth of the other. An articulation of the form of knowledge that constitutes self-consciousness is not the description of a stance toward a reality to which one may with equal justice take other stances. Rather, as this manner of knowledge is internal to the reality that is known in this manner, a description of it gives the *metaphysics* of the self-conscious subject.

The above description of the account of self-consciousness expounded in this book shows it to be faithful to the principle of Kant's and Hegel's philosophy; and yet, it is materialist: it represents spontaneity, or self-consciousness, as the character of a material reality. According to Marx's Theses on Feuerbach, the flaw of "all hitherto existing materialism" is its empiricism: its conceiving of material reality "only in the form of *the object or of contemplation,* but not as *sensuous-human activity*". Empiricism is the principle obstacle to a true materialism. We will recognize the truth of this diagnosis in our treatment of action in Chapter 2, of receptive knowledge in Chapter 5, and of thought of a second person in Chapter 6. The empiricism that pervades contemporary philosophy produces a flawed materialism, which is unable to think a self-conscious material reality: a movement that is thought, a receptive relation that is essentially self-conscious, and a material substance that is known through an order of reason.

This is my second attempt at the topic. The first was published in 1998 under the title "Selbstbezug und Normativität" by mentis (Paderborn). When, in 2000, I set out to produce an English translation of that book, it seemed to me that I could go further and do better, so I wrote a new book. Whether I have done better remains for the reader to judge.

I am grateful to many colleagues and friends. First among them is Robert Brandom, without whose generous support over the years this project would not have started and could not have been completed. James Conant's early interest in my work and his philosophical friendship helped me find my way into anglophone philosophy. Alice Crary commented encouragingly on an early version of the book. Anton Ford read early versions of the first chapters, helping me to clarify my ideas and correcting my English. I frequently discussed the material on action with Doug Lavin; it grew as we spoke. Matthew Boyle went with me through the penultimate draft of the entire manuscript; his advice was extensive and invaluable. Parts of the book were presented at the University of Chicago, Auburn University, and the Université de Bordeaux. I thank the audiences for their comments and questions; in particular I am grateful to Eric Marcus and Gabrielle Richardson Lear for extended discussions of my presentation. Kieran Setiya wrote very helpful comments on some chapters. The discussion of these comments and a seminar he taught on reason and action afforded me much insight into the dialectical location of the position I seek to defend in this book. Various conversations with Steve Engström helped me place my ideas in relation to Kant. John McDowell criticized meticulously the penultimate draft of the first two chapters. The exchange that ensued greatly improved this material.

I do not think there is a single thought in this book that was not at some time or other the topic of conversations I have had with Michael Thompson. If a thought in this book is of value, I shall not know that it is not his.

Self-Consciousness

1

First Person Thought

What is self-consciousness? What is it to be conscious of oneself? She who is self-conscious has the power to think of and refer to herself. But this is not a sufficient description. I may refer to myself without realizing that it is I to whom I am referring. Such was the fate of Oedipus, who ordered the murderer of Laius to be found without imagining that the search would lead back to him. When Oedipus spoke of the murderer of Laius, he was referring to himself, but not, as we might put it, as himself. The man whom he banished was he who banished him, but only *per accidens*, not in virtue of the manner in which he referred to the man. For Oedipus said, "The murderer of Laius shall be banished", not "*I* shall be banished". Someone manifests self-consciousness in the sense that will interest us when she refers to herself *as herself*, i.e., in a way such that she would express her thought with the first person pronoun. Self-consciousness is properly described as the power to think of oneself only if we lay it down that "oneself", here, is a form of "I".[1] Hence, approaching self-consciousness through its linguistic expression, we must reflect on the use of the first person pronoun. Let us rephrase our question what self-consciousness is accordingly and ask how one refers with "I".

Sense and Reference

This does not seem too difficult: "I" is used to refer to her who is using it.[2] But although this is true, it does not answer our question. This becomes apparent when we follow Gottlob Frege and distinguish the

1. See Hector-Neri Castañeda, " 'He': A Study in the Logic of Self-Consciousness".
2. See Hans Reichenbach, *Elements of Symbolic Logic*, p. 284: "The word 'I', for instance, means the same as 'the person who utters this token'."

sense of an expression from its meaning. The Fregean meaning of a referring expression is the object to which one refers in using it; its sense is the way in which one refers to this object. One may refer to the same object in different ways, e.g., with "the President of Russia" and "Vladimir Putin". Frege says "a" and "b" differ in sense if and only if "Fa" and "Fb" express distinct thoughts.[3] So the way in which one refers with "a" is different from the way in which one refers with "b" if and only if thinking Fa is not the same as thinking Fb. This condition plainly needs elucidating. But it is clear and will suffice for our purposes that someone who thinks Fa does not *ipso actu* think Fb if there is room for a thought, distinct from Fa and Fb, which she may fail to affirm even as she affirms Fa and Fb, that a is identical with b. The distinction of sense and meaning relates to the distinction between referring to oneself per accidens and as oneself in this way: in Oedipus' mouth, "I" and "the murderer of Laius" have the same meaning, but not the same sense. Oedipus thinks, "The murderer of Laius shall be banished", but he does not thereby think, "I shall be banished", for he does not yet know and will learn only later that he is the murderer of Laius. Asking what self-consciousness is, we are concerned with the sense, rather than the meaning, of "I". We do not want to know *what* one refers to with this word, but *how* one refers with it. Explaining that "I" refers to the person uttering "I" thus misses the point, for the way in which one refers with "I" is not the same as the way in which one refers with "the person uttering 'I'". "I am F" does not express the same thought as "The person uttering 'I' is F". I may think the latter and not the former if I fail to notice that I am uttering "I".[4]

A proposition of the form "With t, one refers to b" may be intended to specify only the meaning of t or also its sense. In the former case, t and "b" must have the same meaning; in the latter case, they must bear the same sense as well.[5] The proposition "With 'I', one refers to the speaker" satisfies only the first condition. It provides only the meaning of a given

3. Gottlob Frege, "Über Sinn und Bedeutung", p. 32.

4. Compare Ludwig Wittgenstein, *Philosophische Untersuchungen*, 2:x: "Horchte ich auf die Rede meines Mundes, so könnte ich sagen, ein Anderer spreche aus meinem Mund." In "The First Person", G. E. M. Anscombe describes a practice of using a name in such a way that the referent is the person using the name. She shows that this does not entail that the name bears the same sense as "I".

5. See John McDowell, "On the Sense and Reference of a Proper Name".

use of the first person pronoun. In order to specify its sense, we must replace "the speaker" with an expression that also satisfies the second condition. One might try "With 'I', one refers to oneself", where "oneself" is a first person pronoun. But this does not get us anywhere, as it is a tautology. And even if there were an expression different from "I" that could be used to specify the sense of "I", this would be irrelevant. After all, we do not want to know whether there is an expression that is used in the same way as "I"; we want to know how "I" is used. So we face a problem of method. We seek to understand how one refers with "I". But what is it to understand this? We are asking after the sense of the first person pronoun, but what form of answer do we envisage? The rule that "I" refers to her who is uttering it provides for every use of "I" an expression that, used in the same context, would have the same Fregean meaning. Yet this tells us nothing about the sense of "I". Furthermore, I may know what expression is used in French for "I" and say, "With 'je', one refers to oneself." A speaker of French may know a corresponding fact about "I". Knowing this, neither she nor I know what we seek to know. A proposition that relates the first person pronoun to an expression of the same sense does not answer our question. In that case, what does?

This methodological question is sometimes denied the attention it deserves. Consider the view John Perry expounds in "Frege on Demonstratives" and "The Problem of the Essential Indexical". A singular thought, or, as Perry puts it, a "proposition", is composed of the sense of a name and the sense of a predicate. Perry inquires what the first person pronoun contributes to the proposition expressed. He inquires into the sense of a first person reference. How does Perry conceive of this question? What form of answer does he seek? He writes:

> There is a missing conceptual ingredient: a sense for which I am the reference, or a complex of properties I alone have, or a singular term that refers to no one but me. To identify the proposition [. . .], the advocate of the doctrine of propositions must identify this missing conceptual ingredient. ("The Problem of the Essential Indexical", p. 171)

Perry requires that the sense of a given use of "I" be identified by a "singular term that refers to no one but me", an expression which, as he says later on the same page, "gets at the missing ingredient". Presumably, a term "getting at" a sense is one that expresses, or has, this sense. Now, the specification of the sense of "I" must not be circular. It would not answer our question if we said that with "I" one refers to oneself, for here the term getting at the sense is the first person pronoun. Since first person reference is involved in the use of any indexical, the term Perry seeks must not contain any indexicals; it must be an indexical-free description. Thus he says this about demonstratives:

> How can we extract from a demonstrative an appropriate completing sense? Such a sense, it seems, would have to be intimately related to the sense of a unique description of the value of the demonstrative in the context of utterance. ("Frege on Demonstratives", p. 485)

By Perry's lights, then, the sense of a first person reference is to be identified by an indexical-free description of the same or an "intimately related" sense. So he proceeds from the following methodological presuppositions. First, identifying the sense of a first person reference is providing an expression with the same sense. Secondly, this expression must be a pure definite description. That is, Perry conceives of his question as asking for another expression, and he understands the notion of sense in such a way that only definite descriptions have a sense in their own right, while other expressions have a sense only to the extent that there are definite descriptions that can replace them *salvo sensu*. It is unsurprising if Perry, on such premises, finds that an "I"-reference does not have a sense. Replacing the first person pronoun by a definite description invariably alters the sense of the statement. We learn from his reflections that his premises are misguided and that the sense of "I" differs *in form* from the sense of a definite description.

Sense and Ways of Knowing

John Perry is unable to find a sense for the first person pronoun, or indeed any indexical, because, for him, "sense of a referring expression" means "sense of a definite description". We need a more abstract conception of sense, which allows us to recognize the sense of a definite description as one kind of such a sense alongside other kinds. To this end, we turn to Gareth Evans, who in *The Varieties of Reference* explains the sense of certain forms of reference in terms of *ways of knowing* how things stand with the object referred to.

Sense as Logical Perspective

Frege calls the sense of a singular term "die Art des Gegebenseins des Gegenstands", the way in which the object is given.[6] He also says that referring to an object is an aspect of thinking a thought about it. So when one refers to an object, the object is given in this sense: it is given to be brought under concepts. The sense of an act of reference, how one refers, may then be seen as consisting in how the object, thus referred to, is apprehended to fall under concepts. Call this the logical perspective on the object afforded by the reference. We must develop this metaphor: what does it mean that a reference affords a perspective on an object from which it is apprehended as falling under certain concepts?

In order to explain this, we must distinguish identification-free from identification-dependent judgments. A judgment is identification-free if it does not rest on an identity judgment, identification-dependent otherwise. My judgment *Fa* is identification-dependent if and only if my ground for thinking it true is that $a = b$ (and *Fb*). We shall also speak of mediated and unmediated judgments, meaning judgments mediated or unmediated by an identity judgment. An example: I hold that the Palace of the Republic is beautiful because I think, "This building is beautiful" and "This building is the Palace of the Republic". The judgment "The Palace of the Republic is beautiful" is identification-dependent; it rests on an identity judgment. The judgment "This building is beautiful" is identification-free.

We are suggesting that the sense of an act of reference is a logical perspective on the object, i.e., the way in which the object, thus referred to, is apprehended to fall under concepts. We can explain this as follows. Suppose I make an identification-dependent judgment *Fa,* based on an identification-free judgment *Fb*. Then I bring *a* under the concept *F* only because I refer to it also as *b*. By contrast, as *b*, the object is given to me in such a way—referring to it with "*b*" makes it available to me in such a way—that I am able to determine it to be *F*. In order to ascertain whether the object comes under the concept, I need not refer to it in any other way. We can express this by saying that it is from the perspective of "*b*" that I place the object under the concept. In general, an act of reference

---

6. Gottlob Frege, "Über Sinn und Bedeutung", p. 26.

affords a perspective on the object from which I know it to be *F* if my thinking that it is *F* involving the act is identification-free. This yields the following abstract conception of the sense of an act of reference: it is the logical perspective on the object the act affords, which in turn is what delimits the range of unmediated judgments of which it is a part, or the principle of unmediated knowledge articulated by its means.

The Account Applied to Descriptive and Demonstrative Reference

Let us apply this notion of sense to definite descriptions. An example of a judgment made from the perspective of a definite description is the following. I think, "The author of this article is brilliant", and my judgment that she is brilliant rests solely on the ground that she wrote this article. Then I do not need to refer to her in any other way in order to judge that she is brilliant. My judgment is unmediated. With a definite description, I refer to an object as the only one that satisfies a certain concept. And I characterize the object from this perspective when I infer from its satisfying this concept, or from its being the only one that satisfies it, that it is to be thus characterized. Here an individuating concept delimits the range of unmediated knowledge: a judgment that refers descriptively is identification-free if and only if it follows from the object's satisfying, or from its uniquely satisfying, the description. In this way, an individuating concept is the principle of unmediated knowledge expressed by a definite description.

Demonstrative judgments are often unmediated. When I say, for example, "This tomato is ripe", my judgment need not be based on an identity judgment. What delimits the range of unmediated knowledge that involves this form of reference? Obviously, no individuating concept does; no concept is such that the object's falling under it is the principle of unmediated demonstrative knowledge of this object. But a principle of unmediated knowledge need not be a piece of knowledge, knowledge that the object (uniquely) satisfies a certain concept. It may be *a relation to the object* by which one is *in a position to know* how things stand with it. Here we reach Gareth Evans's doctrine. According to Evans, the sense of a demonstrative reference is constituted by a perceptual relationship with the object.[7] This relationship delimits a range of unmediated knowledge

---

7. *The Varieties of Reference*, chap. 5.

in this way: a demonstrative judgment is identification-free if and only if it rests, directly or indirectly, on a sensory nexus with the object—directly if one thinks it true on the ground that one perceives that it is true, and indirectly if one thinks it true on the grounds of something one knows in the former way.

As perceptual demonstrative judgments are identification-free, demonstrative reference and predication based on perception are internally related. We can describe their nexus from the angle of demonstrative reference and from the angle of perceptual predication. On the one hand, referring to an object demonstratively, I perceive this object. And it is not that I happen to perceive it; rather, perceiving the object is the way in which I refer to it. I may perceive the Palace of the Republic, referring to it by name, when, for example, I stand in front of it and judge, on the basis of perception, "The Palace of the Republic is beautiful". Here, although I perceive the object, this does not constitute the sense of my statement wherefore the thought is mediated; it is based on my identifying the building I see with the Palace of the Republic. By contrast, when I think, on the basis of what I perceive, "This building is beautiful", I need not, in order to make the judgment, refer to the object in any other way; as I refer to it, it is an object I perceive. On the other hand, as perceptual judgments "This is F" are identification-free, there is no room for an identity judgment "This is the object I perceive" on which a judgment "This is F" could be based. An object I perceive as such is one to which I refer demonstratively. If I perceive that something is F, then I perceive that *this* is F.[8]

The Account Applied to First Person Reference

According to John Perry, the sense of an act of reference is, or is intimately related to, an individuating concept. Following Gareth Evans, we expounded an alternative: the sense of an act of reference is the logical perspective it affords on the object, which is the principle of unmediated knowledge involving this act. An individuating concept, or piece of knowledge, is one kind of such a sense; another kind is a relation to the object that is a source of indefinitely many pieces of knowledge. There are

8. Analogously, Evans writes, "We cannot understand [. . .] the possibility of its appearing to a subject by the unmediated exercise of his senses that it is *F somewhere* without its appearing to the subject that it is *F in his vicinity*" (*The Varieties of Reference*, p. 187).

distinctions within this latter sort of sense, nondescriptive sense, if there are distinct relationships with an object by which one may be in a position to know how things stand with it, relationships that differ with regard to *the form of knowledge* they make possible. And there are such distinctions.

As Perry observes, first person reference is not descriptive. As its sense is not an individuating concept, it will consist in a knowledge-providing relationship with the object. The relationship is not perception; first person reference is not a species of demonstrative reference. Consider this analogy: Aristotle explains that, although a doctor may heal herself, it is not in the nature of the art of healing that she who heals is identical with her who is being healed. If doctor and patient are the same person, then this is so only per accidens. Aristotle expresses this by saying that the art of healing is a principle of change in something other or in oneself *as other*.[9] Now, a sensory representation of an object depends on this object, which, on its part, exists independently of being so represented. It follows that, although it is possible to perceive oneself, it is not in the nature of perception that she who perceives is she who is being perceived. If the identity obtains in a given case, then it is not on account of the nature of perception; the perceiving subject and the subject perceived are identical only per accidens. Using Aristotle's words, we can say that perception is a way of knowing something other or oneself *as other*. So it is external to a demonstrative thought if the object it is about is the subject thinking it. As demonstrative reference is to an object as perceived and thus as other, the identity is the content of a *separate judgment*. The form of demonstrative reference, viz. its being sustained by a sensory relationship with the object, fixes it that there is no concept F such that "I" could be explained as "this F". Even when, in despair, we try "this self" or "this I", it will not be internal to the sense of the reference that she to whom one refers in this way is oneself. Recognizing this will be thinking a further thought, identifying the referent with oneself: "I am this one (this man, this self, this I)". It is often said that unmediated first person knowledge is not perceptual. Rarely is the true account of why this is so being given: sense perception is a way of knowing something as other.

First person reference depends on a knowledge-providing relationship with the object. This relationship must differ from perception in that it must follow from its nature that she to whom one bears it is oneself. It is

9. *Metaphysics,* Δ 12, 1019a15–18.

easy to say in the abstract what that relationship is: it is identity. First person reference depends on a way of knowing an object such that I know an object in this way by being this object. Unmediated first person thoughts articulate knowledge I possess, not by *perceiving*, but by *being* their object. If I know without mediation that I am *F*, then I know it, not by perceiving that I am *F*, but by being *F*. Our question after the sense of "I" becomes: How does being an object enable me to refer to it? Equivalently, how does being an object put me in a position to know how things stand with it?

A first person judgment may pass through a demonstrative reference and be based on a demonstrative judgment and an identity judgment, "This one. . . . I am this one. So I . . .". For example, after a crash, I may see an arm waving in a pile of bodies and think it is mine. Here, my first person thought involves, as Wittgenstein put it, "the recognition of a particular person".[10] It is natural to say that, in such a case, I know the movement of my arm "from the outside", whereas when, in normal circumstances, I make the judgment without passing through a demonstrative reference, I know it "from the inside". So let us call knowledge associated with first person reference "knowledge from the inside". When I know how things stand with an object by being this object, I know it "from the inside". At this stage, this is but a methodological claim: investigating first person reference is inquiring into a kind of knowledge, the kind articulated in unmediated first person thought. "From the inside" is a name we give to this manner of knowing an object. We must replace the name with an account.

In unmediated first person thought, the object is characterized "from the inside". Thus first person reference and predication "from the inside" are internally related in the same way as demonstrative reference and predication based on perception. Again, we can describe the relation from the angle of reference and from the angle of predication. On the one hand, referring to an object first personally, I am in a position to know "from the inside" how things stand with it. It does not so happen that I know the object "from the inside". Rather, this is how I refer to it. When I think on the basis of what I know "from the inside" that I am *F*, I need not refer to the object in any other way, for, as I refer to it, it is an object I know "from

10. Ludwig Wittgenstein, *The Blue Book*, p. 67. Wittgenstein calls the use of "I" to express identification-dependent thoughts "use as object" and its use to express identification-free thoughts "use as subject".

the inside". On the other hand, if I know "from the inside" that someone is *F*, then there is no room for the question whether *I* am the one of whom I know this. To someone whom I know "from the inside" I refer first personally. So when I know "from the inside" that someone is *F*, I know that *I* am *F.*

There must be a way, or perhaps ways, of knowing that stand to first person reference as perception stands to demonstrative reference; they deliver, as we call it, "knowledge from the inside". As perception is the way of knowing such that the sense of a demonstrative reference consists in a relationship with the object by which I am in a position to know it in this way, so is knowing "from the inside" a way of knowing such that my first person reference is constituted by a relation I bear to the object—identity by which I know it in this way. We must solve this equation for "knowledge from the inside". Understanding first person reference—understanding self-consciousness—is understanding this form of knowledge.

The Course of Our Inquiry

We ask what self-consciousness is; that is, we inquire after the sense of "I", the logical perspective that this form of reference affords on an object. I refer to myself first personally, not through an individuating concept, but through a relationship with the object by which I know how things stand with it. Since first person reference is reference as to oneself, the relation is identity. First person knowledge is knowledge one has not by perceiving but by being its object. In order to explain the sense of "I", we must describe this form of knowledge.

Where to Begin: Thought or Sensation?

If I am in a position to know that an object is *F* by being this object, then this must be on account of the nature of what I thus know myself to be. There must be concepts of being *F* such that being *F* places me in a position to know that I am, and reflection on these concepts must yield a description of ways of knowing that sustain first person reference. Hence we must study concepts that figure in unmediated first person thought and their form of predication.

Among the concepts that fit our formula, concepts of acts of sensibility perhaps first come to mind: I feel warm and thereby know that I do. I am in pain and in this way know that I am. Here it is by being the object that I know how things stand with it. It might seem, then, that we must inquire into thoughts representing acts of sensibility. We must seek insight into first person reference by inquiring how, for example, I know that someone is in pain, when I know it by being in pain, or how I know that someone feels warm, when I know it by feeling warm. But in fact we cannot proceed in this way. Although it is true that by feeling warm I know that I do, we shall not, from reflecting on this type of case, understand how that can be. Reflection on the nature of sensation cannot reveal how it is that sensation is represented in first person thought, because sensation is present in animals that are not self-conscious. If, in animals with thought, sensation is represented first personally, then this is because, first, the power of thought includes a power of first person knowledge and, secondly, sensation is caught up in thought in such a way as to be brought within the purview of this power. Therefore, the first thing we must consider in order to understand self-consciousness is thought, not sensation.

One might attempt to explain how I know, or perhaps, can say, that I am in pain by being in pain, by observing that saying "I am in pain" may be expressing pain. There is no denying this observation. But it affords little comprehension until we know how pain acquires this peculiar form of expression: judgment or thought. It does not suffice to say that this form of expression is available when the creature in pain has, in addition to a faculty of sensation, the power of thought. For, this does not explain how an act of the power of thought can be an expression of pain, an act of sensibility. We must know how thought and sensation are joined so that their union yields first person thought of sensation. It is impossible that we understand that, unless we first investigate thought and its link to first person reference.[11]

11. Recent treatments of first person statements that seek an account of them in the fact that they may express what they represent fail to consider the possibility that first person knowledge of acts of thought differ in form from first person knowledge of acts of sensibility. An example is Dorit Bar-On's *Speaking My Mind: Expression and Self-Knowledge* and its critique of Gareth Evans. In the relevant chapter of *The Varieties of Reference,* Evans describes a way of knowing oneself that provides knowledge of acts of thought, e.g., knowledge that one believes or perceives or remembers that such-and-such is or was the case, but not knowledge of sensations, e.g., knowledge that one is hungry or in pain. Bar-On, calling the rele-

An investigation of self-consciousness cannot start with sensation because sensation does not constitute the kind of subjectivity we call self-consciousness. A sentient creature bears a special nexus to her sensations, which we may call consciousness. Its description would be an account of the subjectivity of the sentient living being, the animal. This subjectivity is not self-consciousness. Self-consciousness is a relation a subject bears to herself by virtue of being a subject of thought. This means that it is in the first instance a character of the nexus a subject bears to her acts of thinking, of the way in which she represents herself as thinking. Acts of sensibility of a thinking subject are part of the content of her self-consciousness, which shows that, in her, the nexus of subject and sensation has a different form from the one it has in an animal without thought. An inquiry into the nexus that a subject bears to her sensations in virtue of being able to think them inquires into the sentience of a *thinking* subject and presupposes an understanding of the subjectivity of such a subject. Hence, thoughts about sensations are not the place to

---

vant way of knowing "the transparency method", objects that, "since Evans's transparency account applies to some non-avowals (such as perceptual self-reports and memory reports), it is too inclusive. But, in another way, it is too exclusive. [. . .] The relevant notion of transparency is applicable only to intentional avowals [. . .]. Since not all avowals are of this kind, any account that uses the transparency-to-the-world as the central notion will fail to explain the security of all and only avowals" (p. 122). In the text Bar-On discusses, the term "avowal" does not appear, which suggests that its topic is not avowals. In fact, it is first person reference. That his account of first person reference does not deploy the concept of avowal, and that his description of a central way of knowing associated with first person reference "fail[s] to explain the security of all and only avowals" shows that Evans holds that the first concept of the theory of self-knowledge unites acts of belief and experience and does not apply to sensations. It shows that he holds that the concept of avowal, which unites statements of belief and pain, but does not apply to the self-ascription of experience, holds no interest for her who desires to understand self-knowledge. Bar-On does not seem to realize that the challenge Evans puts to her is not that he might have a better account of "the security of all and only avowals", but that he might deny that the concept of avowal is capable of providing comprehension of what is gathered under it. In the introduction to her book, Bar-On lists features of avowals she believes demand explanation. But that avowals share certain features requiring explanation does not entail that the explanation of these features is one for all avowals. It does not entail that the concept of avowal is suited for deployment in a philosophical account of anything. Perhaps it designates something that lacks the unity of an object of understanding. There is no effort in Bar-On's book to justify the presumption that the concept of avowal is a concept of philosophy. She appears unconscious of this task.

begin when investigating self-consciousness.[12] The primary topic of a theory of self-consciousness is thought about thought.[13]

The Spontaneity of Thought: Practical and Theoretical

Of it, there are two kinds: thought about theoretical thought and thought about practical thought, or thought about acts of the intellect and thought about acts of the will, or again, thought about belief and thought about action. While we cannot hope to understand from the nature of pain why and how someone in pain as such knows herself to be in pain, we can expect to understand from the nature of action how and why someone who is doing something intentionally as such knows that she is. And while we cannot hope to understand from the nature of sensory affection how one can know that one feels warm by feeling warm, reflection on the nature of belief will reveal how believing something places one in a position to know that one does.

First person knowledge does not rest on observation, for perceptual knowledge is of something as other and involves a demonstrative reference to its object. We shall argue that first person knowledge of action and belief springs from reasoning about what to do and believe. So this is our account of the kind of knowledge that sustains the "I"-reference in thought about thought: it is knowledge from reflection. What action and belief, the will and the intellect, have in common, in virtue of which both are thought, is this form of knowledge: self-consciousness. We treat of action in Chapter 2, of belief in Chapter 3. In Chapter 4, we give a more ab-

12. In saying this, we remain neutral on whether the same methodological order should govern an investigation of *first person authority* (which is the topic, e.g., of David Finkelstein, *Expression and the Inner*). First person authority does not concern us. Our topic is the way in which one knows oneself without mediation by another manner of referring to oneself. An act of a power to know in this way bears the authority of knowledge: it is a nonaccidentally true thought. This does not distinguish first person thought. Someone else may have knowledge of a fact that I know first personally, in which case her thought bears the same authority: it is true and nonaccidentally so.

13. That it is the primary topic does not mean that it is the whole topic. As first person thoughts about thought and first person thoughts about sensation differ with regard to how one knows what they represent, there is a plurality of ways of knowing associated with "I". A complete account explains them all and demonstrates their unity. We shall not be able to do this within the present treatise. We shall make a beginning with the beginning, which is thought about thought.

stract description of the contrast between knowledge from observation and knowledge from reflection: the former is *receptive,* while the latter is *spontaneous.* What I know receptively is not the same reality as my receptive knowledge of it. It is an independent object, which must be given to me and which I must receive. By contrast, my spontaneous knowledge and what I thus know are *one reality.* When I know an object through spontaneity, the idea of the object's affecting me, and being taken in by me, does not apply. There is no room in this case for something that connects me with the object and through which I know it.

It will transpire that action concepts and the concept of belief bear an inner nexus to first person reference: they essentially figure in first person thought; their sense depends on this form of thought. Hence, actions and beliefs are such as to be known from spontaneity. They are the kind of thing that *is* its subject's knowledge of it. This explains why it is, and what it means, that the "I do" must be able to accompany all my actions and the "I believe" all my beliefs. Actions and beliefs are acts of spontaneity. The concept of spontaneity is broad; it applies to the sentient life of animals and perhaps even to the vegetative life of plants. The spontaneity of thought is of a special kind: it is a spontaneity whose acts are knowledge of these very acts. Our reflections will enable us, in Chapter 4, to explain the idea that such is the spontaneity of *reason.*

True Materialism

It is transparent that our inquiry can be read as an attempt to comprehend a principle of German Idealism. At the same time, we seek to give an account of self-consciousness that is truly materialist in a sense implicit in Karl Marx's Theses on Feuerbach. Marx maintains that all hitherto existing materialism failed, as it conceived of material reality merely as an object of intuition, not as human activity. That is, existing materialism is flawed by being empiricist. And indeed, a true materialism must show how first person knowledge, which is nonreceptive, nonempirical, can be of a material reality. Our theory reveals the subject of action and the subject of belief to be, *in such a way as to know herself to be,* material, which knowledge is first personal and not empirical. As we shall explain in Chapter 4, a subject of practical thought brings herself under a material substance concept in first person thought; she applies this concept not by perceiving instances of it, but by *being* an instance of it. Chapter 5 shows that the spontaneous knowledge of a subject of theoretical thought equally includes a material reality, as first person thought extends to the sensory nexus to an object by which one is in a position to acquire receptive knowledge of it. Contemporary epistemology is largely empiricist and to that extent incapable of appreciating the self-conscious nature of receptive knowledge. A sound account of receptive knowledge of an object of demonstrative thought depends on a proper understanding of spontaneous knowledge of an object of first person thought.

Other Subjects

There is a material reality that is knowledge of itself: a material subject of intentional action and receptive knowledge. This explains the unity of first person and second person thought; it lets us see that thought about oneself and thought about someone else are guises of one form of thought. It is customary to say that, in contrast to one's own beliefs and actions, one knows someone else's actions and beliefs through observation. So long as we say no more than this, the unity of first person and second person thought remains a mystery. Clearly, observation will bear a rather peculiar form when it turns to the self-conscious. We argue in Chapter 6 that there is a sense in which "observation", i.e., immediate apprehension, of actions and beliefs of another subject is an act not of receptive, but of spontaneous knowledge.

This explains why the fundamental form of reference to another subject is such that its linguistic expression requires the use of a *second person* pronoun, "you". Reference to a self-conscious subject is never a species of demonstrative reference. Second person reference, like first person reference, is not demonstrative reference governed by a special concept, "This man (person, thinker, self, I)". On the contrary, the relevant concept—be it "man", "person" or "self"—can only be explained in terms of a form of reference, which, formally, is to a self-conscious subject and is sustained by a different sort of knowledge from that which underwrites reference to a nonrational substance. As one power is a power to know oneself and a power to know others who are self-conscious like oneself and possess this same power, the spontaneity of reason, being a material reality, is a unity of first person and second person thought. In this way, our account of "I" yields a metaphysics of the self-conscious that is as idealist as it is materialist.

2

Action and the First Person

Certain forms of reference must be understood in terms of ways of knowing how things stand with the object, acts of which are unmediated thoughts involving the relevant form of reference. This applies to first person reference, and it is clear how to characterize in the abstract ways of knowing that sustain it: I know in a first person way that an object is F by being that object, i.e., by being F. If and only if I know that someone is F in a way that satisfies this formula, I know without mediation that I am F. In order to identify such ways of knowing, we must investigate concepts that figure in unmediated first person thoughts. Although concepts of acts of sensibility belong with these, they are not the place to begin, for acts of sensibility are self-conscious only in a thinking subject. Therefore, we must investigate the subjectivity of thought. In this chapter, we discuss practical thought, or action; in the next we discuss theoretical thought, or belief. An inquiry into the nature of action must reveal how actions conform to the first person knowledge formula, i.e., how I know that I am doing something when I know that by doing it.

We shall approach action through practical reasoning. Practical reasoning and action are one topic: practical reasoning is thought on which movement rests, while action is movement that rests on thought. From the nexus of thought and movement in action springs a special form of knowledge. G. E. M. Anscombe saw this. Of my own actions I have, she says in *Intention, practical* knowledge. She introduces the idea of practical knowledge, observing that understanding it requires investigating practical reasoning: "The notion of 'practical knowledge' can only be understood if we first understand 'practical reasoning'."[1] At the end of her in-

---

1. *Intention,* p. 57.

quiry she finds that the order of practical reasoning, of thinking about what to do, *is* the order of action explanation, of explaining why someone is doing something.[2] It will transpire that this identity is the source of a way of knowing that defines the first person reference of a subject of action and practical thought.

The chapter proceeds as follows: the first section expounds a theory of practical reasoning, the second section explains how practical reasoning is internal to intentional action, and the third section shows how this nexus of intentional action and practical reasoning is the ground of self-consciousness of the acting subject. So, we first describe practical reasoning, giving a system of forms of answering the question it addresses, the question what to do. Then, following out Anscombe's claim that the concept of action designates a form of explanation, or kind of causality, we argue that an action *is* an answer to that question, a conclusion of practical reasoning. Finally, we explain how this gives rise to a way of knowing: I may know that I am doing something from ascertaining what to do. When I know in this way that someone is doing something, I know that *I* am doing it. Being positioned to know myself in this way sustains my first person reference.

The Question What to Do

Practical reasoning aims to answer the question what to do. So its conclusion joins a subject with an action-form in a manner that represents the latter as to be done. We use "*" to signify this form of predication. "I * do *A*" expresses the posture of mind in which practical reasoning comes to rest. Our theme in this chapter is this form of predication, which will turn out to be a manner of predicating a concept that stands to first person reference as perceptual predication stands to demonstrative reference.

We must make some preliminary remarks about the conclusion of practical reasoning, "I * do *A*". It is sometimes said that practical reasoning concludes that there is reason, or most reason, to do such-and-such. This is strictly nonsense. As a reason for doing something is something from which one may reason practically to a conclusion, this describes practical reasoning as reasoning from a reason for doing something to the conclusion that there is reason to do it. We cannot employ the concept of a

---

2. *Intention*, p. 80. Anscombe appears to limit the claim to the form of action explanation whose counterpart in practical reasoning is the instrumental syllogism (see "The Will").

reason for doing something, of something's speaking in favor of doing it, when we seek an account of practical reasoning. This concept formally describes to what it applies as a term of practical reasoning; we comprehend it precisely to the degree to which we know what practical reasoning is.

It is better to say that practical reasoning concludes in an action. But this, too, is no account of practical reasoning. A term of reasoning is an act of applying concepts, i.e., a thought in the broad sense in which we speak of practical and theoretical thought. Hence, that practical reasoning concludes in an action means that it concludes in *a thought that is a movement*. Our aim is to understand the nature of such a thought or, equivalently, the nature of such a movement. We can define an intentional action as a movement that is a conclusion of reasoning, defining it as a unity of thought and movement. Comprehending this unity is comprehending practical reasoning. If we explain what practical reasoning is by saying it concludes in an action, we fail to make it clear that we lack this comprehension.

We are not denying that practical reasoning concludes in an action. Indeed we explain what this means and why it is true in the second section of this chapter. And already in this section we shall rely on the abstract and undeveloped idea, contained in the concept of practical reasoning, that practical reasoning arrives at the kind of thought on which movement may rest. That is, the unity of subject and action-form "I * do A" must have the power to be the ground of their unity in "I am doing A". We shall exclude ostensible ways of answering the question what to do that yield thoughts whose form of predication does not satisfy this condition.

"To do" in "what to do" is a gerundive and belongs to a family of forms we may call imperatives. English has no synthetic first person imperative forms, but analytic forms such as "Let me do A" or "I should do A"; these are guises of "I * do A".[3] (A first person imperative is not an imperative addressed to oneself. Second person thoughts address someone; first person thoughts do not.) Immanuel Kant explains that an imperative subsumes under a normative order something that is liable to fall from it. When we abstract from this liability, we use "good" and speak not of what is to be done, but of what is good to do: "Sie [Imperative; SR] sagen, daß

---

3. I have heard people say that "I should do A" means "There is most reason for me to do A". This is a claim about the English language, which as such is without philosophical interest. I do not believe it is true; but if and where it is, "I should do A" does not express a conclusion of practical reasoning.

etwas zu tun oder zu unterlassen gut sein würde, allein sie sagen es einem Willen, der nicht immer darum etwas tut, weil ihm vorgestellt wird, daß es zu tun gut sei."[4] We shall employ both modes of expression.

Imperatives and "good" depend on a suitable order; "what to do" is a schema that acquires a sense as a determinate order interprets it. Now, something may fall under an order in two ways. It may be that its own kind, or what it is, is its measure. For example, we explain that a house provides shelter for men and goods, and say that our house is not as it should be because its roof leaks. Our house falls under a measure in virtue of what it is: a house. In other cases, we place something under an order not contained in its nature, or what it is, as when a grocer thinks his apples ought to be shinier, or a farmer that his swine have too few ribs. In the former case, the order is internal to the thing, external in the latter. We said we would argue in the next section that an action is an answer to the question what to do, a conclusion of practical reasoning. If this is right, then an order that provides a sense for this question is internal to the actions that it governs.

This does not decide the nature of this order. Perhaps there is an order internal to action as such, a measure to which one is subject simply in virtue of being an agent. Kant holds this when he maintains that the bare concept of the will supplies a sense for "good" in "good will".[5] This measure then is *the* measure that everywhere interprets the question what to do. By contrast, Philippa Foot argues that only a more determinate concept such as, e.g., the concept of a human will contains a measure internal to its instances. According to Foot, "good will" is a schema, "good will of an *X*", where values of "*X*" are *life-forms*.[6] If she is right, then the question what to do acquires a sense as it is asked by, for example, a man. In his mouth, it is to be interpreted by the order internal to the human will. Should there be other life-forms whose bearers confront our question, it will have a different sense in their mouths.—In claiming that being human is being under an order that governs one's will, Foot opposes an empiricist

4. *Grundlegung zur Metaphysik der Sitten*, p. 413. "They [imperatives; SR] say that to do or to omit something would be good, but they say it to a will that does not always do something because it is represented to it that that thing is good to do."

5. We are attributing to Kant the claim not that the concept of action contains a normative standard (which he denies), but that we know *synthetically a priori* that actions as such fall under a certain measure. This is synthetic knowledge a priori, as it is contained in any application of the concept of action in an act of *knowledge*. See our discussion in Chapter 6.

6. Foot, *Natural Goodness*.

orthodoxy according to which the standard that interprets the question what to do is a *totality of desires*. Terms that take the place of "*X*" in "good will of an *X*" then signify such a totality. But perhaps even this goes too far. Perhaps the standard is *an end that one is pursuing* (perhaps on account of some desire, which is strongest just now). A particular end then defines the sense of the question what to do asked by her who is, and while she is, pursuing it. When later she is pursuing a different end, the question she poses with "what to do?" will be a different question; a different measure will interpret the gerundive.

The phrases "what to do" and "good will" designate a concept only if there is an order that is internal to action as such; otherwise, they are schemata and designate a form of a concept. Accounts then differ over what kind of thing provides them with content: a life-form, a totality of desires, an end being pursued. If we call an order under which a subject places herself in asking what to do an order of practical reason, then there may be no such thing as *the* order of practical reason. The definite article is legitimate only if "what to do" identifies a question independently of any character of her who is asking it other than her being a subject of action. Otherwise, there are as many orders of practical reason as there are, e.g., rational life-forms, totalities of desires, or ends being pursued.[7]

An inquiry into practical reasoning is an inquiry into the sense of the question it addresses. This in turn is an inquiry into the kind of thing that supplies the question with a sense on an occasion of its being posed. So we inquire after the form of what interprets the question what to do, *the logical category of an inner measure of action*. In general, the sense of a question transpires from statements that answer it, and the form of its sense from the form of the answers. Thus our procedure will be to develop a system of forms of statements that answer the question what to do, statements that fill the blank in "I * do *A* because ____".

The Will

The following seems a basic form of reasoning about what to do: I want to do *B* and reflect on how to do it. I realize that doing *A* will take me

7. An account of practical reason, or intentional action, or moral obligation, that uncritically relies on phrases such as "*S* rationally ought to do *A*" or "*S* should do *A* in the sense that she has a reason (or most reason) to do it" to have a meaning *simpliciter* cannot be certain that it has a topic.

some way, perhaps even all the way, toward doing B. I conclude that I should do A. So here is a form of ascertaining what do to: I should do A because I want to do B. Call this an *instrumental syllogism*.

This form of reasoning may be thought to be invalid because, as there may be other ways of doing B, I cannot, by recognizing doing A to be *a* way, single out A as what I should do. If this objection is based on the notion that, concluding I should do A, I conclude that I have most reason to do A, we can disregard it. But there is a deeper error. It may be thought that I cannot reason from wanting, e.g., to get a box of cereal to taking this one here, because I have no grounds for choosing this one here over that one there. Reasoning from wanting *a* box cannot connect me to this box in a manner in which it does not connect me to that box. But this is wrong. While I might have derived, from wanting a box of cereal, "I should take that box over there", without my reasoning having been defective, this does not show that I cannot derive, from wanting a box of cereal, that I should take this box over here. Since that box does not figure in my reasoning from wanting to take a box to taking this one, my reasoning does not leave me stuck between boxes. This is a feature of practical reasoning in all its forms. Practical reasoning proceeds from something general, and its office is to arrive at a specification. It is in the nature of the case that there may be more than one way of doing this. Inferring from this fact that practical reasoning fails to reach a definite action is refusing to consider the idea of *practical* reasoning.[8]

So let us return to the instrumental syllogism: I should do A because I want to do B. This is peculiar. How, we must ask, can the fact that I want something pertain to the question what to do? What is wanting if representing something as a means to something I want is representing it as to be done?

One might respond that, in "I should do A because I want to do B", "do B" specifies *the measure* to which doing A is said to conform. The action-form B defines the sense of the question what to do that I answer in thinking I should do A. Let us rewrite the syllogism so as to represent this nexus of A and B: "I should do A in the sense that it is a means of doing B", or, "I should$_{do\ B}$ do A". On this account, the order that inter-

---

8. Compare Anselm Winfried Müller, "How Theoretical Is Practical Reasoning?", p. 104.

prets my question what to do is an end I am pursuing as I ask the question.[9]

We must reject this doctrine because it fails to represent practical reasoning as arriving at an action. Suppose I think I should$_{\text{do } B}$ do A and I think I should$_{\text{do } B*}$ not do A. On the present account, no thought about what to do brings these thoughts into contact, for such a thought would have to employ a gerundive defined by neither end, B or $B*$. The difficulty this poses for the account is not that it has no space for a thought that resolves a conflict in which I may find myself, thinking that I should$_{\text{do } B}$ do A and that I should$_{\text{do } B*}$ not do A. Rather, the problem is that *there is no conflict.* "I should$_{\text{do } B}$ do A" does not contradict "I should$_{\text{do } B*}$ not do A". Thinking I should$_{\text{do } B}$ do A leaves me free to think I should$_{\text{do } B*}$ not do A. In thinking I should$_{\text{do } B}$ do A, I attach myself to doing A in a way that places no obstacle in the way of my attaching myself in the same manner to not doing A. It follows that my doing A cannot rest on the nexus I bear to doing A, thinking I should$_{\text{do } B}$ do A. For, to be doing A is to bear a nexus to doing A that excludes bearing the same nexus to not doing A.[10]

Perhaps the doctrine, while false of us, describes the thought of a creature that never thinks she should do something, in a sense defined by an end she is pursuing, which she should not do in a sense defined by another end. The unity of her will, which according to the current hypothesis is not

9. That is, I reflect on what to do only if a specific end has conferred a meaning on this question; my reflection proceeds under this end. I may reflect now under one end and then under a different end. But these reflections proceed in isolation. No thought belongs to both, for if it did, it would employ (or implicitly refer to) a concept of "should" not defined by either end. Therefore, "should" bears an index; the notation must not recognize the same concept in both courses of reflection. It follows that someone who thinks that the instrumental syllogism is the only form of practical reasoning thereby denies that the instrumental principle ("If you pursue an end, you should take the necessary means") is a practical law as opposed to a *law schema.* If a subject's practical reasoning is confined to the instrumental syllogism, we can describe *the form* of her practical judgment by saying that she thinks she should do what serves her ends. In saying this, we employ the formal concept of an end, which does not figure in her practical thought. Recognition of this fact would have to complicate Christine Korsgaard's argument in "The Normativity of Instrumental Reason".

10. It does not help to aggregate the indices. Then it will be true that I both should$_{\text{do } B \text{ and } B*}$ do A and should$_{\text{do } B \text{ and } B*}$ not do A. We may rule this out, stipulating that aggregated ends must be instrumentally coherent: achieving one must not be incompatible with achieving any other. But the representation of this requirement deploys an imperative not defined by any end; hence, someone whose practical thought is confined to indexed imperatives does not represent this unity of ends. Compare the parallel discussion in Chapter 3.

the work of thought, may be the work of a nonrational principle, instinct or appetite, say, that supplies her ends. However, as the problem of the doctrine is not that ends may conflict, ensuring that they do not conflict does not solve it. It is irrelevant whether she who thinks she should$_{\text{do } B}$ do A at the same time thinks she should$_{\text{do } B*}$ not do A, or whether this never happens on account of a cause external to her thinking. Such a cause regulates when and whether she thinks certain thoughts, but does not alter the logical character of these thoughts. What ruins the doctrine is that thinking I should$_{\text{do } B}$ do A peacefully coexists with thinking I should$_{\text{do } B*}$ not do A. This it does no matter whether another thought, that I should$_{\text{do } B*}$ not do A, is present. Since it tolerates a thought that I should$_{\text{do } B*}$ not do A next to it, thinking I should$_{\text{do } B}$ do A is not affixing myself to doing A to the exclusion of not doing A. But to be doing A is so to affix myself to doing A.

The second term of an instrumental syllogism is not the order to which the first term conforms. Rather, the former *conforms to the same order* to which the latter conforms. Not only the conclusion of an instrumental syllogism, already its premise responds to the question what to do. This is apparent from the fact that the conclusion of one syllogism may be the premise of another. When I think about how to do B and recognize that doing A is a way, I will straightway do A only if I know how. Otherwise, my reasoning will conclude not in my doing A, but in my wanting to do it. "I want to do A because I want to do B", I will say. I could have expressed the same thought by saying, "I should do A because I want to do B". This shows that premise and conclusion of an instrumental syllogism share a logical form. "Should" and "want to" signify the same form of predication—both are guises of "*".

The instrumental syllogism extends the status of being good to do from one action-form to another. It subsumes its terms under the same measure: its premise represents something as good in the same sense in which its conclusion does so. Hence, the question what to do is not defined by the end that figures in the premise of an instrumental syllogism. On the contrary, an end from which one may reason to a conclusion about what to do is something to be done in that same sense. Instrumental reasoning leads from one answer to the practical question to another; it does not make explicit the measure of this question. Therefore, there must be a form of answering the question what to do that is not a case of deriving one answer from another answer. From this form of answering the question, its sense—the order that interprets it—must transpire. It is important to be clear why this is so. There must be another form of practical reasoning not because, otherwise, practical reasoning would not come to a close—I reason that I want to (should) do A because I want to (should) do B, that I want to (should) do B because I want to (should) do C, and so on—but because, otherwise, we would not understand a single member of this potentially infinite sequence.[11] We would not understand the form of predication "*". For, we cannot explain the idea of something to be done by saying one should do what is a means of doing what one should do. We understand what an instrumental syllogism is only if we know what kind of thing interprets the question it addresses. And we cannot gather what that is by attending to this form of reasoning alone. There must be another way of answering the question that the instrumental syllogism answers, which reveals the measure the question invokes.

Desire

The measure that defines the question what to do cannot be an end the subject is pursuing, for this allows to exist side by side thoughts about what to do that propose actions that cannot exist side by side. It is useless to invoke a nonrational principle like appetite as that which provides for the unity of ends. For the problem is not lack of unity, but lack of *representation* of unity (or its absence). Appetite or desires can be a principle of the will only if, and in the form in which, they enter practical reasoning, i.e., only as represented. They can govern the will only through thought. Now, there is a manner in which appetite, through its representation, is taken to inform the will. We call this way of founding an act of the will on appetite, which, among others Donald Davidson describes, *calculation from desire*.

Davidson describes practical reasoning as proceeding from prima facie judgments to all-out judgments.[12] An all-out judgment is a judgment about what to do. It is a wanting or, as we say to avoid this awkward noun, an *intention*. A prima facie judgment, by contrast, expresses a *desire;* it is the form in which desire enters practical reasoning. It joins a subject and an action-form A in a manner weak enough not to amount to an act of thinking one should do A, yet strong enough to suggest that some-

11. In *Zettel,* p. 693, Ludwig Wittgenstein notes that, in philosophy, the problem posed by a regress is not its infinity, but the impossibility of understanding any one of its steps.

12. See, for example, "Intending", p. 98.

thing speaks in favor of doing it. Let us use "#" to signify this form of predication. English guises of "I # do A" are, e.g., "I feel like doing A", "It would be nice to do A", or, perhaps, "I desire to do A". We do not say, "I should do A because I feel like doing B"; nevertheless, if I feel like doing A, that may speak in favor of doing it.[13] Davidson maintains that "I want to do A" expresses a prima facie judgment. But the phrase can state the premise of an instrumental syllogism and then expresses an all-out judgment. It is true that the same form of words may express a desire. This is a peculiarity of English. "Ich will A tun", e.g., never expresses a prima facie judgment.[14]

"I # do A" does not express an act of the will, an intention, but an act of appetite, a desire. While acts of the will are essentially capable of linguistic expression, this is not true of desire; the faculty of desire does not depend on the power of thought. Therefore desire in general cannot be defined in terms of a form of thought. However, our interest is in desire as it enters practical reasoning, and this topic can be defined in terms of a form of predication. It might seem that prima facie judgments express a variety of attitudes, desire being only one of them. Davidson gives these examples: a conviction that pornography is wrong, love of children, a distaste for salt cod, a sudden desire to touch a woman's elbow. He says about these "desires, principles, [. . .], obligations", that "the 'logical form' of the propositional expression [. . .] is the same".[15] So Davidson does not use "principle" and "desire" to designate a difference in logical form, i.e., in the manner in which these things figure in practical reasoning. This is an idiosyncratic and unhappy employment of these terms. First, philosophy would have no use for the concept of a principle if it did not designate a logical form. Secondly, in its application to animals

---

13. Davidson's notation of prima facie judgments is "pf(a is intention-worthy, a is a case of doing A)". The notation is based on ideas a discussion of which would be a distraction. They are these: Davidson holds that, while "I intend" does not express an intention, "It is intention-worthy" does ("Replies to Essays", p. 209), and that intentions include reference to an event, wherefore he writes, "a is intention-worthy" instead of "It is intention-worthy to do A". So while we define the conclusion of practical reasoning by a *form of predication* of action-forms, Davidson defines it by a *predicate* that applies to events. If we ignore this otherwise all-important difference, we can write a prima facie judgment, "pf(I * do X, doing X is a case (means, part) of doing A)", or shorter, "I # do A".

14. Compare Michael Thompson's distinction of two senses of "want" in "Naïve Action Theory".

15. "Replies to Essays", p. 202; "Actions, Reasons, Causes", p. 4; "Intending", p. 102.

without thought the concept of desire is defined in terms of a *form of explanation of movement*, which thus explained is self-movement. Thus desire as it enters thought should be defined by the way in which it figures in practical reasoning and thus, presumably, in *action explanation*.

Davidson describes reasoning from prima facie judgments to an all-out judgment as follows. In a first step, desires expressed by various prima facie judgments are integrated into one such judgment, an all-things-considered judgment. It represents a desire that brings all desires to a unity.[16] The unified desire is constituted by the calculation; it is essentially represented and cannot exist in an animal without thought. In the shape of an all-things-considered judgment, appetite bears a unity mediated by and represented in thought. In a second step, an all-things-considered judgment is made the ground of an all-out judgment according to a principle Davidson calls the principle of continence. As an all-things-considered judgment considers all given desires, the principle counsels doing what best satisfies these. On Davidson's view, this principle is not a substantive judgment about what to do. If it were, it would be neither prima facie nor all out, and his account of practical reasoning would be incomplete. The principle must be analytic and *define the sense of the question that all-out judgments answer:* the order that defines this question is a totality of desires. Thus there is no asking whether one should do what best satisfies given desires; this would be an attempt to employ an imperative not defined by a totality of desires, of whose sense no account can be given. We shall see, however, that the principle of continence cannot be analytic and define the question of practical reasoning. Desires do not define that question.

We are considering calculation from desire as a form of reasoning that yields an answer to the question what to do that does not rest on an answer to that same question. However, if intentions rest on desire eventually, there is no deriving an intention from an intention. The manner of reasoning we thought would yield a starting point of instrumental reasoning does away with the instrumental syllogism. This reduces the idea that appetite unified by calculation is the order of practical reason to absurdity. For, practical reasoning arrives at a thought on which movement may rest, and without the instrumental syllogism there is no such thing as movement resting on thought.

16. We need not inquire how the calculation proceeds; what we shall say will be indifferent to this. According to Davidson, the calculation conforms to the calculus of decision under uncertainty ("Replies to Essays", pp. 199, 214).

It is easy to see that intentions cannot rest on intentions if they rest on desires eventually. Suppose I calculated that, considering all given desires, I should do B. I reasoned that I should do first A_1 and then A_2, took the first step and did A_1. Now, it need not be that doing B still best satisfies my desires now that I have done A_1; new desires may have sprung up. Hence, it need not be that doing A_2 best satisfies my desires now that I set out to do A_2. Thus instrumental reasoning may lead me to act against what, all in all, I desire.

It looks as though, having formed an allout judgment to do B, I can judge on that basis all out to do A_1 and A_2. One intention to do B seems to ground my intention to take the first step and do A_1 and my intention to take the second step and do A_2. But this is not so, if my intention to do B, formed before I take the first step, is based on the thought that, in view of all desires then, doing B is best. For, this does not settle that now that I have taken the first step, doing B is best in view of all my desires now. Were I to derive an intention to do A_2 from the intention I formed before I took the first step, it would be an accident and not guaranteed by the form of my reasoning if I did not flout the principle of continence and acted counter to what, considering all my desires now, is best. An intention to do A_2 cannot rest on a judgment that desires earlier were best served by doing B. It can rest only on a judgment that doing B is best given all desires now. If appetite unified by calculation is the order of practical reason, then she who conforms to it forms *two* intentions to do B: one is the ground of her intention to take the first step and do A_1, another the ground of her intention to take the second step and do A_2.

One might think that there are not two intentions, but one that remains, if the desires on which the intention is based remain. (We imagined they remained.) But this is wrong. The ground of an intention is a judgment that desires, all in all, speak in favor of doing A. As desires come and go, that judgment contains a reference to a time. It is a judgment that desires now present all in all speak in favor of doing A. Such a judgment made at t_1 bears no logical connection with the judgment expressed by the same words at t_2, no matter whether the same things are present at t_1 and t_2, no matter whether it was probable or even necessary that the same things would be present. On Davidson's account, the same holds true of all-out judgments, or intentions, as their basis is an all-things-considered judgment: judging all out at t_1 to do B and judging all out at t_2 to do B are different judgments, regardless of whether desires changed in the meantime, whether it was unlikely or even impossible that they would change.

If intentions eventually spring from a calculation from desire, then the instrumental syllogism is not a valid form of reasoning.[17] We said this would reduce the antecedent to absurdity, that appetite, unified by calculation, is the order that interprets the question what to do, as without the instrumental syllogism there is no such thing as thought on which movement rests. This is so because a thought that is the proximate principle of a movement must have an object that itself has the form of temporality of a *movement*. But the object of a thought that concludes a calculation from desire bears a different form of temporality: it is a *changeable state*.

Let us first consider these concepts, the concepts of movement and changeable state, in abstraction from their application in practical reasoning. They are logical concepts, designating a form of predication.[18] A state is a determination that joins a thing under a contrast of past and present tense, "was/is", while a movement is the object of a thought whose predication exhibits not only this contrast, but also the contrast of progressive and perfective aspect, "was doing/did". For example, "the house is white" contrasts with "the house was white", while "the chair is

---

17. Michael Bratman argues that, as calculation takes time and effort (we are not "frictionless deliberators", *Intention, Plans, and Practical Reason*, p. 28), and as therefore the chance of superior desire satisfaction will often be too slight to offset the cost of recalculating, it is beneficial to cultivate a habit to keep going once one has formed an intention, and reason from it to further intentions. This presupposes that the instrumental syllogism is not a valid form of reasoning, i.e., that it may conclude in an intention to do A when doing it is bad according to the measure of desire satisfaction.—Davidson appears to hold that an intention to do B is based, first, on the calculation that desires present now that I begin doing B all in all speak in favor of doing B and, secondly, on an estimate that this will not change before I shall be done. ("Replies to Essays", pp. 214–215. One might find the same idea in the description of an intention as an "interim report" ["Intending", p. 100], but the passage is less conclusive, as it does not thematize the temporal extension of the action.) This does not justify deriving from an intention to do B, when the time comes to take the second step and do A_2, an intention to do A_2. According to Davidson, an intention to do B is based, in part, on an estimate that, when the time comes, things all in all will favor doing A_2, so that at that time I shall intend, or shall have reason to intend, to do A_2. But resting an intention now on an earlier estimate that I shall form, or have reason to, this intention is not a valid form of reasoning, for the form of reasoning does not guarantee the truth of the estimate.

18. The system of forms of predication, and thus of formal concepts or categories, through which an object is apprehended as temporal are the topic of my *Kategorien des Zeitlichen*.

falling over" contrasts not only with "the chair was falling over", but also with "the chair fell over". We see how the aspectual contrast affects the temporality of the object when we compare "x is F"—tense predication— with "x is doing A"—aspect predication. We shall describe the difference in three, equivalent ways.

It is suggestive to say, metaphorically, that "x is doing A" looks forward; it looks forward to x's having done A. No such anticipation is present in "x is F". The content of the metaphor is this: when x has done A, it is doing it no more. Or if it is, then it is doing it again, which is a different movement. Thus "x is doing A" specifies an end of what it represents. It need not be the end in fact; x may stop doing A before it has done it. So there are two ways in which x may no longer be doing A: it has done A, or it stopped doing A short of completion. But these ways of no longer doing A—incomplete, short of having done A, or complete, having done A—are not on a par. The movement's ending with x's having done A belongs to it in the sense that this end is singled out by the concept of doing A, through which the movement is apprehended in the progressive thought. In the same sense, any other end is accidental to it: it is not contained in the predicative material of the progressive thought. A progressive thought looks forward in the sense that it designates *a certain end as proper to what it represents.* By contrast, the predicative material of "x is F" does not designate a terminus of what the thought represents. The concept of being F is indifferent as to when x will no longer be F. In this sense, no end is accidental to x's being F; no end of its being F is premature. It may be no accident if something that is F remains F for a given time, but not on account of the logical nature of the predicative material, but on account of the real nature of the thing of which it is said. To a changeable state *any duration is accidental.*

From this we can derive a further way of describing the contrast of state and movement. Consider an interval during which x was F. If we divide this interval into intervals, then it is accidental to being F that any one of these subintervals was followed by the next, which in fact followed it. An interval during which something was in a changeable state is *an aggregate* of such intervals. By contrast, suppose something is doing A. It has done something toward this, as it is on its way. But it is not there yet; it has not yet done A. Now there are two possibilities: the movement may end incomplete, or it may continue and progress toward its completion. These possibilities are not on a par. If they were, the concept of doing A, which singles out one of them, would not bear on the situation. It would not be true that x is doing A, but only that it has done what it has done so far. Thus there is a nonaccidental unity of the phase it has completed and the phase following it by which it progresses toward having done A. An interval during which something was doing A is *a unity* of such intervals.

Our third and final way of articulating the contrast is the following. As any duration is accidental to a changeable state, a sentence "x is F", representing a changeable state, invariably expresses *distinct judgments at different times*. At any time, it will be a further truth that x still is F then, a truth not contained in the truth that it was F earlier. By contrast, consider x, which did A. It may have taken it time to do it. But if we hold that "x is doing A" expresses distinct judgments during this time, we pretend that the interval during which x was doing A is an aggregate of such intervals and that any duration is accidental to it. And then we do not register that the concept of doing A singles out an end of what is represented by "x is doing A", an end that thus is proper to it. So "x is doing A" does not invariably express a distinct judgment at different times. It expresses *the same judgment all the while x is doing A and until it has done it*.

We can now return to practical reasoning. I reason instrumentally, "I want to do B. So let me do A_1", and, "I want to do B. So let me do A_2", from *the same premise*. The premise is the same throughout my doing B and until I have done it, which means that its object has the temporality of a movement. By contrast, the conclusion of a calculation from desire represents a changeable state. Now that I begin doing B and do A_1, the sentence "All in all, things now present speak in favor of doing B" expresses a different judgment from the one it will express later as I continue doing B and do A_2. Calculation from desire does not yield a premise for instrumental reasoning because its conclusion represents a changeable state, while an instrumental syllogism proceeds from a thought that represents something with the temporality of a movement.[19] But the instrumental syllogism is a *necessary* form of practical reasoning, for practical reasoning arrives at a thought on which a movement may rest. And if a movement rests on thought, then the unity of its phases, which constitutes it as a movement, must rest on thought. So it does if I reason from the same thought now, "I want to do B. So let me do A_1", and then, "I want to do

---

19. In "Naïve Action Theory", Michael Thompson concludes that "I want to do B" does not represent a changeable state from the fact that it can serve as cause in an action explanation "I am doing A because I want to do B."

B. So let me do A_2", and so on. As "I want to do B" expresses the same thought all the while that I am doing B and until I have done it, the unity of the phases of my doing B consists in the fact that they all hang on that thought. By contrast, if "I want to do B" represented a changeable state, I would not reason from the same thought, now to doing A_1, and then to doing A_2. In consequence, my doing A_1 and my doing A_2 would bear no unity. These would not be phases of a movement, and I would not, in doing A_1 and A_2, be doing B.

This is where we left Davidson: I calculate that, all things considered, I should do B, follow the principle of continence and decide all out to do B. I observe that doing A_1 is a means, arrive at an action, and do A_1. As I have done A_1, I ask what to do, considering all things now present. I calculate that, all in all, I should do B, follow the principle of continence and decide all out to do B. I realize that this requires doing A_2, arrive at an action, and do A_2. No *one* intention is the ground of my doing A_1 and my doing A_2, but one underlies my doing A_1, another my doing A_2. But then I am not doing B. Suppose I walked from a to c, via b. It may be that I decided to walk from a to b, and, having got there, decided to walk from b to c. Or I decided to walk from a to c, and did. In the former case, I was walking from a to b, and then I was walking from b to c. But only in the latter case, not in the former, was I walking from a to c.[20] As a movement, an action is not an aggregate, but a *unity* of phases. Davidson cannot mark this distinction.

And this reduces his position to absurdity, for, being unable to represent an action as a unity of phases, Davidson is unable to represent the phases, which exhibit the same unity. If I am doing A, I have not yet done A, but there is something that, in doing A, I have done, call it A'.[21] But if I have done A', I was doing that earlier. So the thought applies to A' and thus reapplies indefinitely. Davidson's account of practical reasoning entails that, when I am doing B by first doing A_1 and then A_2, separate intentions underlie these actions. But then not only am I not doing B, I am not doing anything at all. As I was doing A_1, I had not done it, but I had done something, call it A_{11}. When I had done that, it was an open question whether, considering all things then, I should do A_1, and thus A_{12}.

20. Here I am indebted to Doug Lavin.
21. It may be doubted that this is always true when "I am doing A" describes an intentional action. But in any case, if I did A, there was a time when I was doing it such that, in being doing it, I had done something else. Our argument can proceed from there.

Suppose my answer was yes. If I did A_1, then no one intention underlay my doing it, but one my doing A_{11} and another my doing A_{12}. So on this view, no action can be traced to *one* intention. If an action is in progress, another has been completed, and the intention that seemed to underlie the former underlies only the latter.

Calculation of desire does not yield an intention. For, an intention is a thought on which a movement may rest and therefore has the temporality of a movement: the interval during which I intend to do something is a unity of such intervals.[22] By contrast, the conclusion of a calculation from desire expresses a state to which any duration is accidental. In his illuminating book *Intention, Plans, and Practical Reason,* Michael Bratman seeks to describe the peculiar temporality of intentions by saying that they are states of the mind that have inertia: they put up a certain resistance

22. Christine Korsgaard may seem to be onto that point, that desire cannot be the ground of intention because of the temporal mismatch of an action in progress and a changeable state of desire (see "The Normativity of Instrumental Reason", p. 247n64). In fact, she makes it clear that she thinks that irrelevant: "If I am to work I must *will* it—I must resolve to stay on its track. [. . .] Desire and temptation will also take their turns. 'I am not a shameful thing like terror', desire will say, 'follow me and your life will be sweet'. But if I give in to each claim as it appears *I* will do nothing [. . .]. For to will an end is not just to cause it, or not even to allow an impulse in me to operate as its cause, but, so to speak, to consciously pick up the reins, and make *myself* the cause of an end. And if I am to constitute *myself* as the cause of an end, then I must be able to distinguish between *my* causing the end and some desire or impulse that is 'in me' causing my body to act. I must be able to see *myself* as something distinct from any of my particular, first-order, impulses and motives. [. . .] Now, I need to clarify these remarks in one important way. In the above argument I appealed to the possibility of being tempted away from the end on another, temporally later occasion. But the argument does not really require the possibility of a later occasion. It only requires that there be two parts of me, one that is my governing self, my will, and one that must be governed, and is capable of resisting my will" (ibid., pp. 246–248.) The essential point is, she says, that I distinguish myself from my inclinations. If I am working on account of my desire to work, then it is not I who am working. My desire is working or makes me work. In, "If I give in to each claim as it appears I will do nothing", Korsgaard emphasizes "I": if I follow my desires, I (better: the thing that would be I, if I weren't governed by desire) may do many things, but *I* won't have done any of them. But why is that so? I do not seem to misuse the first person pronoun when I say, "I am doing *A* because I like it". Emphasizing the first person pronoun is not understanding it. But suppose we inquired into first person thought and associated ways of knowing and could show that first person knowledge springs from reasoning defined by forms beyond calculation from desire. Suppose, that is, we could establish that, if someone's thinking were confined to "I should do *A* because, all in all, I desire to do it", then she could not think without mediation, "I am doing *A*". We could express this result by saying: Were I ruled by desire alone, *I* would not act. Such is the form of our argument.

against being pushed out.[23] The inadequacy of this way of stating the point comes out when we notice that it makes it quite surprising that the inertia gives out, all of a sudden, when I have done what I intended to do. At this point, my intention gives way without the slightest resistance, its inertia reducing to zero. Bratman might as well have said that a movement in progress is a state with inertia. He is trying to capture the nonaccidental unity of phases, which is the logical character of movement, and therefore of intention, which is the proximate principle of a movement.

Calculation from desire does not arrive at an action. It yields thoughts that represent changeable states and therefore cannot be the source of a movement. The principle of continence, counseling doing what best satisfies given desires, does not define the question what to do. We do not understand its imperative; we have yet to describe the order to which it refers. Appetite unified by calculation is not this order.

Infinite Ends

The second term of an instrumental syllogism does not give the order to which the first term conforms, but something that conforms to the same order. Therefore, the measure that defines the question what to do that an instrumental syllogism answers is not an end the subject is pursuing; on the contrary, an end that provides the premise of an instrumental syllogism is something good. Hence, there must be a different way of answering the question what to do, the form of which will determine the category of the relevant order. We considered the idea that calculation from desire is this form and calculated unity of appetite the order that defines the sense of the relevant "good" or imperative. It seemed that, in this way, a representation of appetite could represent the unity (or lack of unity) of ends, which representation we found necessary in reasoning that arrives at action. Our hope was disappointed; all-things-considered judgments represent changeable states and therefore cannot be the ground of an intention, which is the principle of a movement. So the necessarily represented unity of ends must bear a different kind of temporality. We shall now suggest that the relevant unity is a unity not of desire, but of what we shall call *infinite ends*. Just as the concept of desire, so is our concept of an infinite end defined by the form of a thought that constitutes adherence

---

23. *Intention, Plans, and Practical Reason*, pp. 14–18.

to it. As a man may desire noble things, so may his infinite ends be base, if base things figure in his thoughts of the relevant form. All-things-considered judgments join subject and action-form *at a time*. An intention, "I * do *A*", joins them *progressively*, guiding the progress of the action. If the representation of an infinite end is to provide the principle of temporal synthesis of an action, it must join subject and action-form neither at a time nor progressively, but in a way that, metaphorically speaking, always already contains the whole of a temporally extended action. We shall see that this means that its predication is *time-general*.

"I am getting my tools because I want to repair my bicycle", I say. "Why do you want to repair your bicycle?," you ask. "I want to go cycling." "But why go cycling?" you insist. "It is healthy", I respond. Is this an instrumental syllogism? It appears so. Does not it represent health as an end and cycling as a means? It is true, we call health an end. But it is an end in a different sense from repairing a bicycle; the end and what is done in its service relate differently in these cases.

Suppose I want to repair my bicycle. I do various things because I want this: I gather the tools, put my bicycle upside down, make sure it is stable, and so forth. These actions lead up to my eventually having repaired the bicycle; they cover a distance that separates me from my end. When I have traversed the distance and repaired the bicycle, my want to repair it expires. As long as I want to repair it, I have not yet repaired it, whereas once I have repaired it, my want ceases to be and moves me no more. My want exhausts itself in explaining what it explains. In this sense, its object is a *finite end*.

Now suppose I want health. I do not want it in the way a sick man does; I do not want to *become* healthy. Imagine me perfectly healthy: I may still want health. Perhaps I want not to be healthy but to *remain* healthy? I will have remained healthy in the future; my end is at a distance and I can take steps toward it. But if my having remained healthy is future, when in the future is it? When will I have reached it? It seems I must lay it down that I want to remain healthy, say, until next Sunday. On this day, I will have reached my goal, if I have not fallen ill in the meantime. I can then set myself a new end, e.g., to remain healthy for another week. This is possible, but need not be what I mean when I say I want health. I may say this in a sense such that I do not expect the question "How long do you want to remain healthy?" as I expect the question "How long do you want to remain in the bathtub?" when I say that I want to be in the bathtub. Perhaps it is understood that I want to remain healthy as long as I live? But what would it mean to want to be healthy beyond one's death?[24] Once I have repaired my bicycle, I no longer want to repair it. I may want to repair another bicycle, but then I have set myself a new end, as when I remained healthy for one week and resolve to do so for another week. A finite end is something I have not yet got. Wanting health is not like this. In full health, I want to be healthy. One feels like saying that health is an end *I have already achieved while being after it.*

But one may also want to say that health is an end *I never achieve.* If I want health, I do various things for the sake of it. I go running one day, buy wholesome food the next day, and refrain from lying in the sun at midday the day after. I do not thereby diminish a distance that separates me from my end in the way in which gathering the tools, putting my bicycle upside down, and so on, brings me closer to a repaired bicycle. I never seem to be done with my health; I can never mark it off as completed and move on to new projects. My want to repair a bicycle exhausts itself in explaining my actions; it is the cause of its own extinction. An end such as health, by contrast, does not expend itself in explaining what it explains. As long as I adhere to it, it does not lose its power to explain what I do. It seems this must mean that I never get there.

We want to say that health is an end I have already achieved while I am pursuing it,[25] and that it is an end I never achieve as long as I am pursuing it. Is wanting health a paradox, then? No; but it is not a finite end. It does not admit of the contrast that defines finite ends: of being on the way toward and having reached the end. A paradoxical description suggests itself when we attempt to conceive of health through this contrast and thus attempt to represent it as a finite end. An end to which the contrast of pursuing and having got does not apply is an *infinite end.*

This is the negative concept of an infinite end, the negative description of the relation of the end to what is done in its service that defines it. We need a positive account of that relation. She who cares about her health does certain things: she eats dry food, exercises, and so forth. These thoughts—she eats dry food, exercises—join subject and action-form *ha-*

---

24. For analogous reasons, survival usually is not a goal, and certainly not "the ultimate goal", of the living, as claimed, e.g., by Daniel Dennett in "Three Kinds of Intentional Psychology" (p. 53). In great peril, I may think "I want to survive this", which is a finite end. She has a terrible life who constantly seeks to survive something.

25. This is Aristotle's definition of *energeia;* repairing a bicycle fits his definition of *kinesis* (*Metaphysics,* Θ 6).

bitually; they are *time-general* in the sense that thoughts of all tenses exemplify them. She went running yesterday, is playing tennis today, and will
go swimming tomorrow: all of this shows that she exercises. If "I want to
be healthy" expresses an infinite end, then it is not true if I merely think it
would be nice to exercise and eat dry food. If I never, or rarely, did any of
these things, then that would show that I do not want to be healthy. (It
might show that I like to say that I do).[26] As thoughts representing infinite
ends entail time-general thoughts about what one *does*, they are themselves time-general. She went running yesterday, is eating wholesome
food today, and will refrain from lying in the sun at midday tomorrow: all
this manifests that she cares about her health.[27]

"I want to go cycling for the sake of my health" is not an instrumental
syllogism. It represents cycling as a means and health as an end, but the
relation of means to end has a different form. A finite end explains an action as a *part of itself.* When I am doing *A* because I want to do *B*, then I
think that, in doing *A*, I am doing part of doing *B*. An infinite end explains an action as a *manifestation of itself.* When I am doing *A* because it
is healthy, then I think that, in doing *A*, I am doing something such that
she who does it (habitual aspect) is healthy. This explains the infinity of infinite ends: while a whole is exhausted by its parts, what is manifested is
not exhausted by its manifestations.

Infinite ends are time-general; this distinguishes them from desires. I
may one moment feel like going to the movies, the next moment feel like
staying home, and a minute later again think that going to the movies
would be nice. But it makes no sense to say that, one moment, I cared
about my health, was completely indifferent to it the next moment, and a
bit later again cared greatly about it. If I want health, then this manifests
itself in actions at various times; wanting health is time-general and not
tied to a moment. Of course, concepts that designate infinite ends may
figure in fleeting thoughts: a man may one moment be excited by the idea
that he submits to the discipline of a healthy life and the next moment de-

26. Compare G. E. M. Anscombe, "Thought and Action in Aristotle", pp. 70–71.
27. Anscombe says this about the difference between finite and infinite ends: "The reck-
oning what to do or abstain from in particular circumstances will constantly include reference, implicit or explicit, to generalities. [. . .] Because of it human conduct is not left to be
distinguished from the behavior of other animals by the fact that in it calculation is used by
which to ascertain the means to perfectly particular ends. The human wants things like
health and happiness and science and fair repute and virtue and prosperity, he does not
simply want, e.g., that such-and-such a thing should be in such-and-such a place at such-
and-such a time" ("Authority in Morals", p. 48).

light in seeing himself under a Genetian ideal of expenditure. Such momentary thoughts do not represent one's infinite ends, but are wishful thinking or vain declaration.

Desires are impotent to explain an ongoing action, since they are changeable states. An infinite end, by contrast, is neither a state, nor is it a movement. It is time-general and thus manifests itself throughout an action and up to its end. In this way an infinite end contains the whole temporal extension of actions it explains. Infinite ends have the right temporality to be the principle of progress of an action.

Practical Life-Form

An instrumental syllogism answers the question what to do on the basis of another answer to this question. It follows that there must be a different way of answering the question, which yet gives something that has the right temporality of a principle of action and thus reveals a measure that can define the practical question. Now we found a way of answering our question that satisfies this description: thinking such-and-such is something to do upon seeing that it manifests an infinite end to which one adheres. Infinite ends are the order that defines the question what to do. More precisely, the order of this question is an *objective unity of infinite ends*, which we shall call a *practical life-form*.

It transpires that not infinite ends, but a unity of infinite ends is the order that defines our question, when we consider this: I want to be healthy, which means, among other things, that I protect myself from untoward weather. I also want to be just, and thus keep my promises. "I protect myself" and "I do what I have promised" are habitual, time-general thoughts; they represent me as adhering to certain infinite ends. Now suppose that on a particular occasion I can keep a promise only by exposing myself to hours of rain. It appears I should do one thing in the light of one end, another thing in the light of another end. But then I cannot reason from an infinite end to an action. I want to be X and thus do A; I want to be Y and thus do B. Since I may, in a given case, fail to do B if I do A, and vice versa, I cannot establish that I should do A on the ground that in doing it I would fall under a concept that describes me as someone who wants X. If I could, I could by the same form of reasoning establish that I should do B. But a valid form of reasoning does not yield incompatible results. So even if I do A (habitual aspect), X being my infinite end, I cannot infer that such-and-such is a good thing to do from the premise that thereby I would do *A*.

It might seem to follow from these reflections that I can never reason from an infinite end to an action. I must weigh the end against others. When, for example, keeping a promise might endanger my health, I arrive at an action, thinking, for example: "I should do *A* with regard to my health. I should do *B* with regard to justice. I attach more importance to justice than to health. Hence, all things considered, I should do *B*. Let me do *B*." I speak elliptically when I say that I intend to do *B* because I promised to do it. A complete statement of my ground would determine the desirability of my action with respect not only to justice, but to a totality of ranked infinite ends. This totality defines the question what to do that I ask.

This view will appear natural to someone who, like Davidson, does not distinguish principles and desires by their logical form. Indeed, the view rests on a failure to recognize this distinction. The predicative nexus of subject and infinite end is time-general. But the predicative nexus of a subject and a totality of ranked infinite ends is not. Since a ranking of ends is to be the order under which practical reasoning proceeds, practical reasoning imposes no limits on the possibilities for changes of the ranking. It follows that it does not characterize the *form* of practical reasoning that the same ranking may manifest itself at various times, in movements represented in the past and the present tense, and through the progressive and the perfective aspect.[28] As the nexus of a subject and a ranking of ends is not progressive either—a ranking does not contain a measure of completion, it has no proper terminus—*a ranking of infinite ends is a changeable state;* judgments representing it, made at different times, invariably are different judgments, even if they have the same content. Thus placing infinite ends within the scope of a subjective ranking is assigning to them the logical character of desires. Our argument that desires do not have the right temporality to be the ground of an answer to the question what to do, which must be capable of issuing in an action, applies to ranked infinite ends, as these are desires.

The idea that the order to which the question what to do refers is a totality of ranked infinite ends of her who is asking the question is, anyway,

---

28. I am grateful to Matthew Boyle for suggesting to me the possibility of an argument of this shape.

absurd. A system of ranked infinite ends, if there were such a thing, would be a *subjective unity* in the sense that the unity of the ends of a subject would consist in the fact that she happens to hold them. An explanation why the ends have come together in her would have to look beyond the ends themselves; we might explain that she grew up in a society that prizes such ends. If two people have the same ends, they could not account for this congruence by reflecting on their shared ends. An explanation of their agreement, if there were one, would refer to materials external to their practical thought. We have grown up in the same village, they might say. So the view entails that each subject has her own order to which she implicitly refers in asking what to do. There is no community of practical thought among subjects: no two people ever share a practical thought. This destroys the idea of a wrong infinite end. When I say, e.g., that you should not seek to outdo others and that this should not be your end, I employ an imperative we have not explained; neither your nor my system of ends defines its meaning. It is sometimes thought a consolation that we can yet bestow honorific titles upon this sublime imperative, calling it, perhaps, a moral imperative or the ought of reason. This does not change the fact that the imperative is *practically irrelevant,* as, ex hypothesi, no one employs it in thinking about what to do.[29]

Some will think this absurd; others will think it true. We cannot think together practically, critique of infinite ends is empty, it presupposes a religious framework in which we have lost faith: so they preach. But our reflections show that the subjective account of the unity of infinite ends not only excludes practical unity of subjects, but undermines the unity of *a* subject. The weight someone assigns to a certain end may change at any time, as nothing in the nature of such weighing singles out any duration as proper to it. And on the present account, the subject before and the subject after the change share no practical thought in common. But then the

29. Candace Vogler wonders why one should want to call the vicious man irrational if one can express one's disapprobation by calling him vicious (*Reasonably Vicious,* pp. 194–195, 199, 201). But "irrational" signifies the form of the reproach, not its content; it says that the relevant "you should not" employs the imperative of the addressee's practical reasoning. The point is not that one wants to call the vicious man irrational *in addition to* calling him vicious, as if that made him worse and were harder to take. It is that thought of virtue and vice must be *practical.* If no practical order joins me and you—if no shared order defines the sense of "to do" in which we think about what to do—then "vicious" and "virtuous" either bear different senses in your mouth and mine or do not figure in practical reasoning.

alleged subject is one of which no action can be predicated, for she thinks no *progressive* practical thought, which may be the principle of the progress of an action.

If the unity of infinite ends were subjective, principles would be desires. Davidson assigns the same logical form to principles and desires because he has no concept of an objective unity of principles, and hence no concept of a principle. The necessary, and necessarily represented, unity of infinite ends must be an objective unity, a unity that is internal to its elements. We find an explication of the objective unity of infinite ends in John McDowell's "Virtue and Reason". He discusses the infinite ends of the virtuous man, but his argument does not depend on the content of virtue; we can read it as employing a formal notion of virtue equivalent to our concept of an infinite end. Then his argument says that infinite ends exhibit a unity in virtue of their *form of generality:* a unity of ends is implicit in the relation of *instantiation* that actions bear to infinite ends they manifest.

An infinite end is described in time-general statements about someone who adheres to it: she who is *X* does *A, B, C;* the concepts *A, B, C* articulate the content of *X*. But it is not sufficient to recognize that one would fall under one of these concepts in doing something in order to ascertain that it is good to do. For, an incompatible action may fall under a concept that articulates another infinite end. This need not mean that one can never reason from an infinite end to an action (as thought by those who postulate a subjective ranking of ends). It may mean that manifesting an infinite end is more than falling under a concept that articulates this end.[30] McDowell argues that, in order to ascertain what to do, it does not suffice to establish that in doing such-and-such one would fall under a concept that articulates a certain infinite end. In addition, one must ascertain that this end bears on the situation here and now. Consider again the case in which I can keep my promise only by exposing myself to hours of rain. When I say I should keep out of the rain for the sake of my health, I not only state that in keeping out of the rain I fall under a concept that describes the actions of someone who cares about his health. I also represent health as the end that pertains here and now. As McDowell puts it, I recognize the danger to my health, not the disregard of my promise, as

30. Compare John McDowell's critique of "the deductive paradigm", "Virtue and Reason", §§4–5. See also "The Role of *Eudaimonia* in Aristotle's Ethics", pp. 17–18 and note 24.

salient. Thus I do not calculate from relative values I assign to health and justice. I do not assign a merely relative value to either; I do not think that health is more important than justice.[31] When I recognize the demands of health to be pertinent here and now, I do not compromise my love of justice. I am not acting according to a concept that describes what it is to be just, but this need not mean that I fail to be just. It does not mean that if the end of justice does not bear on the situation.

When an action falls under a concept that articulates an infinite end that does not bear on the situation here and now, then it falls under the concept, but does not manifest the end. Instantiating a concept does not suffice for manifesting an infinite end. An infinite end X manifests itself in my doing A only if X bears on the situation. And only then is it true that I should do A for the sake of X. So it must be, if an infinite end is to be a source of answers to the question what to do. For, this requires that representing an action as manifesting an infinite end is representing it as good, as in accord with the order of the question what to do. This describes the *form of generality* of infinite ends, i.e., the relevant relation of instantiation. In virtue of this form of generality, an infinite end contains a reference to a unity of infinite ends. That an action cannot manifest one's being X and yet manifest one's failure to be Y, if X and Y are infinite ends, defines a sense in which X and Y are *one* thing, a thing that may be described as X and as Y and is manifested in actions that manifest X as well as in actions that manifest Y. We shall call such a thing a *practical life-form* in view of a logical analogy. Statements that describe an animal life-form form a system the principle of which is the life-form they describe; judgments that describe an animal as exemplifying a form of behavior characteristic of its life-form presuppose a grasp of this life-form as a unity of forms of behavior.[32] On the current account, infinite ends form a system in this way: thoughts that represent an action as exemplifying an infinite end presuppose a grasp of a unity of infinite ends because an action manifests an infinite end if and only if it manifests the practical life-form that includes this end.

31. Indeed, on the present account, it is unclear what that would mean. It could mean that there may be situations when demands of health are salient and requirements of justice do not pertain, or it could mean that the demands of health eclipse the requirements of justice in any situation. On the first rendering, health would be both more and less important than justice; on the second, it would be neither.

32. See Michael Thompson, "The Representation of Life".

A practical life-form is included in the infinite ends that are its elements as the form of their generality: an action manifests an infinite end only if it manifests the practical life-form of which it is a part. In contrast to subjective rankings, a practical life-form is an objective unity: an account of infinite ends includes an account of their unity as aspects of a practical life-form. Therefore, an explanation why ends gathered in a practical life-form have come together in a subject need not reach beyond the ends themselves; their unity transpires from any one of them. People sharing a practical life-form who find themselves with the same infinite ends can explain this by reflecting on their ends. So a practical life-form underwrites community of practical thought of its bearers and it makes room for the possibility of wrong infinite end thoughts, as these presume to represent a practical life-form, which they might misrepresent.

We seek the sense of the question what to do that is answered by an instrumental syllogism, which we said would transpire from the mode of answering that question that represents an action as manifesting an infinite end. We found that, in ascertaining what to do by deriving an action from an infinite end, I represent the action as manifesting my practical life-form. The order of the question what to do is the practical life-form of her who poses it.

Conclusion

In the beginning of this section, we listed kinds of things one might think interpret the question what to do on an occasion of its being asked: a finite end, a totality of desires, a rational life-form, reason itself. We excluded the first possibility in the first subsection, the second in the second. What we said does not decide between the third and the fourth. While a rational life-form exhibits the logical characteristics of a practical life-form, so does reason itself, if it is the order of practical reasoning. We shall return to this in Chapter 6.

We have nothing to say on the content of our practical life-form—if we all fall under the same one and share a sense of the question what to do. Knowledge of the content of a practical life-form comes, not from reflection on the form of practical reasoning, but from practical reasoning the imperative of which is interpreted by that practical life-form. Thus we would need to reflect on the content of our practical thought in order to describe our practical life-form substantially. This would lead us away from our topic, which is the nexus of action and self-consciousness.

Acting and the Question What to Do

We have described a system of forms of answering the question what to do and specified the logical form of its principle: a practical life-form. In this section, we shall argue that an action *is* its subject's answer to this question; it is the conclusion of her practical reasoning. From this it follows, so we shall see in the third section, that there is a special way of knowing one's own actions.

In *Intention*, G. E. M. Anscombe explains the concept of intentional action in terms of a form of explanation, or sense of the question "why?", which she defines by describing ways of answering this sense of the question. Intentional actions, she writes, "are the actions to which a certain sense of the question 'why?' is given application." And: "This question 'why?' can now be defined as the question expecting an answer in this range. And with this we have roughly outlined the area of intentional action."[33] Let us call an explanation of the relevant form an "action explanation". An action explanation not just explains something that is an action, but what it explains is an action in virtue of receiving this kind of explanation. In the next section we shall see that this form of explanation, action explanation, which the concept of intentional action designates, contains the first person reference of the acting subject. In order to bring this out, we develop in this section the nexus of practical reasoning and action explanation.

The Place of Practical Reasoning in Action Explanation

Anscombe delimits the question "why?" that asks for an action explanation by a list of ways of answering it. She does not explain how these spring from a principle and constitute a system. Thus she fails to establish that they define one sense of "why?", and thus one concept of action, as opposed to many. Now, the principle of the relevant question "why?"— the principle of action explanation—transpires when we reflect on the nexus of intentional action and practical reasoning. Practical reasoning is

33. *Intention,* pp. 9 and 28.

practical in that it arrives at an action. It may remain idle; I may decide to do something and yet never do it. Yet it is the kind of reasoning that issues in action. Now when, thinking I *should do A* because ____, I arrive at an action, then I not only think this, I *do A* because ____. That practical reasoning arrives at an action means at least that a ground for thinking that such-and-such is good to do is the kind of thing that may explain why someone is doing it. What fills the blank in "I should do *A* because ____" is capable of filling the blank in "I am doing *A* because ____". This specifies a *kind of reasoning:* practical reasoning. Inverted, it characterizes a *kind of explanation:* that which in the intended manner explains why someone is doing something is the kind of thing in the light of which she may apprehend it as good. While practical reasoning is reasoning that arrives at an action, an action is a movement at which reasoning arrives. Thus a condition by which reasoning is practical is, read in the other direction, a condition by which explanation is of action. Reasoning arrives at an action and is practical if that on account of which the subject thinks she should do something explains why she is doing it. Conversely, an explanation of why someone is doing something represents her movement as resting on thought and is an action explanation if the cause given is something on account of which she thinks it something to be done. So the same system which, looked at from one side, is the system of answers to the question what to do of practical reasoning is, seen from the other side, the system of answers to the question "why?" of action explanation.

Anscombe reports that she found, after she had described the order of action explanation, that it was the same as the order of practical reasoning that Aristotle describes. This does not mean that the two descriptions of this order, as of practical reasoning and as of action explanation, can be given in isolation. Our derivation of forms of answering the question what to do relied on the idea that practical reasoning arrives at an action, wherefore we fully understand the "because" of practical reasoning—"I should do *A* because ____"—and the nature of its conclusion, a thought about what to do, only as we understand this idea. Conversely, an account of action explanation shows how such explanations represent a movement as resting on thought. Hence, it is only through comprehending its connection with practical reasoning that we understand the "because" of action explanation—"I am doing *A* because ____", and the kind of movement it explains, intentional action.

Let us consider, then, how practical reasoning figures in the causality of action explanation. When an action is arrived at by reasoning, then that which explains why the subject is doing what she is doing is something in the light of which she thinks it good. *The same thing* is the cause of her doing it and the ground of her thinking that she should do it. This identity is *no accident*; rather, it characterizes the *form* of action explanation.

In order to see what this means, it will be helpful to consider a case in which the cause of a movement and that on account of which its subject thinks it good have come together per accidens. Someone is falling ill because he wants to lose weight. It may be that he did something with the result of falling ill and did it in order to lose weight, in which case the explanation is like: "His house is on fire because he wants the money from the insurance." But it may also be that his falling ill is caused by his desire to lose weight in a manner not mediated by his doing something toward this end: he has been wanting to lose weight for a long time, nothing he tried worked, finally his anxiety manifests itself in somatic symptoms, his digestive system revolts, and he loses weight. He might be so desperate as to think he should fall ill. "I want to lose weight. I shall if I fall ill. It would be good if I fell ill", he might think. So he is falling ill because he wants to lose weight, and he thinks he should fall ill because he will lose weight in consequence. Yet, the explanation is no action explanation: it does not represent his falling ill as an intentional action; his falling ill is not intentional on account of receiving this explanation.[34]

Someone who thinks he should do *A* because he wants to do *B* may yet do *A* because he wants to do *B* without doing it intentionally. Donald Davidson seeks to say what is missing:

> Wanting to do something of type *x* may cause someone to do something of type *x*, and yet the causal chain may operate in such a manner that the act is not intentional. [. . .] Beliefs and desires that would rationalize an action if they caused it in the *right* way— through a course of practical reasoning, as we might try saying—may cause it in other ways. ("Freedom to Act", p. 79)

---

34. Perhaps this is because falling ill is something that happens, as opposed to something one does, wherefore one cannot speak of it as something one should do? But we cannot stipulate that the values of "do *A*" in "should do *A*" be confined to actions. We seek to describe a form of thought that so restricts the values of the variable. If we want to elucidate the distinction of doing something intentionally from having things happen to one in terms of a form of explanation, we must not rely on this distinction in describing this form.

Describing the right way of causing is describing the "because", or the "why?", of action explanation.[35] Davidson imagines "we might try saying" that the relevant causality consists in "a course of practical reasoning". We shall indeed try to say that, and try to say what it means.

Consider him who is falling ill because he wants to lose weight in the way we imagined: nothing works, great anxiety, and so on. And suppose he thinks he will lose weight on account of his illness. Now, it is not necessary that he think this in order for it to be true that he is falling ill because he wants to lose weight. By contrast, an *action explanation* "She is doing *A* because she wants to do *B*" is true only of someone who thinks that doing *A* is a means of doing *B* and to be done on that account. The same holds of explanations in terms of the representation of an infinite end. "She is doing *A* because she promised to do it" is an action explanation only if she thinks that, in doing *A*, she is keeping her promise. (We could devise a story in which someone did *A* because she promised, thought she should do *A* on that account, and yet did not do *A* intentionally, as her thought was external to the truth of the explanation.) So an action explanation is true only of someone thinking a certain thought. This is not an empirical fact, but a feature of this form of explanation. It does not so happen that someone who is doing *A* because she wants to do *B* in this sense of "because" can be relied on to think that her action is leading up to her doing *B* and is therefore and to that extent good. Rather, that she thinks this *is the same reality* as that described in explaining that she is doing *A* because she wants to do *B*. In the same way, it does not so happen, by coincidence or friendly disposition, that someone who is doing *A* because she promised to do it thinks she is keeping her promise. If this is an action explanation, then her thought is contained in the fact that the explanation represents. Of course, she who thinks that doing *A* is a step toward doing *B*, need not be doing *A* because she wants to do *B*, and she who thinks that doing *A* is keeping her promise may not be doing it on that account. It may be that no explanatory nexus links her action to her want or her promise, or none that involves this

35. Donald Davidson is wrong in thinking that his incapacity to spell out the right form of causation is due to ignorance of empirical fact. (Compare "Freedom to Act," p. 80: "To improve on this formulation in turn, in a way that would eliminate wrong causal chains, would also eliminate the need to depend on an open appeal to causal relations. [. . .] Unavoidable mention of causality is a cloak for ignorance; we must appeal to the notion of cause when we lack detailed and accurate laws." See also "Psychology as Philosophy", pp. 232–233.) We do not seek laws, but a form of explanation. Our problem is logical.

thought. The man who falls ill because he wants to lose weight in the manner we imagined is an example, and we could concoct a story in which a promise acts as a desire to lose weight does in that story. But, *if* someone is doing *A* because she wants to do *B*, and this answers Anscombe's question "why?", then her instrumental thought constitutes the causality the explanation represents. And *if* someone is doing *A* because she promised to do it, and this is an action explanation, then her thought that she is keeping her promise by doing *A* is the described causal nexus. Her wanting to do *B* and her act of promising cause the action "through a course of practical reasoning", as Davidson rightly suspected "we might try saying".

We said that practical reasoning arrives at an action means at least that a ground on which someone thinks such-and-such is to be done must be the kind of thing to explain why she is doing it. In fact it means more. It means that an action explanation "She is doing *A* because ____", is true only if she who is doing *A* thinks "I should do *A* because ____". If someone is doing *A* because ____, then her thought that she should do it because ____ is the causal nexus that the first "because", the "because" of the action explanation, represents.[36] A way to express this is to say that, in the fundamental case, practical reasoning *concludes in an action*.[37]

At the beginning of the previous section, we considered the attempt to capture the practicality of practical reasoning by saying its conclusion is an action. As an account of practical reasoning, this is unhelpful; under the name of "action", it presupposes the idea of a unity of thought and movement, which is what is to be understood. We comprehend this unity, and with it the idea of a kind of reasoning whose conclusion is a movement, through the unity of action explanation and practical reasoning. When someone is doing *A* intentionally, then what explains why she is doing it is something on account of which she thinks it good to do. And it is not per accidens that the ground of her thinking it good is identical with the cause of her doing it; rather, this identity defines the kind of causality that action

---

36. In "How Theoretical Is Practical Reasoning?" Anselm Winfried Müller observes that practical reasoning is intrinsically for the sake of action in the sense that no thought is needed nor possible that represents it as a means to action as an end. The account of the practicality of practical thought as the causality of action explanation, I think, captures this.

37. Compare Aristotle, *On the Movement of Animals*, 701a17–20: "I need a covering, a coat is a covering: I need a coat. What I need I ought to make, I need a coat: I make a coat. And the conclusion 'I must make a coat' is an action."

explanations represent. And this can be put by saying that an action *is* the acting subject's answer to the question what to do. Of course, someone may think he should do something without doing it, or without doing it intentionally (as he who is falling ill and thinks he should). But if someone's doing something has a true action explanation, then her doing it and her thought that it is good to do are *the same reality.* An action expresses a thought about what to do, not in the sense of being its effect, but in the sense of being this thought. Actions do not point to a state of mind as to their cause. Acting intentionally *is* being of a certain mind.

Empiricist Objections

In the empiricist milieu of contemporary philosophy of action, our account of action explanation as representing a causality of thought, entailing that doing something intentionally is thinking it good,[38] is bound to meet with opposition. We shall discuss certain objections in order to bring out that indeed we radically break with empiricism.

Davidson says that an action is caused by a belief and a desire: someone is doing *A* because he wants to do *B* and because he thinks that doing *A* is a means to this end. Christine Korsgaard observes that this may express an account that is not an action explanation and bears no inner nexus to the concept of action, as when someone is doing *A* because he is "conditioned" to do *A* whenever he wants this and thinks that. She discusses Thomas Nagel's example of someone who "has been conditioned so that whenever he wants a drink and believes the object before him is a pencil sharpener, he wants to put a coin in the pencil sharpener".[39]

---

38. The proposition that intentional action is under the guise of the good has been attacked recently (cf., e.g., David Velleman, "The Guise of the Good", and Kieran Setiya, *Reasons without Rationalism*). The attack does not appreciate the nature of the proposition it attacks: it is a synthetic judgment a priori, describing the form of representation of action, a form of explanation, or kind of causality. In "Goodness and Desire", Matthew Boyle and Doug Lavin mount an effective defense of the guise-of-the-good thesis.—It is sometimes held that the phenomenon of weak will shows that doing something intentionally cannot be thinking it good. It is unnecessary for our purposes, and would be a distraction, to give an account of weakness of the will. Even if it were true that the weak-willed man is doing something intentionally while thinking he should not (which is too simple an account), it would not follow that thought and action are not one when the will is not weak.

39. Thomas Nagel, *The Possibility of Altruism*, pp. 33–34.

Neither the joint causal efficacy of the belief and the desire, nor the existence of an appropriate conceptual connection, nor the bare conjunction of these two facts, enables us to judge that a person acts rationally. For the person to act rationally, she must be motivated by her own recognition of the appropriate conceptual connection between her belief and her desire. We may say that she herself must combine the belief and the desire in the right way. A person acts rationally, then, only when her action is the expression of her own mental activity. ("The Normativity of Instrumental Reason", p. 221)

Now, we must know how the mental activity figures in the account. It may be a further cause. An action would then be an expression of mental activity in the sense of being its effect. However, adding causes does not settle the sense of the "because".[40] Action explanation differs from explanation by "conditioning" not in that, in addition to thought and desire, it cites mental activity as a further cause of the movement. Someone may be conditioned to do A whenever she wants this, believes that, and engages in a certain mental activity. Of course Korsgaard wants a notion of mental activity that renders the last sentence ungrammatical. But she does not explain that notion. In fact, action explanations do not cite further mental causes, but represent a different configuration of thought, will, and action. When we explain that someone is doing A because she wants to do B, and add that she thinks that doing A is a means of doing B, we do not give a further cause; rather, we specify *the kind of causality*. We give the sense of the question "why?" that we answer. If the explanation is true, then the subject's thought constitutes the causal nexus. The causality of the will is thought.

It is common to suppose that actions are movements with special causes, mental states or normative attitudes. An action will then be caused by, but not be, a thought.[41] But the concept of action designates not spe-

40. The idea that there is an irreducible agent causality distinct from event causality registers that it is not possible to identify the "because" of action explanation by special causes. However, the idea is useless because the nexus of subject and action is not causal; the question "why?" is never answered by the name of a subject. The nexus is predicative; the concept of intentional action designates a form of predication.

41. Consider, e.g., Robert Brandom: "Action depends on reliable dispositions to respond differentially to the acknowledging of certain sorts of commitments [...] by bringing about various kinds of states of affairs. A competent agent [...] responds to the acquisition of a commitment to flip the light switch by flipping the light switch" (*Making It*

cial causes, but a kind of causality. It designates a causal nexus that is thinking. Now, if one takes "thinking" to refer to mental events or processes, then one will not be able to conceive of thought as anything but a cause. However, while saying something—the sensory appearance of thinking—is an event, thinking something is not. Cato said many times that Carthago was to be destroyed. This does not show that there is more than one act of thinking he expressed on all of these occasions.[42] We shall say more about the temporality of thinking in the next chapter. Here it suffices to note that when we say that she who is doing A because she wants to do B thinks a thought connecting the terms of the explanation, we do not say that something is going on in her mind while she is acting. We do not speak of what occupies her mind. She may be contemplating the cosmic order or be dreaming of her lover while she is doing A. Her instrumental thought may appear in her saying to herself, "Now I need to do A because ____". But it may appear in countless other ways, for example in her answer to the question "why?" or in her ceasing to do A when it is pointed out to her that it does not help her attain her end. Reasoning is representing items as ordered as ground to grounded, and "representing", here, does not signify an event or episode.[43]

It may seem extravagant to speak of kinds of causality, especially of a causality that is thought. But it is an extravagance of a different order altogether to believe in a causality that bears no inner nexus to ways of an-

Explicit, p. 235). According to Brandom, someone is doing something intentionally if and only if her doing it manifests a disposition to do something whenever she undertakes a commitment to do it. So a movement is an action if its subject thinks it good and if it is caused by her thinking this, a suitable disposition underlying the causality. Within the class of movements thus circumscribed, we find those of Nagel's madman and of the man who falls ill from his desire to lose weight. (We can expand the stories to include reference to a disposition.) Brandom says, "That a practical commitment elicits a performance by the exercise of such dispositions is another way of putting the condition on action that the performance not only be caused by the intention but be caused by it 'in the right way'" (*Making It Explicit*, p. 261). This seems false. It is no part of the concept of a reliable disposition that explanations in terms of it represent its acts as intentional actions.

42. That thought is distinct from its appearance in speech does not exclude that it is essential to human thought so to appear.

43. G. E. M. Anscombe suggests that "reasoning" is not a psychological verb in the sense that it does not describe mental motions ("Practical Inference", pp. 3–4). This is not to deny that there are episodes of reasoning, or silent soliloquy. The point is that, speaking of someone as, e.g., resting one thought upon another, we speak of something that need not manifest itself in such an episode. What we say is not disproved if there is no such episode.

swering the question "why?". A cause is a "because", and until a sense of "because" (a sense of "why?") is specified, talk about causes is empty. One may stipulate that only answers to a certain sense of the question "why?" give causes. But then one must not confuse terminological legislation with metaphysical insight.[44]

It is often maintained, and more often implied, that only causes in a certain restricted sense of "because", which joins an event to a subsequent event according to a law or disposition, are the *real* explanation of what happens. When action explanation is forced into this mold, it is distinguished by content, not by form, by its causes, not by its causality.[45] But the causality represented by action explanations, a causality of thought, is metaphysically fundamental, for it is internal to its terms. As Anscombe observes, most concepts of what may be done intentionally would be empty if they did not figure in action explanations.[46] Let us call these action concepts, in analogy to substance concepts: concepts that depend on the form of thought that the concept of substance signifies. As "man" is a substance concept, so is "making breakfast" an action concept. It is no accident that there are concepts such as "man", whose sense depends on the form of thought that the concept of substance signifies. Just so, it is no ac-

---

44. Donald Davidson confuses the ordinary with a restricted sense of "cause" in "Actions, Reasons, Causes". He observes that a reason may be "the because" of an action—"If [. . .] causal explanations are 'wholly irrelevant to the understanding we seek' of human action [. . .] then we are without an analysis of the 'because' in 'He did it because . . . ' where we go on to name a reason" (p. 11)—and infers that an action and its cause fall under a physical law (pp. 15–17). Richard Moran writes: "The basic point can be expressed in a loosely Kantian style, although the idea is hardly unique to Kant. The stance from which a person speaks with any special authority about his belief or his action is not a stance of causal explanation but the stance of rational agency. [. . .] Anscombe's question 'why?' is not asking for what might best explain the movement that constitutes the agent's action, but instead is asking for the reasons he takes to justify his action" (*Authority and Estrangement*, p. 127). This way of expressing the point is un-Kantian and unhappy. The opposition of causes and reasons is as foreign to Kant as the opposition of explanation and justification is to Anscombe. Anscombe holds that rational agency manifests itself in movements that fall under a special form of explanation, or, as Kant puts it, exhibit a special kind of causality.

45. There is a vague idea that this view is demanded by, and expresses, proper respect for the sciences. In fact it shows poor respect for the sciences to represent them as a source of metaphysical dogma.

46. *Intention*, §49. There is reason to doubt that there can be concepts of action that are not action concepts. For our part, we would be prepared to delete the word "most" from the sentence to which this note is attached. We need not pursue this, though, because Anscombe's weaker claim is sufficient for our purposes.

cident that there are movement concepts to which the form of thought that the concept of action designates is internal. If there were not, the relevant form would not get a grip on what is and what happens, since nothing the apprehension of which does not involve the deployment of a given form of thought can justify its application.[47] This holds of forms of thought and formal concepts generally. For any form of thought, there is a range of material concepts to which that form is internal.

This may be thought to be a verbal point, pertaining to the description, not to the reality of action. Perhaps it is impossible to describe a movement *as* making breakfast unless it figures in action explanations. But the same movement may be available through other concepts whose sense does not depend on this form of explanation.[48] However, we saw in the subsection on desire that an action concept is not a classification defined upon an independently constituted domain. It signifies the principle of temporal unity of its instances.[49] As an action is no aggregate, but rather a unity of phases, instances of an action concept are apprehended only through it, the principle of that unity. Even if one could apprehend all the phases of someone's making breakfast without employing action concepts, one would not thereby apprehend her making breakfast. For, one could not raise the question whether the phases had come together per accidens or on account of her deploying the concept of making breakfast in instrumental reasoning. And only in the latter case would she be making breakfast. (Remember him who was walking from *a* to *b,* and was walking from *b* to *c,* but never was walking from *a* to *c.*) Hence, bereft of action explanation, and with it of action concepts, we would not be giving different explanations of the same movements. We would not be confronted with the movements that action explanations explain. Conversely, with action explanation, we can explain why someone is, e.g., making breakfast, explaining all the phases of her action. We thus give the true explanation of these, as they are phases of her making breakfast.

The unity of thought and movement in action is metaphysical, not verbal. There will be those who are tempted to think that the reason why

47. As Immanuel Kant observes in *Kritik der reinen Vernunft,* §13.

48. This idea is a crucial component of Donald Davidson's argument for Anomalous Monism in "Mental Events".

49. This holds true of movement concepts, i.e., concepts whose predication is informed by a contrast of progressive and perfective aspect, in general. See my *Kategorien des Zeitlichen,* chap. 5.

she who is acting intentionally thinks an appropriate thought is that we impute to her such a thought when we *count* her movement *as* an action, while we would not so count it if she did not think this thought. This presupposes that there are substances and movements, apprehended otherwise than through action explanation, some of which substances are classified as subjects and some of which movements are classified as actions, as they are brought under this form. And this denies the validity of the concept of intentional action in the way in which Hume denied the validity of the concept of substance: by representing the unity that the formal concept makes explicit as imposed on a reality to which it is external in the sense that apprehending this reality does not require deploying the corresponding form of thought. Now, if the concept of substance is not valid, then neither is any substance concept; analogously, if the concept of intentional action is not valid, then neither is any action concept. But what allegedly was counted as an action is apprehended only through action concepts. Since they depend on action explanation, there is in general no step from apprehending a movement to knowing it to be an action, thus no space for an act of counting the movement as an action.[50]

A theory that conceives of intentionality as a feature picking out a class from an independently constituted domain of movements takes the following as given: something is moving in accordance with a concept—x is doing A—and deploys that concept in thought—x thinks [. . . do A . . .]. The theory explains the concept of intentional action by a predicate joining

---

50. I take it that this is Anscombe's point in *Intention*, §4: "The greater number of the things which you would say straight off a man did or was doing, will be things he intends. [. . .] I am sitting in a chair writing, and anyone grown to the age of reason in the same world would know this as soon as he saw me, and in general it would be the first account of what I was doing."—Concepts of wanting and intending, of practical commitment and thinking one should do something, depend on action explanation as well. It is internal to these notions that someone's wanting or intending to do B (his being committed to doing it or thinking it good) is capable of explaining why he is doing A in a way that includes his thought that, in doing A, he is making progress toward having done B. (Cf. Michael Thompson's definition of wanting in "Naïve Action Theory".) Of course, his wanting to do something may explain in a different way, as when he is falling ill because he wants to lose weight, or when he has acquired a disposition to do certain things whenever he has certain beliefs and desires. Here the explaining term is not understood as wanting in virtue of the form of the explanation. Such explanations depend on the deployment of the same concept in action explanations. We no longer understand the phrases "wanting to do A" or "thinking it good to do A" if we abstract from their use in this form of explanation.

these materials: INT(. . . x is doing A, x thinks [. . . do A . . .] . . .). The predicate is to represent a relation that obtains between the mind of a subject and her movement, her thought and what happens, when she is acting intentionally. A agreeably simple account of "INT" would be: it describes the subject's doing A as an act of a disposition to do what she thinks is good to do.[51] Naturally, there is no limit to the complexity that counterexamples will bring to accounts of "INT". All such theories fail because the concepts on which they rely—instances of the schema "do A"—depend on action explanation. And when an action explanation is true, then the subject's thought about what to do need not be linked to what happens; *it is what happens*.[52] If doing A is an action concept, then it cannot be necessary, e.g., to be disposed to do A in response to thinking it good to do A in order to do it intentionally. The disposition would come too late; if it were needed, the concept of doing A would be empty.[53] If someone asks what to do and exemplifies action concepts, then some of her movements have action explanations. And when they do, her thought that what she is doing is good to do is her doing it. It is impossible to isolate what happens when someone is acting intentionally from the mind of the acting subject.

Action and Self-Consciousness

Actions fall under a form of explanation such that she who is acting thinks what she is doing is to be done. We will see that this entails that, if a movement can be explained in this way, its subject is able thus to explain it. From this it follows in turn that she expresses action explanations by a first person pronoun. When she does, she states knowledge not from observation, but from practical reasoning, which way of knowing sustains her first person reference. In this manner, self-consciousness, action, and practical reasoning are internally related.

51. Compare Robert Brandom, *Making It Explicit,* as quoted in note 41.

52. We are echoing G. E. M. Anscombe, *Intention,* "I *do* what *happens*" (p. 52).

53. Our reflections cast doubt on the coherence of the notion of language-exit that Robert Brandom inherits from Wilfrid Sellars. What allegedly exits language and thought is contained within it. If this is true, then language and thought are something very different from what Brandom and Sellars believe. In *Mind and World,* John McDowell aims to undermine the analogous notion of a language-entry by arguing that, if reliable dispositions were needed to tie beliefs to the sensible world, they would come too late, for then the concept of belief would be empty.

The First Person Nature of Action Explanation

If a movement has an action explanation, then its subject thinks a thought that constitutes the causal nexus that the explanation represents. If, for example, she is doing *A* because she wants to do *B*, then she thinks doing *A* is a step toward doing *B* and to be done on that account. Now consider the subject herself, explaining why she is doing *A* and reasoning that it is to be done. It may seem that there is her thought, "I am doing *A* because I want to do *B*", which *represents* the causal nexus, and her thought, "I should do *A* because I want to do *B*", which *is* the causal nexus. In fact, there is but one thought: the thought that represents the causality is the thought that is the causality. In the acting subject, reasoning toward and explaining the action are *one act of the mind*. In order to see this, we must again reflect on what it means that practical thought is the causality as opposed to a cause of action or, equivalently, that it characterizes the form as opposed to the content of action explanation.

An action explanation "She is doing *A* because she wants to do *B*" is true only if the subject thinks doing *A* is a means of doing *B*. It may seem that this must mean that the fact that she thinks this is part of the content of the explanation. In this case, if she herself were to explain, "I am doing *A* because I want to do *B*", she would *assert*, among other things, *that she thinks* that doing *A* is a means of doing *B*. But her explaining why she is doing *A* would not *be* her thinking that. However, we said the thought is *not* part of the content of the explanation; rather, it defines its form. In order to see what this means, consider a simple case of a form of thought. We describe the form of a thought *Fa,* i.e., the manner in which it conjoins *a* and *F,* when we say that it brings an *object* under a *concept;* the relevant form is *Fregean predication.* When we say that *a* is an object, we describe the matter of the thought as constituted in such a way as to be thought in this way: as the logical subject of a Fregean predication. And apprehending someone as thinking *Fa,* we apprehend *a* to be of a logical nature that permits this way of thinking it; that is, we apprehend it to be an object. Like "Fregean predication", "action explanation" signifies a form. The subject's practical thought linking the terms of the explanation defines this form. Its logical analogue is the copula, not any part of the predicate. That is, the subject's doing *A* because she wants to do *B* includes her thinking that doing *A* is a means of doing *B*, not because the explanation contains further material over and above doing *A* and doing

B, but because it is by her thinking this that that material is such as to be thought in this manner: in action explanation. Again, when we apprehend someone thinking, "She is doing *A* because she wants to do *B*", we apprehend what she thinks as such as to be thought in this way, and that is, here, we apprehend doing *A* as represented by the acting subject as a means to her end of doing *B*. Now consider what this entails when the subject herself explains that she is doing *A* because she wants to do *B*. The logical character of her doing *A* in virtue of which it is thus thought involves her taking it to be a means of doing *B*. Apprehending her thinking, "I am doing *A* because I want to do *B*", we apprehend doing *A* as of the right logical nature to figure in this thought, and that is, we apprehend her thinking that *A* is good to do, as it serves her end of doing *B*. Hence, apprehending her thinking the former *is* apprehending her thinking the latter. We apprehend her thinking but *one* thought.

We reach the same result from the side of the normative thought. In the case we are considering, the acting subject's thought that *A* is good to do because it serves her end of doing *B* is a causal nexus of its terms. This is no part of the content of that normative thought; it characterizes the manner of thinking, the mode in which, thinking this, the subject joins doing *A* and doing *B*. But what does that mean? Consider again our simple example. She who thinks *Fa* ipso actu thinks that the object *a* falls under the concept *F*. To be sure, it requires reflection to grasp this, in the course of which suitable words, such as "object" and "concept", will be introduced. But what this reflection reveals is that thinking *Fa is* thinking that the object *a* falls under the concept *F*. That reflection is necessary to see this does not make that two thoughts. Analogously, she who thinks that doing *A* is a means of doing *B*, when her thinking this is the causality of an action explanation, apprehends doing *A* as bearing the logical character to be thought in this manner. And this means she apprehends herself as doing *A* because she wants to do *B*; for, this characterizes the manner in which her practical thought joins these materials. So again, her thinking the former *is* her thinking the latter.

"I am doing *A* because I want to do *B*" and "I should do *A* because I want to do *B*" express one act of thought—if the former is true and an action explanation. In the first section, we found that "I should do *A*" and "I want to do *A*" exhibit the same form of predication, "I * do *A*". The unity of action explanation and practical reasoning is the source of a third guise of this form: "I am doing *A*". We shall now find that what bears this form is known in a first person manner.

"I should do *A* because I want to do *B*" and "I am doing *A* because I want to do *B*" express the same thought. According to the preceding section, the acting subject thinks this thought if the explanation is true. So if someone's doing something has an action explanation, then she is in a position to give it. The causality represented by action explanations contains the subject's representation *of this very causality*. Such explanations, then, when given by the subject, satisfy the formula of first person knowledge: a subject is able to give the explanation by being its object. This means that action explanations by the acting subject deploy the first person pronoun and are unmediated first person thoughts. Compare a case in which thought and movement are externally related, as in the case of the man who is falling ill because he wants to lose weight. He may be able to give this explanation, but need not be able to give it in order for it to be true. Subject and object of the explanation are identical only per accidens, so that their identity is the content of *a separate judgment*. By contrast, if someone gives an action explanation of why she herself is doing something, then the identity of the moving subject with the explaining subject follows from *the form* of the explanation. So there is no space for an identity judgment and the explanation is given from the first person perspective. A first person thought represents the thinking subject as the object of which she thinks, and since the form of an action explanation settles it that it satisfies this description when it is given by the acting subject, its first person character pertains to it originally and need not be conferred on it by an identity judgment.

The Way of Knowing Actualized in First Person Action Explanation

It is easy to characterize in the abstract the knowledge-providing relationship with an object that underwrites first person thought: it is identity. But, so we asked, how does one know an object when one knows it by being it, and how does being an object enable one to think about it? We said that, in order to answer this question, we must investigate concepts predicated in the relevant manner, first among them concepts of thought, and in the present chapter practical thought, or action.

It is often said that one knows what one is doing intentionally without observation, which suggests that such knowledge is first personal. Anscombe writes:

Certainly in modern philosophy we have an incorrigibly contemplative conception of knowledge. Knowledge must be something that is
judged as such by being in accordance with the facts. The facts, reality, are prior, and dictate what is to be said. And this is the explanation of the utter darkness in which we found ourselves. For if there
are two knowledges—one by observation, the other in intention—
then it looks as if there must be two objects of knowledge; but if one
says the objects are the same, one looks hopelessly for the different
mode of contemplative knowledge in acting, as if there were a very
queer and special sort of seeing eye in the middle of the acting. (*Intention*, p. 57)

The darkness of which Anscombe speaks is the darkness that occludes first
person reference. First person reference is tied to a kind of knowledge that
differs from perception more radically than the postulation of special
modes of awareness can account for. But we cannot rest content with a
negative description—without observation. This tells us only that reference to the object as known in this way is not demonstrative; but we want
to know how one refers to an object first personally, how one knows it in
unmediated first person thought.

Part of the answer must lie in the nature of action, and since the concept of intentional action designates a form of thought, action explanation, it must transpire from an inquiry into this form. And so it does. In
action explanation, the cause of the action is, at the same time, and not
per accidens, something from which its subject reasons to the conclusion
that it is good. Since that conclusion expresses the same thought as the "I
am doing *A*" of her action explanation, it follows that *the cause of her action is the ground of her knowledge of her action*. What a true action explanation gives as the *ratio essendi* of the action is at the same time the subject's *ratio cognoscendi* of her action. Her knowledge that and why she is
doing *A*, which her action explanation articulates, does not come from *observing what she is doing*. It comes from *ascertaining what to do*. First
person knowledge is not from the senses, but from thought.

But does not reflection about what to do conclude only in wanting or
intending to do something? Whether I am in fact doing what I intend to
do depends on whether I have the power to do it. It is *no accident* that I
am doing what I intend to do only if I know how to do it, and only then

is my conclusion of practical reasoning *knowledge* that I am doing it. So the source of my knowledge that I am doing something is not the mere thought that it is a good thing to do, but this thought in the context of a power to do it. Now, this is not wrong, but misleading, as it portrays thought about the good as "mere thought". We quoted Anscombe saying: "The notion of 'practical knowledge' can only be understood if we first understand 'practical reasoning'." She also describes practical knowledge as an act of a skill, of knowledge how to do something.[54] She can say both, for these are not independent accounts. The power to reason about what to do *is* a power to do things. For, in the fundamental case, thinking that such-and-such is to be done because _____ is the causality of an action explanation that one *is doing it* because _____. Since practical thinking is, fundamentally, acting, the power of practical thought is a power to act.[55]

We seek an account of first person reference, of the logical perspective it affords on an object, which consists in a relationship with the object by which one knows how things stand with it in such a way that acts of knowing the object in this way are unmediated first person thoughts. So we are looking for a way of knowing that satisfies this condition: When I know an object in this way, then there is no room for asking whether I am that object; that is, first person thoughts articulating such knowledge are identification-free. Now we have described a way of knowing of which this holds true: knowing that I am doing something by concluding I should do it. When I know that someone is doing something through reasoning about what to do, then there is no room for the question whether it is I of whom I know this. One way of knowing "from the inside" that someone is doing something, which founds the first person reference of a subject of action, is knowing it from reasoning about what to do.[56]

It can be no surprise that the unity of action explanation and practical reasoning is a source of first person reference. If it were only per accidens that

54. *Intention*, §48.

55. One manifestation of this, which Aristotle observes, is that deliberation about how to do something terminates in things one can do (*Nicomachean Ethics*, 1113a). Another, which Kant notes, is that recognizing that one must do something is recognizing that one has the power to do it (*Kritik der praktischen Vernunft*: "Er urteilet also, daß er etwas kann, darum, weil er sich bewußt ist, daß er es soll" [p. 30].) On the inner nexus of intention and practical powers compare Annette Baier, "Act and Intent", and my "Practice and the Unity of Action".

56. There is another way of knowing that one is doing something from the inside, which affords, as Anscombe puts it, "patient conceptions of actions" ("The First Person", p. 36).

I am doing what I determine as good, how would my "This is good to do" have anything to do with *me*? As it would not be a character of the manner in which I think about what to do that I who am answering the question am the one who, if all goes well, is acting in accordance with the answer, practical reasoning would not be expressed by a first person pronoun. Conversely, if it were only per accidens that I am doing something upon thinking that it is to be done, how would I represent my doing it in the first person manner? I could only know from experience that, upon my thinking that such-and-such is to be done something tends to happen that satisfies this description. And then I would not know without mediation that it happens to *me*. It is obvious that the nexus of thought and action founds the first person reference of the acting subject. We have explained how.[57]

First person knowledge of action is from thinking. First person reference is shrouded in darkness so long as, and to the extent that, this form of knowledge is. Anscombe finds a source of this darkness in a conception of knowledge on which "knowledge must be something that is judged as

---

57. David Velleman maintains that self-knowledge is the constitutive aim of intentional action (*The Possibility of Practical Reason*, p. 26). But on his account, the representation of one's own actions is neither knowledge, nor is it of oneself, if "oneself" is a first person pronoun. Concerning the first point, the relevant representation is said to be a belief about a "future action" (p. 25): I believe I will do *A*. It is to be knowledge because my believing I will do *A* is the cause of my doing it. But from the fact that I, in whatever way, know I will do *A*, it does not follow that I know that I am doing it while I am doing it. Knowing I will do *A*, I do not know whether I have begun and whether I am still at it. It is obvious what is missing: the manner in which the subject's thought of doing *A* guides her doing it. As our discussion in the second subsection of the first section of this chapter revealed, there can be no account of *this* in terms of events causing events, for it is a character of the unity of *one* event. Moreover, it does not seem that, on Velleman's account, I know I will do *A*. I am said to know this by knowing an explanation: I will do *A* because of a certain desire, say. But according to Velleman himself, this explanation is false. The desire does not move me to do *A*, not if I am doing *A* intentionally. Rather, my thinking that I will do *A* because of this desire does. As the explanation is false, it is not knowledge. Hence neither is any term of it. Concerning the second point, the explanation is not of oneself; it is no unmediated first person thought. For, even if we grant that I know I will do *A*, as I will do it because I think this, this knowledge does not satisfy the first person knowledge formula: I do not know the movement by being its subject. I know it by being the subject of a thought that is its cause. And the subject of the thought and the subject of the movement are identical only per accidens and *not in virtue of the way in which the thought represents the movement*. Of course, there may be all manner of reason why the subject of a thought that causes a movement must be identical with the subject of that movement. But this fact, if it is one, will not affect the logical nature of the thought in question; it will not characterize the manner in which the subject, thinking the thought, refers to its object.

such by being in accordance with the facts. The facts, reality, are prior, and dictate what is to be said." Indeed, what sets first person knowledge apart from sensory knowledge is that what is known first personally *is not an independent reality of the first person knowledge of it.* For, first person reference is a way of referring such that the object referred to is the subject referring to it, wherefore a way of knowing associated with this form of reference must fix it that an object thus known is the subject knowing it. And this it does only if knowing in this way that an object is F is knowing it *by being F.* Obviously, what is known in accordance with this formula includes the subject's knowledge of it. Practical knowledge satisfies the formula. Knowing that one is doing A by reasoning about what to do and doing A intentionally are *one reality.* This is a character of the form of predication "I * do A": that subject and action-form are joined in this way includes the subject's representing them as so joined. The facts are not prior and dictate. They are not prior and cannot dictate, as they include and are included in the subject's knowledge of them.[58]

Another obstacle to comprehending first person knowledge is that its content is equally well expressed by "I am doing A", which describes what happens, and "I should do A", which depicts what happens as conforming to a normative measure. This registers the unity of action explanation and practical reasoning, which defines first person predication of action. "I * do A because ____", which is "I am doing A because ____" or, equivalently, "I should do A because ____", expresses knowledge that I am doing A that I have, not by experiencing what I am doing, but by ascertaining what to do. First person thought of action has a *normative significance;* it represents its subject as conforming to a normative order. It describes the subject in such a way as to position her in relation to that order. The same holds of "I want (intend) to do A": the phrase expresses a thought about what to do and rests not on (inner) observation, but on reasoning.

One might admit that "I am doing A", when it is a term of an action explanation, represents A as to be done, but explain that this is so because, in uttering these words, I perform two speech acts: I describe what

---

58. Does not this mean that speech acts expressing first person knowledge make it the case that things are as they say? On a certain use of that term, such speech acts are performative and do not express knowledge. We need not decide if performative speech acts express knowledge. Clearly, first person descriptions of intentional actions are not performative. Saying that one is making breakfast does not make it the case that one is.

happens, and I evaluate, recommend, or praise it, the description being based on observation, the praise on practical reasoning. I say "I am doing A because ____", describing what happens, and in addition think "I should do A because ____". Thought and action are distinct realities; perhaps a predicate "INT" represents their connection. But first person thought cannot be analyzed in this manner. On the one hand, most concepts of what may be done intentionally depend on action explanation. And as it is a feature of this form of explanation that the subject is in a position to give an explanation of this form if it is true, it follows that someone falls under action concepts only if she deploys them in action explanations, in which context her thought that she is exemplifying the concept has the normative significance we described. On the other hand, although someone may think that A is good to do and yet not do A intentionally, a subject of such thoughts is a subject of movements that receive action explanations, and when her movement has such an explanation, then her thought that what she is doing is a good thing to do is not a distinct reality from her doing it. If first person thoughts were compounded of independent speech acts—description and assessment—then the description would not be true, for the subject would not fall under the concept that allegedly describes her, and she would not make the assessment, as she would not possess the idea of something good to do. In this way, the reduction reduces to absurdity: isolating a descriptive from an evaluative component is rendering the components unintelligible.

If doing A is an action concept—if its sense depends on action explanation—then someone possessing it has the power to know in the way that underwrites first person reference. In acquiring these concepts, she acquires the power to know in this way: she acquires the power to know why and how to do what these concepts describe, and, as an inseparable part of this, the power to think of herself first personally. It has been held that, since its essential normativity cannot be accommodated within the natural sciences, we might be forced to throw the concept of action and with it action concepts on the trash heap of outdated theories. With action concepts a logical basis of first person thought disappears. Renouncing action concepts is a form of self-annihilation: logical self-annihilation. It annihilates a source of the power to think and say "I".

3

Belief and the First Person

We inquire into the sense of first person reference, and therefore into ways of knowing acts of which are unmediated first person thoughts: ways of knowing such that if I know that someone is *F* in such a way, I know that I am *F*. In order to describe ways of knowing that satisfy this condition, we investigate concepts that are predicated accordingly. As self-consciousness is the form of subjectivity of a thinking subject, the concepts we must consider first are concepts of thought. Thought is theoretical and practical, and while, in the preceding chapter, we discussed practical thought, or action, our topic now is the "I" internal to theoretical thought, or belief. So we ask how I know that I believe something when I know it in a way that satisfies our abstract description of first person knowledge, i.e., when I know that I believe something by believing it.

We approach belief through theoretical reasoning, reasoning about what to believe. As an action is a movement that rests on practical reasoning, so is a belief an act of the intellect that rests on theoretical reasoning. Doing something intentionally is answering the question what to do, wherefore I can know that I am doing something by ascertaining what to do. This is the source of an inner nexus of action and the first person: knowing an action through practical reasoning, I know it as my own. In this chapter, we shall expound a parallel nexus of first person thought and belief. Believing something is answering the question what to believe. Therefore I can know that I believe something by determining what to believe. When I know that I believe something in this way, I have unmediated first person knowledge; I do not need to recognize a person in order to tie the belief to myself.

The chapter follows our treatment of action. The first section gives a theory of theoretical reasoning, expounding a system of forms of answering the question it addresses, the question what to believe, while the second section argues that believing something is answering this question, developing a claim put forth by John McDowell, that the concept of belief depends on a certain form of explanation, or kind of causality. Finally, the third section explains how this gives rise to a way of knowing: I may know that I believe something from ascertaining what to believe. When I know in this way that someone believes something, I know that *I* do. As the thought is identification-free, the way of knowing that it exemplifies constitutes the sense of its first person reference. By thus running parallel to the preceding chapter, our exposition of the self-conscious nature of belief paves the way for the next chapter, which describes the structure of self-consciousness that action and belief share.

The Question What to Believe

Theoretical reasoning addresses the question what to believe; she who answers it affixes herself to a proposition in a way that represents it as something to believe. Let us use "°" to signify this unity of subject and proposition. "I ° p" expresses the posture of mind I reach completing a course of theoretical reasoning.

As "to do" in "what to do", "to believe" in "what to believe" is a gerundive or, more generally, an imperative. A variety of forms may express it. We can say, e.g., that theoretical reasoning concludes in a thought that represents a proposition as something one should believe or as something it is right to believe. "I should believe that p" and "It is right to believe that p" are guises of "I ° p". It might be said that this cannot be true of "It is right to believe that p", for it contains no "I". But it certainly does, if it answers the question what to believe that I put to myself.

As an imperative brings its object under a normative order, representing it as bound to, yet liable to fall from, this order, elucidating the question what to believe requires describing the relevant order. This may seem easy: asking what to believe is asking what to believe is true, or what is true. The relevant measure is the truth. And indeed, we can specify the sense of "right" in "It is right to believe that p" by writing "It is true that p". However, we thus do no more than introduce "truth" as a name of the measure of theoretical reasoning. It is all right to give our topic this name, but we must not confuse giving something a name with comprehending its nature. We might have said that the question what to do asks what to do is good, or what is good. This would have been correct because and insofar as "good" is the name of the order of practical reasoning. So used, "good" refers to a formal concept signifying the manner in which an action-form is represented in a conclusion of practical reasoning: as to be done, and that is, as good. It signifies the form of predication for which we adopted the sign "*". Understanding this formal concept requires describing the system of forms of answering the question what to do. In the same way, "true" designates a form, viz. the manner in which a proposition is represented in a conclusion of theoretical reasoning: as something to believe, and that is, as true. It designates the unity of subject and proposition that characterizes the conclusion of theoretical reasoning. In order to understand this formal concept, we must describe the system of forms of thought on which an answer to the question what to believe may rest. By nominal definition, the good is the theme of an inquiry into the question what to do and the order it invokes. Just so, by nominal definition, does an inquiry into the question what to believe and its measure inquire what truth is.

We said we would argue in the next section that believing that something is the case is answering the question what to believe. If that is so, then the order that interprets the imperative of this question is internal to belief, and comprehending this order is comprehending what it is to believe something. Thus we understand Gottlob Frege's claim that the concept of truth signifies the nature of judgment.[1] Frege also propounds that the concept of a thought, or, as we put it, a proposition, must be understood together with the concept of truth.[2] If "truth" signifies the order of the question what to believe and hence the unity of subject and proposition in an answer to this question, we can put this by saying that this unity is constitutive of its elements: from the unity of subject and proposition "I $^\circ p$", we must comprehend the nature of the object as well as the nature of the subject of belief. (Analogously, we found in the previous chapter that

1. "Meine grundlegenden logischen Einsichten", p. 272: "So scheint das Wort 'wahr' das Unmögliche möglich zu machen, nämlich das, was der behauptenden Kraft entspricht, als Beitrag zum Gedanken erscheinen zu lassen." As "true" signifies the form of assertion, it is not a predicate and does not refer to a Fregean concept. Frege maintains that, in this regard, "true" differs from "good". He is wrong. "Good" signifies a formal concept, the form of an object of the will.

2. "Der Gedanke", p. 33.

action-forms, values of the variable "do A" in "I * do A", depend on that form of predication.) An inquiry into the order of the question what to believe is an inquiry into the nature of belief, the nature of truth, and the nature of the proposition. Frege was right in holding that this is one topic.

In the preceding chapter, we asked whether there is an order internal to action as such, an order that governs the question what to do independently of any characteristic of her who is asking it other than her being a subject of practical thought. A parallel question arises here, whether there is an order internal to belief as such and thus a sense that the question what to believe bears regardless of the character of the subject confronting it over and above her being a subject of theoretical reasoning. It might be thought that the measure of someone's question what to believe is provided by what she already believes, or by a privileged subset of her beliefs, those that, say, she does not think of doubting. Or one might hold that the measure of what to believe is a totality of sensory impressions. If one of these views is right, then there is no such thing as *the* order of theoretical reasoning, and "true" designates a kind of measure, not a measure. For, the notion of a set of propositions that are beyond doubt and the notion of a totality of sensory impressions admit of a manifold of instances.

We said that "true" does no more than name the measure of the question what to believe. But it may seem to contain a claim about this measure: calling it "truth" is saying that it governs belief as such. It is excluding any character of the subject other than her possessing the power of theoretical reasoning from being relevant to the order under which she brings herself in asking what to believe. In this regard, "true" appears to differ from "good", of which it seems possible to hold that it designates a mere form. However, this appearance reflects a prior philosophical doctrine and has no independent standing. (What it says about "true" can be, and has been, said about "good".) When we call the order of theoretical reasoning "truth", we do not *assume* that there is an order that governs theoretical reasoning as such. That cannot be the premise of our inquiry. It may be its result. Richard Rorty holds that it makes no sense to conceive of the question what to believe as referring to an order independent of local and historical characteristics of her who is asking it.[3] It is useless to object that the question asks for the truth, which transcends any such characteristics. Without an analysis of the modes of answering the question that shows that she who answers it conceives of herself as conforming

---

3. Compare, for example, the first two essays of *Truth and Progress*.

to a standard that joins her to *any* subject with the power of theoretical reasoning, insisting on the transcendence of truth is worshipping a name.[4]

We said that theoretical reasoning arrives at belief. Even where it remains idle, it is the kind of reasoning that issues in its subject's believing something. In the next section, we shall develop this character of theoretical reasoning by describing the unity of theoretical reasoning and belief explanation. Already in this section, we shall rely on the abstract idea that a belief must be capable of resting on a conclusion of theoretical reasoning. That is, the nexus of subject and proposition in "I ° *p*" must be such as to be the principle of their nexus in "I believe *p*". We shall exclude accounts of theoretical reasoning on which its conclusion does not satisfy this condition.

Inference

The first way of determining what to do that we considered in the preceding chapter represents an action as a means to a finite end. As instrumental articulation is essential to action, so does inferential articulation seem essential to belief. Hence, statements representing this articulation are the place to begin: I think that *q* and consider what follows from it. I realize that *q* implies *p* and conclude that *p* is true. This is the first form of answering the question what to believe: *p,* because I think *q*. Call it an *inference.*

I conclude that I should believe one thing because I believe another thing. But how can the fact that I believe something be relevant to what it is right to believe? How is it that, by representing something as entailed by something I believe, I represent it as something it is right to believe? An analogous question arose with regard to, "I should do *A* because I want to do *B*": how is it that representing something as a means to something I want is representing it as to be done? There the explanation was that an instrumental syllogism represents the action of its premise as conforming to the same order to which it reveals the action of its conclusion

---

4. Jürgen Habermas and Albrecht Wellmer, swayed by Rorty's claim that the measure of the question what to believe can only be set by features of the subject that go beyond her being such as to confront it, attempt to maintain the purity of truth by distinguishing it from that measure. (Compare Jürgen Habermas, "Zur Kritik der Bedeutungstheorie"; Albrecht Wellmer, "Wahrheit, Kontingenz, Moderne" and "Was ist eine pragmatische Bedeutungstheorie?") This is hopeless. It renders the notion of truth empty and the epistemology skeptical. An account of truth *is* an account of the order of reasoning about what to believe, and vice versa.

to conform. Wanting to do something is viewing it as to be done. The same is true here. She who reasons from her belief that q to the conclusion that it is right to believe p takes q to be something it is right to believe. It is because the premise of her inference expresses her view about what to believe that she can rest a verdict about what to believe upon it. An inference extends the status of being something it is right to believe, i.e., by nominal definition, of being true, from premise to conclusion. The expression of inference reflects this, as this manner of answering the question what to believe is equally well expressed by "p, because q". "I believe" can drop out, not because it is not contained in that nexus of the propositions p and q, but because the proposition of the premise is represented as something it is right to believe, or true.

An inference leads from one answer to the question what to believe to another. It follows that there is a different manner of answering this question. Again, let us be clear why this is so. One might think that, unless there is another way, theoretical reasoning reaches no end: I reason that (it is right to think) p because (it is right to think) q; and that (it is right to think) q because (it is right to think) r; and so on. But that is not the problem. The problem is not that, without another manner of determining what to believe, we are launched on a regress. Rather, without another form of answer to our question no regress commences, because we do not understand its first step. An inference leads from one thing it is right to believe to another, and we cannot explain the notion of something it is right to believe by saying that it is right to believe what follows from what it is right to believe. There must be a way of arriving at an answer to our question that is not a case of deriving it from another answer. It will reveal the order under which I bring myself in asking what to believe. Unless there is such a form of answer, the notion of inference is empty.

In the preceding chapter, we discussed the suggestion that a chain of instrumental reasoning terminates in a finite end that no longer *falls under* the normative order under which the conclusion is brought, but *is* that order. This end then defines the question what to do asked by her who is, and while she is, pursuing it. An analogous idea is popular with regard to inference, on account of a certain epistemological assumption. We shall discuss this assumption in Chapter 5; here we concern ourselves with the view of inference it contains. We said: if an inference represents its premise as conforming to the same order to which its conclusion is shown to conform, then it is not the only way of answering the question what to believe. The epistemological assumption in question is that the consequent of this conditional is false. The view is known as "coherentism", which Donald Davidson defines as follows:

> What distinguishes a coherence theory is simply the claim that nothing can count as a reason for holding a belief except another belief. ("A Coherence Theory of Truth and Knowledge", p. 426)

Coherentism, being the negation of the consequent of our conditional, entails the falsity of its antecedent. If coherentism is true, then it cannot be true that an inference, as such, subsumes its premise under the same order under which it brings its conclusion. A chain of inferences must terminate in beliefs that no longer conform to, but *are* the order to which beliefs inferred from them conform. Accounts of the source of these beliefs may vary. Perhaps they result from sensory affection, or perhaps they are beliefs that those who are immersed in a certain form of life do not doubt.[5] In fact it is irrelevant how the propositions that are to constitute the measure of belief come to the subject. It is equally irrelevant whether the set of propositions playing that role changes over time. The essential point, which defines coherentism, is that the subject does not, in an act of theoretical reasoning, recognize them to be something it is right to believe.

This view is untenable for reasons analogous to those we mounted against the corresponding account of instrumental reasoning. Suppose the normative order of the question what to believe, on an occasion of its being asked, is a set of propositions Σ. In order to indicate this, we give the imperative an index specifying that set; we write, not "It is right to believe p because Σ" but "It is right$_\Sigma$ to believe p". Now, nothing we said about Σ excludes that it may be right$_\Sigma$ to believe p and right$_\Sigma$ to believe *non p*. Thinking it is right$_\Sigma$ to believe p peacefully coexists with thinking it is right$_\Sigma$ to believe *non p*. This shows that, thinking it right$_\Sigma$ to believe p, I have not determined what to believe. For, thinking this is not having affixed myself to p in a manner that excludes affixing myself in the same way to *non p*. But thinking it right to believe p—thinking it true—is so affixing myself to p.

It looks as though the difficulty is that nothing we said about Σ excludes that it may be right$_\Sigma$ to believe p and right$_\Sigma$ to believe *non p*. So why not say something that excludes it? Let us require that the measure of

---

5. This view is often associated with Ludwig Wittgenstein, *Über Gewißheit*. Andrea Kern critically discusses this manner of invoking the notion of a form of life in an account of knowledge in "Does Knowledge Rest upon a Form of Life?"

the question what to believe be a coherent set of propositions. But what does that mean? Presumably, it means that it is not ruled out that it is *right* to believe all propositions in the set. But now we are deploying a "right", an imperative, that is not defined by any set of beliefs. We said that, without another manner of answering the question what to believe, the notion of inference is empty. So is the notion of coherence. The requirement of coherence we are imposing on propositions that are to serve as the measure of the question what to believe on an occasion of its being asked *is not represented* by her whose question receives its sense from these, or any set of, propositions. Therefore, it remains that, in her, thinking it right$_\Sigma$ to believe p coexists peacefully with thinking it right$_\Sigma$ to believe *non p*.[6] It is irrelevant if some cause other than her reasoning should guarantee that she never thinks both. Such a cause does not alter the logical character of her thoughts, which is such that each tolerates the other. As in the practical case, it is useless to ensure, or stipulate, unity— there of ends, here of beliefs—if the subject does not represent the unity. And in both cases, it is the representation of the relevant unity that requires concepts that depend on other forms of reasoning.

Sensation

The normative order of the question what to believe is not a set of propositions that she who is asking it believes, for this allows thoughts about what to believe that relate to incompatible propositions to coexist in peace. It is useless to stipulate that the set of propositions that defines the measure be coherent, for the problem is not lack of unity, but lack of rep-

---

6. Robert Brandom gives the following account of how rules of inference may be "subject to empirical criticism": "It may happen that one uses the term 'acid' in such a way that a substance's tasting sour is a sufficient condition for applying it, and that it will turn litmus paper red is a necessary consequence of applying it. Finding a substance that both tastes sour and turns litmus paper blue shows that such a concept is inadequate" (*Making It Explicit*, p. 225). How does it show that? I find myself committed to the claim that the substance is acid as well as to the claim that it is not. As it is irrelevant that I acquired one of these commitments noninferentially, we can simplify: Following given inferential norms, I come to be committed to p and I come to be committed to *non p*. This is supposed to show, and show *me*, that I deploy an inadequate concept, i.e., that the norms of inference that constitute it are inadequate. If indeed it shows me that, then the order under which I know myself to be having these commitments cannot be identified with given norms of inference. Inferentialism, the doctrine that the quoted passage defends, can give no account of this order.

resentation of unity (or its absence). It might anyway have seemed desperate to try to think of believed propositions as the order of theoretical reasoning. Is it not obvious that the senses are the final judge of what to believe? Sensation must be the order of theoretical reasoning.

In order for sensation to be that measure, it is not enough that sensory impressions cause beliefs, which then serve as premises of inferences. Since the unity of these premises must be represented, sensation can be the principle of the intellect only as it enters theoretical reasoning. Indeed, it may seem that the senses inform the intellect in a manner parallel to that in which, according to Davidson, appetite informs the will. After all, Davidson modeled calculation from desire after a method of empirical confirmation. In view of this parallel, we call the relevant manner of founding an act of the intellect on sensory affection *calculation from sensation*.

Calculation from sensation is modeled after (a certain theory of) inductive inference, but it is not inductive inference. An inductive inference proceeds from propositions accepted as true, wherefore it is of no interest to us, as we seek a manner of answering the question what to believe that yields a starting point for inference, inductive or deductive. It is sometimes said that empirical beliefs as such are justified inductively. If that is so, then there is an analogue to inductive inference that rests beliefs on sensory affection. This is calculation from sensation.

Modeling it on inductive inference, with sensory impressions taking the place of accepted propositions, we can think of calculation from sensation as follows. It proceeds from prima facie judgments that represent certain impressions as pertinent to whether it is right to believe a given proposition. We write such a judgment "pf(p, e)", "p" signifying the proposition and "e" the impressions speaking in its favor. In a first step, these judgments are integrated into an all-things-considered judgment, which says that, all in all, given sensory impressions speak in favor of believing that p. We write "pf(p, E)", "E" signifying a given totality of impressions. As in the practical case, we can be indifferent to how the integration is supposed to be effected. Again, as in the practical case, while sensation exists in animals without thought, the unified state of sensory affection represented by an all-things-considered judgment depends on its unification and thus is essentially represented in thought.

The second step of the calculation is from the all-things-considered judgment to an all-out judgment that it is right to believe p, or that p is true. It is licensed by a principle analogous to the principle of continence, which we therefore call the principle of epistemic continence. About this principle, we must say what we said about its practical counterpart. It states that it is right to believe p (or to assign p a certain subjective probability) if given sensory impressions all in all speak in favor of believing p. This is an *analytic* statement. It gives the sense of the word "right" that its consequent deploys and specifies the order that interprets that imperative. It cannot be a substantive claim that a belief all in all favored by sensation is, or is likely to be, true, where we credit ourselves with an independent grasp of what we call "truth". A grasp of this order that was independent of calculation from sensation and thus could found a substantive assessment of its validity would have to come from reflection on another form of answering the question what to believe, which we have not yet specified. Our interest is in the principle of epistemic continence and in calculation from sensation only as representing sensory impressions as the measure of the question what to believe.

The following phrases appear to express prima facie judgments in English: "It looks as though p from here" or "These appearances suggest that p". By contrast, "I perceive that p", e.g., does not express a prima facie judgment. That I perceive that p does not speak in favor of thinking that p is true. It *establishes* that p is true. Therefore, no calculation is needed to integrate "I perceive that p" with judgments of the same form. It is a formal feature of these judgments, which distinguishes them from prima facie judgments, that they do not conflict. It is possible that it looks as though p from here, while from there it looks as though *non p*. But it is impossible that I perceive that p and perceive that *non p*. Calculation from sensation proceeds from impressions, not from acts of perceiving that something is the case. We shall return to such acts in the next subsection.

In the preceding chapter, we found that desire, or practical sensibility, cannot determine the will, as it bears too low a form of temporality. We shall see now that, for the same reason, sensation, or theoretical sensibility, cannot determine the intellect. An all-things-considered judgment unifying sensation represents a changeable state. It says that sensory impressions given *so far* all in all speak in favor of believing p, which is a distinct judgment from one that would be expressed by these words later. Judgments made with this form of words at different times bear no logical connection between them. It follows that an answer to the question what to believe—"It is right to believe that p" or "It is true that p"—if it rests on an all-things-considered judgment according to an analytic principle, represents a changeable state as well. This proves that calculation from sensation is not a way of answering the question what to believe and that sensations are not the order of theoretical reasoning.[7]

Suspicion arises when we notice that, if an answer to the question what to believe rests on sensation eventually, then inference is not a manner of arriving at such an answer. For, something it was right to believe yesterday, in the sense of being all in all favored by sensory impressions then, may not be right to believe today, in the sense of being all in all favored by sensory impressions now. Inferring something today from a premise established yesterday may lead me to believe something that, in the relevant sense of "should", I should not believe. As this is so regardless of the length of the temporal gap, there is no such thing as establishing what to believe through inference. My hold on the rightness of the proposition gives out before I can draw a conclusion from it. So again, in a manner analogous to the practical case, the form of reasoning that was to provide a starting point for inference does away with inference.[8]

7. The reflections to follow owe a great debt to Stephen Engström's essay "Understanding and Sensibility".

8. We can imagine ways of responding to the difficulty parallel to those encountered in the preceding chapter. One might give a pragmatic rationale for not reconsidering a verdict on what to believe when it is improbable that a new assessment of the evidence will result in a change of mind, so that the cost of reconsidering would not be offset. As a pragmatic rationale for not reconsidering intentions entitles us to keep going even as we may act counter to what, all in all, desire recommends, so a corresponding rationale lets us keep thinking what we do even as this may be counter to what, all in all, the senses suggest. Of course this presupposes that inference is not a valid form of reasoning.—Or one might argue that an assessment that it is right to believe *p* is based on present impressions *and* an estimate of the future. Albrecht Wellmer writes: "Whenever we make truth-claims on the basis of [. . .] convincing evidence, we suppose [. . .] that no new [. . .] evidence will turn up in the future that would call our truth-claim into question" ("Wahrheit, Kontingenz, Moderne", p. 163). Wellmer is not concerned specifically with sensory evidence, but he speaks to our topic, as his "convincing evidence" is prima facie. When I think that *p* is true on the ground that I perceive that *p*, I need not suppose that no evidence to the contrary will turn up in the future. If my evidence for thinking something consists in my perceiving that it is the case, then I know, on the strength of this evidence, that there shall not be contrary evidence of the same kind. I need not, *in addition to this evidence,* rest my judgment on an estimate of the future. Now, Wellmer's account of the relation of judgment to convincing evidence entails that inference is not a valid form of ascertaining what to believe. That yesterday I thought that believing *p* would all in all be favored by the evidence today is compatible with its not being so favored today. As the form of my reasoning does not guarantee that my estimate is borne out, I may arrive at something wrong by drawing conclusions from yesterday's premises. (With regard to the temporal reach of the alleged estimate, there is a disanalogy to the

This is a motive for suspecting that thinking it right to believe such-and-such and, in consequence, believing it, may have a different kind of temporality. Gareth Evans gives us a hint. He suggests that a belief is a not changeable state, that is, that believing something is not a determination to which any duration is accidental.

> The acceptance on d_2 of "Yesterday was fine", given an acceptance on d_1 of "Today is fine", can manifest the *persistence* of a belief. (*The Varieties of Reference*, p. 194)

"She believes a is F" said now and "She believes a was F" said later may represent a persisting belief. This does not yet distinguish believing something from a changeable state; "x is white", e.g., said now and again later, may represent persisting whiteness. But Evans goes on:

> No one can be ascribed [. . .] a belief with the content 'It is now ψ', for example, who does not have the propensity as time goes on to form beliefs with the content 'It was ψ just a moment ago', 'It was ψ earlier this morning', 'It was ψ this morning', etc., though of course this propensity can be counteracted by new evidence. [. . .] the thought-units of the atomist are not coherent, independent thoughts at all, but, so to speak, cross-sections of a persisting belief state.

Evans's wording is not happy; he says that the subject must continually be forming new beliefs and that these constitute one belief. He means: no one can be represented as expressing a belief by "a is F" who does not have the propensity as time goes on to express the same belief by "a was F". How are we to understand this propensity?

Michael Bratman seeks to capture the temporality of intention by saying that intentions have inertia. He misrepresents a logical insight as a psychological theorem. Someone's wanting to do A constitutes the nonaccidental unity of the phases of her doing it, wherefore "She wants to do A" expresses the same thought so long as she is doing A. By contrast, as any duration is accidental to a changeable state, any interval during which someone is in a state is an aggregate of such intervals. Thus "x is F", representing a changeable state, invariably expresses different thoughts at

---

practical case, whose source, the temporality of belief, we shall discuss in a moment. Davidson requires only that we expect future desires not to undermine the intention *until it is carried out*, while Wellmer propounds that we suppose future evidence shall *never* undermine our judgment. In "Universality and Truth", Rorty justly objects that supposing this seems mad.)

different times. Now, Evans says beliefs have a propensity to persist. He might have said they have inertia. But he seeks to characterize a logical form, a form of temporality. His point is that there is a nonaccidental unity of my asserting now "*a* is *F*" and my asserting later "*a* was *F*", when these assertions express the same belief, and that this unity of assertions is essential to their expressing a belief. If it were an empirical fact that belief states tend to persist, then we would have to be able to register that fact. Having found that *x* believes *p* at *t*, we would have to be able to find that she still believes *p* at *t'*, which would have to be a different judgment *for any* t' *after* t. Conversely, if the unity of assertions at different times by which they express the same belief is internal to their expressing a belief at all, then "*x* believes *p*" (with the necessary adjustments in the sentence replacing "*p*") *expresses the same judgment so long as* x *believes* p.

Of course, she who yesterday affirmed "It is raining today" need not affirm today "It was raining yesterday". She may have changed her mind or forgotten. And even when she does affirm these sentences on consecutive days, she need not express the same act of belief. She may have forgotten that it was raining yesterday and learned it again from today's paper. In the same way, she who is doing *A* now need not be doing it later even if she has not reached her end in the meantime. She may have changed her mind or encountered insurmountable obstacles. It is not necessarily the case that I want to do *A* until I have done it; neither is it necessarily the case that I still believe today what I believed yesterday. It is not for that reason an accident that I am progressing toward *A* if that is my end, or that I affirm "*a* was *F*" if earlier I affirmed "*a* is *F*". It *belongs to* an intention to govern the progress of the action towards its end, although the progress may be blocked or the end abandoned at any time. And it *belongs to* a belief to stay on, although it may be forgotten or retracted at any time. This is the point: the action must be blocked because it is such as to reach its end, and the belief must be retracted because it is such as to hold out indefinitely. An interval during which someone intends to do something is not an aggregate of such intervals. Evans's point in the last sentence we quoted, about the thought-units of the atomist being not coherent thoughts at all, is that, just so, an interval during which someone believes that something is the case is not aggregate, but a unity of such intervals.

Bratman describes as the inertia of states of intention, and Evans as a propensity of states of belief to persist, a logical character by which intentions and beliefs are not states at all. To a changeable state *F* any duration is accidental, so that "*x* is *F*" invariably expresses different judgments at different times. An act of wanting to do *A* distinguishes its proper end, reached when *A* is done, from any other, wherefore "*x* wants to do *A*" expresses the same judgment so long as *x* is doing *A* and has not yet done it. A belief is neither a state nor a movement. Neither is any duration accidental to it, nor does it have a proper end. It exhibits a yet higher form of temporality: *any limit of its duration is accidental to it.* Thus "*x* believes *p*" expresses the same judgment at all times so long as *x* believes *p*. In order to mark that temporality of belief, we call it a temporally unlimited act.

(This must be limited in one respect. A belief about an independent object, depending on sensory affection, is not without temporal limit altogether, as there is a time when one acquires it. However, the belief is not bound to the time of the affection that makes it possible. When yesterday I came to believe something I expressed by "It is raining", then my saying today "It was raining" may express the same act of belief.[9] It cannot be said of this act as opposed to its linguistic expression that it happened yesterday or today or on both days. While "It is raining" says different things when first said now and then again later (no matter whether it was raining throughout), "I believe it is raining" and "I believe it was raining", said now and again later, may say the same thing.[10] Thinking about the rain has a different manner of being in time from the rain it is about.)

We extracted from Evans's remark about a propensity of beliefs to persist the thesis that a belief is a temporally unlimited act. Now, why is any limit to its duration accidental to a belief? We argued that an intention bears the temporality of a movement because it is the proximate principle of a movement. Now, a belief is temporally unlimited on account of the character of its proximate principle, which is an answer to the question what to believe. We see this when we consider a property of the order of theoretical reasoning that distinguishes it from the order of practical rea-

---

9. An account of observation sentences such as W. V. O. Quine's (see, e.g., *The Pursuit of Truth*), which describes their use as an act of a disposition triggered by current sensory stimulation, does not represent observation sentences as a means of expressing judgments or beliefs (see my *Kategorien des Zeitlichen*, chap. 3). That an act of thinking that something is the case has no temporal limit in the way in which its linguistic expression and sensory affections do so is consistent with the fact that my capacity to think about an independent object depends on my being affected by it and on my being able to express my thought.

10. This sheds light on the concept of memory that applies to a subject of thought. That concept does not apply to nonrational animals, for, in a thinking subject, the power of memory is an aspect of the power of temporally unlimited acts of belief.

soning. If it is right to do something, there may be a time when it is right to do it; what is right to do now may be wrong to do later; one may fail to act well by acting too late or too early. By contrast, there is no such thing as a time when it is right to believe that such-and-such is the case; there is no such thing as a time when something is true.[11] In distinction to the object of an order of practical reasoning, the object of an order of theoretical reasoning does not, *as an object of this order,* attract temporal determinations. Believing something is a temporally unlimited act because an answer to the question what to believe does not impose a temporal limit on the act it propounds. If it is the principle of the act, then the act bears no temporal limit. Its principle is such as not to give out.

This proves that the order of belief is not sensation unified by calculation. Calculation yields all-things-considered judgments, which give out at any moment. No analytic principle links the thought that, all in all, sensations now favor believing *p,* to the thought that it is right to believe *p.* A judgment considering given desires cannot be the ground of the thought that it is *good to do A,* for, while the former represents a changeable state, the latter is the principle of a movement. Even less can a judgment considering given sensations, representing a changeable state, be the ground of the thought that *p is true,* for that thought is the principle of a temporally unlimited act. As the principle of epistemic continence is not analytic, it is a substantive claim about what to believe. We are not asking whether that claim is true. We seek to identify the order that interprets its imperative. Sensations unified by calculation are not this order.

Infinite Grounds

An inference represents its premise as conforming to the same order to which the conclusion is shown to conform; it rests an answer to the question what to believe on an answer to that same question. Hence, there must be a different manner of answering this question, from which the measure that interprets its imperative must transpire. It is natural to sup-

---

11. Tense logic treats of items that are true at a time. This manner of representing temporal thought may be revealing in many ways. But it is a confusion to think it affords insight into the form of the contents of temporal judgment. It is the nature of thought that it provides everything necessary to determine a truth value. A *sentence* may be said to be true at a time, in the sense that, when used at this time, it expresses a thought that is true—not at that time, but without qualification. See my *Kategorien des Zeitlichen,* chap. 2.

pose that sensory affections provide that measure. But affections cannot directly, unmediated by thought, deliver premises of inferences, just as appetite cannot directly provide ends from which to derive actions according to the instrumental syllogism. For, a nonrational cause affords no representation of the unity of its effects. This suggests that sensory affections unified by thought are the order of theoretical reasoning and that calculation from sensation yields a starting point of inference without relying on one. However, affections unified by thought cannot determine the intellect. Calculation from sensation does not yield an answer to the question what to believe, for the conclusion of a calculation from sensation represents a changeable state, whereas an answer to the question what to believe imposes no temporal limit on its object. The necessarily represented unity of premises of inferences, of propositions ascertained to be true, must bear a different kind of temporality. We shall suggest that the relevant unity is a *power of knowledge*. In view of a logical analogy that will transpire in due course, we call such a power an *infinite ground*.

"I perceive that p" is not material of a calculation from sensation. Yet it appears to represent something by virtue of which I am in a position to determine what to believe. For, if I perceive or perceived that p, then p is true. Hence, if the question is posed whether it is right to believe that p, I can respond, "Yes, I perceived that p." In answering the question in this manner, I do not appeal to something else I believe; my answer is not an inference. So here is a form of answering the question what to believe that does not proceed from an answer to that same question. An analysis of its logical form must reveal the kind of measure that interprets its imperative.

There is an impulse to deny that we have come upon a different form of answering our question. We said that, in determining what to believe on the basis of perception, I do not revert to another belief. But, one wants to say, when I think it right to believe that p because I perceive it, then, really, I do not rest my verdict on my perception that p, but on my belief that I perceive it; I reason that it is right to believe that p because *I believe* that I perceive that p, not because I perceive that p. "It is right to believe that p, for I perceive that p" is of the form "It is right to believe that p because q", where q is something I (think it right to) believe.

Even while we lack an account of the present form of answering the question of theoretical reasoning, we know that its reduction to inference is mistaken. For, it makes nonsense of this form of answer. An inference from q to p shows that it is right to believe that p given that it is right to believe that q, which has a point only if I can ascertain that it is right to believe that q independently of recognizing p as true. And in general I cannot determine that I perceive that something is the case independently of ascertaining that things are as I perceive them to be. Perhaps this is inconclusive; philosophers may go so far as to propound that "I perceive that p" does not answer our question. "I perceive that p", they may argue, does not give my ground for thinking that p is true, but only expresses my thinking it true.[12] But now the view reduces to one we have rejected: that the normative order of theoretical reasoning is a set of believed propositions. Thus the reductive interpretation of answers to the question what to believe that appeal to perception undermines its own intelligibility. It leaves us with no way of answering the question that does not revert to an answer to the same question, which means it leaves us unable to accord the question any sense. In consequence, it bereaves us of the very notion of inference, for this notion designates a manner of answering this now senseless question. Answers to the question what to believe that appeal to perception cannot be reduced to inference. We must seek an account that elucidates their distinct form.

In seeking a description of that form, we can let ourselves be guided by our analysis of the form of answering the question what to do that emerged at the parallel juncture in the previous chapter. We found that the will, moving along a chain of means to ends, comes to rest in actions that manifest an infinite end. An infinite end is general and explains an indefinite number of actions, which are ordered to it not as part to whole, but as instance to instantiated. Moreover, the generality of infinite ends includes reference to a unity of infinite ends: the relevant kind of instantiation excludes that doing something manifests one infinite end and frus-

---

12. Donald Davidson appears to be an example. He writes: "The simplest idea is to identify beliefs with sensations. Thus Hume seems not to have distinguished between perceiving a green spot and perceiving that a spot is green" ("A Coherence Theory of Truth and Knowledge", p. 427). It transpires from the context that this is to destroy all hope of justification by perception, because perceiving that a spot is green does not put one in a better position to answer the question whether the spot is green than believing that a spot is green does. Peter Bieri expresses the same view in the following passage: "When I seek to justify my beliefs by *perceptions,* then I refer to the *perception that* something is the case—I refer to *propositional perceptions* or, as one can also say, to *perceptual beliefs.* Pure sensory information states often are the efficient cause of perceptual beliefs, but they are not reasons or evidence for these beliefs. I can epistemically justify a belief only by other *beliefs."* ("Evolution, Erkenntnis und Kognition", p. 123, my emphasis.) The last sentence is the thesis by which Davidson defines the coherence theory of knowledge. It results from a gradual transformation of perception into belief: perception, perception that, propositional perception, perceptual belief, belief.

trates another. If the same structure informs reasoning about what to believe, then answers to this question that do not proceed from another answer will give what we can call an *infinite ground*. An infinite ground will be infinite in the sense in which an infinite end is. Although there is no limit to the number of actions that are means to a given finite end (for there is no limit to the possibility of division), a finite end is finite in the sense that it is exhausted by the means one takes to it. Now, we speak of a proposition containing propositions it entails. This affords a specification of the abstract concept of a part, according to which a proposition is part of a proposition from which it follows. Again, although there may be no limit to the number of propositions one can infer from a given proposition, a believed proposition is a finite ground in that it can be exhausted by propositions following from it. An infinite ground, by contrast, will be inexhaustible by beliefs that it grounds. This means that it will be general: it will ground beliefs that are not contained in it as a part in the whole, but that are subsumed under it as an instance under what it instantiates.

If there is a parallel structure in theoretical and practical reasoning, then the intellect, moving along a chain of inferences, comes to rest in beliefs that manifest an infinite ground. Do answers to our question that revert to perception appeal to an infinite ground? Yes. Compare again the practical case. An instrumental syllogism joins distinct action-forms: "I should *do A* because I want to *do B*." By contrast, an answer to the question what to do that appeals to an infinite end holds on to the same action-form—"I should do *A* because I promised to do *it*"—and gives a different description of my relation to it, representing doing *A* as manifesting an infinite end to which I adhere. In the same way, an inference links different propositions—"It is right to think *p* because *q*"—while an answer to the question what to believe that rests on perception returns to the same proposition: "It is right to think *p*, for I perceived *it*." Instead of offering a new proposition, the answer introduces a new description of my relation to the proposition in question. If answers to the question what to believe exhibit logical forms that correspond to those of answers to the question what to do, then the relevant relation will consist in the belief's manifesting *something general present in the subject*. Now, we can say this about that general item: a belief that manifests it is true, and nonaccidentally so. If I believe something because I perceive or have perceived it, then things are as I believe, and this is no accident. Given that knowledge is nonaccidentally true belief—we will return to this definition in Chapter 5—it follows that instances of the relevant general item are acts of knowledge. A general item whose instances, as its instances, are acts of knowledge is, by nominal definition, a *power of knowledge*. So we are led to the following description of answers to our question by reference to perception. When I determine what to believe in this manner, I represent my believing it as an act of a power to gain knowledge by means of the senses, a power of receptive knowledge. Such a power is an infinite ground: it is a ground of beliefs that manifest their subject's possession of this power.[13]

A power of knowledge not only is the source of its acts; it is the source of the unity of its acts. This unity characterizes the form of generality of the power. We found that doing something cannot manifest one infinite end and frustrate another. Acts of infinite ends as such exhibit a unity, which we called "practical life-form". In the same way, it is impossible that a power of knowledge manifests itself in believing something and yet also manifests itself in believing the contrary. One cannot perceive that p is the case and yet have perceived that it is not the case that p. A power of knowledge confers a necessary unity upon its acts.[14] For this reason, just as I can determine that I should do something simply from the fact that I promised to do it—no unifying calculation is needed—so does my perceiving that p, on its own, place me in a position to establish that it is right to believe that p. There is neither need nor room for a calculation that unifies acts of a power of knowledge. The unity of all answers to the question what to believe of this form is contained in the form of each answer. Hence, the unity is necessary and necessarily represented.

When we consider reasoning about what to believe, we encounter ways of answering this question that revert not to another belief, but to a power of receptive knowledge. The category of a power of knowledge is

13. In his essay "Other Minds", J.L. Austin draws attention to the fact that we may query someone's assertion in two different ways, asking "why do you believe this?" and "how do you know this?". These questions indeed have different uses. But it does not follow that my answer to the question "why do you believe p?" may not show how I know p, as it does when it represents my believing p as an act of a power of knowledge. Conversely, someone may ask "how do you know p?" as opposed to "why do you believe p?" if she expects an answer of this form. This is a matter of implicature and provides no reason for thinking that my answer does not explain why I believe p.

14. The concept of an infinite end or virtue and the concept of an infinite ground or power of knowledge are logically analogous in this way: a virtue manifests itself only in good actions, a power of knowledge only in true beliefs. A theory of knowledge that applied the insight into the centrality of the concept of virtue to the proper understanding of practical thought to its own topic would insist that the concept of a power of knowledge is the first and fundamental concept of epistemology. The book that does that, to which the present chapter and Chapter 5 are deeply indebted, is Andrea Kern's *Quellen des Wissens*.

largely foreign to contemporary epistemology, which, in its stead, employs the very different notion of a habit, or mechanism, or disposition, of belief formation. We will try the patience of the reader who places trust in these concepts by postponing the discussion of her objections until Chapter 5, when we will have described the first person reference internal to acts of thought. Only then will we be able to recognize the neglect of the self-conscious nature of receptive knowledge as the cause of an inability to apprehend the category of a *power* of knowledge and, in consequence, the concept, and possibility, of knowledge.

The Account of Truth Contained in the Present Material

We said an inquiry into the order of theoretical reasoning, of reasoning about what to believe, was an inquiry into the nature of truth. Now, what account of truth is contained in the results of our investigation?

Compare the account of the good of the preceding chapter. "Good" signifies the measure to which something is revealed to conform by an answer to the question what to do. It transpired from the system of forms of answering this question that the category that this formal concept signifies is a practical life-form: *a unity of actions that manifest this life-form and are ordered among themselves as means to ends.* Following the same method, we inquired into the nature of truth: we developed a system of forms of answering the question what to believe in order to see what order interprets its imperative. We found that the relevant order is neither a set of believed propositions nor a totality of sensory affections unified by thought. Rather, the measure of theoretical reasoning is a power of knowledge: *a unity of beliefs that manifest this power and are ordered among themselves as ground to consequence.* How can this be the beginning of an account of truth? It seems so very unlike what one finds in textbooks on conceptions of truth, which will discuss pragmatist theories, correspondence theories, coherence theories, deflationary theories, and so on. But then, neither do such textbooks discuss Frege's claim that the laws of logic "develop the meaning of the word 'true'", or Kant's assertion that the Transcendental Analytic of the *Critique of Pure Reason* is "a logic of truth".[15]

We said that the concept of the true (as the concept of the good) is a formal concept: it designates the manner in which a proposition is repre-

15. "Der Gedanke", p. 31; *Kritik der reinen Vernunft*, A 62/B 87.

sented in an answer to the question what to believe. An account of truth describes what holds of what is true as such, that is, of values of the variable "*p*" in a (sound) answer to the question what to believe, "*p* because _____". Now, we found, first, that a true proposition as such is caught up in an order that links it to other propositions as a sufficient ground of their truth. Perhaps one can go further in the formal description of this order; perhaps there is a necessary form to inferential relations. In this case, explaining the notion of truth involves describing this form. Frege thought so; he thought there was an inferential order that governs thought as thought, a description of which therefore articulates the meaning of the word "true". Our second point was that a truth is not only linked to other truths according to laws of inference. Our inquiry into the forms of theoretical reasoning showed that something true, in a logically fundamental case, is the content of an act of a power of receptive knowledge. Again, it may be possible to take the formal description of the content of such an act further. It may be possible to describe the general form of a truth of which one may acquire knowledge by means of the senses, or, equivalently, the general form of empirical truth, or experience. The description of this form would be part of an account of the notion of truth employed by subjects whose knowledge depends on sensory affection. Kant's Transcendental Analytic seeks to describe such a form, which is why Kant calls it a logic of truth.

In the beginning of this section, we considered the suggestion that calling the order of theoretical reasoning "truth" is more than giving it a name; it is claiming that the same order interprets the question what to believe regardless of any character of the subject asking it other than her confronting this question. We responded that such a claim could not be the premise, but only the result of the inquiry we proposed to undertake. Now, what can we say about the generality of the order of theoretical reasoning? Our reflections on the good, or the practical life-form, left it open whether this category admits a manifold of instances, as it does on the view of, e.g., Philippa Foot, according to which there may be distinct rational life-forms, each of which interprets the question what to do asked by its bearers. This contrasts with Kant's view, according to which the question refers to the same order wherever it is asked. According to Kant, practical reason itself is *the* practical life-form; the category itself signifies an order and thus leaves no room for a manifold of instances. It might appear that, while there may be space for a manifold of instances of the category of a practical life-form, there can be no space for a manifold of instances of the category of a power of receptive knowledge. For, there is only one world to experience, only one world to know by means of the senses. Therefore, any act of a power of receptive knowledge necessarily agrees with any act of such a power, which proves that they are acts of the same power and that there is only one such power. But this argument is unsound. For, how do we know that there is only one world? We do not know it from experience, and any argument from pure thought that there is only one world to experience would as such be an argument that there can be no plurality of powers of receptive knowledge. Saying that there is only one world to experience is not giving the argument, but restating the claim for which an argument is sought. Indeed, Kant, who excludes a manifold of practical life-forms, makes room for a manifold of powers of receptive knowledge in this way. As a power of receptive knowledge depends for its exercise on a faculty of receptivity, powers of receptive knowledge may differ on account of the character of the receptive faculty on which they depend. According to Kant, our power of receptive knowledge is a power of knowing the temporal and spatial; it depends on a corresponding form of sensibility. But a power of receptive knowledge may involve a different kind of sensibility, and then will not be a power to know the temporal and spatial, but rather objects (appearances) of a different form. Again, it is useless to object that there is only one world to experience—temporal and spatial reality. This is not to argue for, but to state the claim that, the nature of the receptive faculty involved in experience can be no ground for a distinction of powers of receptive knowledge in the way in which some hold that the material character of a rational life-form grounds distinctions of the order of practical reasoning that governs its bearers.[16] We must leave it open whether "power of receptive knowledge" signifies a form of order, or an order. But we shall return to this question in Chapter 6.

Belief and the Question What to Believe

We developed a system of forms of answering the question what to believe, thereby specifying the logical category of its principle: a power of knowledge. Now we shall inquire further into the nexus of theoretical rea-

16. Compare the discussion in John McDowell, "Hegel's Idealism as Radicalization of Kant", and Stephen Engström, "Understanding and Sensibility".

soning and belief, in virtue of which theoretical reasoning arrives at belief. This will enable us to comprehend what transpired in our discussion of inference: that believing something *is* answering the question of theoretical reasoning, is taking it to be something it is right to believe. In the third section, we will see that this entails that there is a special way of knowing that one believes something, which underlies the "I"-reference of her who thus knows.

McDowell on Belief Explanation

G. E. M. Anscombe defines actions as movements to which a certain sense of the question "why?" applies. John McDowell finds in Davidson's work a parallel claim about propositional attitudes: propositional attitudes are subject to a special form of explanation.

> The concepts of propositional attitudes have their proper home in explanations of a special sort: explanations in which things are made intelligible by being revealed to be, or to approximate to being, as they rationally ought to be. ("Functionalism and Anomalous Monism", p. 328)

Applied to belief, this is: one explains why someone believes something in the intended way by revealing her to believe something she rationally ought to believe. McDowell says the concept of belief has its "proper home" in this kind of explanation. He means it depends on it for its sense: no one possesses the concept who does not employ it in this form of explanation. So, such explanations do not just explain beliefs; rather, one apprehends what one explains as an act of belief by bringing it under this form of explanation. Therefore we call it a *belief explanation:* an explanation that, in virtue of its form, represents its object as an act of belief.

McDowell says, a belief explanation of why someone believes something gives a cause that reveals her to believe something she ought to believe. Now an imperative—an "ought", a "should", a gerundive—subsumes its object under a normative measure. McDowell identifies the relevant order by the adverb "rationally": the order to which a belief explanation represents its object as conforming is an order of reason. This tells us little. It is a way of saying that this style of explaining why someone believes something gives a reason for believing it. Anscombe was right in finding a parallel account of action explanation not illuminating. In order to articulate McDowell's claim, we must seek the principle of the system of answers to the question "why?" of belief explanation. Then we can name that principle "reason".

In "Functionalism and Anomalous Monism", McDowell confines his attention to "the order of what follows from what", which he says is a part of the order of reason: if p follows from q, then someone who believes q *rationally* ought to believe p. We saw in the preceding section that the order of inference is not self-standing; determining what to believe by joining belief to belief according to this order does not on its own provide a sense of the question it addresses. Rather, inference is governed by an order to which one conforms in acts of believing that something is the case that manifest a power of knowledge. McDowell's "ought" of reason, then, as it pertains to belief, subsumes its object under the measure of theoretical reasoning, of reasoning about what to believe. So the system of forms of answering the question "why?" of belief explanation is the system of forms of answering the question what to believe.

This is no surprise. It follows from the inner nexus of theoretical reasoning and belief. Theoretical reasoning arrives at belief. Even where it remains idle, it is the kind of reasoning to issue in its subject's believing something. When my reasoning is efficacious in this way, then I not only take p to be something *it is right to believe* because ____; rather, I *believe* it because ____. As theoretical reasoning issues in belief, something in the light of which someone determines p to be something it is right to believe must be capable of explaining why she believes it; what figures as ground in her "It is right to believe that p because ____" must be the kind of thing to be given as cause in "She believes that p because ____". This characterizes a kind of reasoning: theoretical reasoning, which arrives at belief. Now, we can turn the formula around and read it as describing a kind of explanation: what explains in the intended way why someone believes something must be capable of being a ground on which she determines it to be something it is right to believe. This specifies a system of answers to a question "why?", that is, a form of explanation; the system of kinds of causes that defines this form is the system of ways of ascertaining what to believe. A form of explanation so defined is belief explanation: what is explained in this way is thereby apprehended to be an act of belief. As believing that something is the case is the kind of act that may spring from reasoning about what to believe, a condition by which reasoning is about what to believe is, inverted, a condition by which explanation is of belief.

Thus the same system which, seen from one side, is the system of answers to the question "what to believe?" of theoretical reasoning is, seen from the other side, the system of answers to the question "why?" of belief explanation.

McDowell gives the following description of belief explanation: that which explains why someone believes something in the intended way reveals it to be something it is right to believe. By contrast, our reflections suggest this account: that which explains why someone believes something in the intended way is something from which she concludes that it is something it is right to believe. We are led to say that the cause of her believing that *p* is something on the basis of which she *takes it to be* something it is right to believe, whereas McDowell says the cause is something that shows that *it is* something it is right to believe. This is not the same, as someone may think *p* true on a ground that does not, in fact, reveal it to be true. And yet, the formulae need not describe different *forms* of explanation. Indeed, it will turn out in Chapter 6 that they designate the same form of explanation. However, in the present chapter, we shall rely only on our apparently weaker formula.

Theoretical Reasoning and Belief Explanation

If the same principle unifies the modes of answering the question what to believe of theoretical reasoning and those of answering the question "why?" of belief explanation, then this must be on account of the way in which theoretical reasoning is involved in the causality that belief explanations represent. So let us consider the role of someone's reasoning about what to believe in explanations of why she believes something. When a belief springs from theoretical reasoning, then what explains why the subject believes what she does is something in the light of which she determines it to be something it is right to believe. The *same* item is the cause of her believing it and the ground on which she judges it to be something to believe. And it does not so happen that cause and ground come together in this way. Rather, this describes the form of belief explanation, or the kind of causality, to which belief as belief is subject.

By contrast, consider a case in which the cause of a belief and the basis on which its subject judges it true come together per accidens. Let us suppose that Julia is disposed to believe that Justus is in the garden whenever she hears her cat purring. (We are supposing for the sake of argument that the notion of such a disposition is coherent. Later we shall argue that it is not.) It may be that she knows of her disposition and, moreover, is of the opinion that acts of it are likely to be true. So she believes that Justus is in the garden because she hears her cat purring, and she thinks that this speaks in favor of thinking that Justus is in the garden. Now, while the explanation of why she represents Justus in terms of her disposition explains a belief, it is not a belief explanation. It is not through giving an explanation of this sort that I apprehend what I explain as a belief. This is clear from the fact that explanations of the same form may explain what is no belief. We might have stipulated that Julia is disposed to imagine Justus in the garden whenever her cat is purring.

It is obvious what is missing. We have set things up in such a way that the causal nexus exists independently of the subject's determining it to be right to believe the proposition in question in the light of the cause. The causality manifests a disposition of association, which operates independently of its subject's recognizing a truth connection of the propositions. The cat's purring gives rise to Julia's belief that Justus is in the garden no matter whether Julia takes it to be a ground for thinking it true that Justus is in the garden. By contrast, a belief explanation "She thinks Justus is in the garden because her cat is purring" is true only if she thinks it right to believe that Justus is in the garden on the ground that her cat is purring.

A belief explanation "She believes p because she believes q" is true only if the subject thinks that p follows from q. Something analogous holds of belief explanations that represent its object as an act of a power of receptive knowledge. Someone who perceives that something is the case is in a position to tell how things stand with an object in virtue of being sensorily affected by it. Now, suppose someone is disposed to believe that such-and-such is the case whenever an object affects her senses in a certain manner. (Again, let us suppose that the notion of such a disposition is coherent.) In an act of this disposition, she believes that p because she has been suitably affected. Clearly, this is no belief explanation. I do not by explaining something in this manner apprehend it to be a belief. Something that is not a belief may be explained in like manner. We might try adding that the subject thinks that the affection of her senses affords her knowledge. Then she believes that p because her senses have been suitably affected, and, in addition, she thinks that it is right to believe that p given that she has been so affected. But adding this does not change the form of the explanation. Her thought remains external to the causality, as the disposition still operates independently of her recognition that its act conforms to a normative measure. By contrast, a *belief explanation* "She believes that p because she perceives it" is true only of someone who thinks she knows, through the sensory affection by the object, that this is how things stand with it. Believing something because one perceives it in this sense of "because" *is* thinking that one acquires knowledge by means of the senses.

Belief explanation and explanation by associative disposition differ in this way: she who believes something through the operation of a disposition of association may think its act is true (or likely to be true). But the causality of the disposition does not depend on her thinking this; her thinking this normative thought is no part of the sense of explanations in terms of the disposition. By contrast, she who believes something because _____, when this is a belief explanation, determines what she believes to be something it is right to believe. It is not a second thought appended to the explanation that she, in the light of the given cause, determines to be true what she believes on account of that cause. That is contained in the explanation. In the case of Julia, "She believes that p because _____" represents an independent reality of "She reasons that it is true that p because _____". We might contend that there are empirical reasons for supposing that, whenever the former state of affairs obtains, the latter does so as well. We may even hypothesize that the relevant disposition, triggered by _____, issues not only in her believing that p, but in addition in her thinking it right to believe p because _____. (We might find it difficult to explain why we should have any confidence in this hypothesis.) None of this will turn the explanation into a belief explanation. If the "because" is the "because" of belief explanation, then it is not an empirical fact that she who believes that p because _____ takes it that it is right to believe this on the ground that _____. A true belief explanation "She believes that p because _____" represents *the same reality* as the description of her theoretical reasoning, "She takes it to be right to think that p because _____". The causality and her reasoning have not come together per accidens. Rather, her reasoning *is* the causal nexus.

We said theoretical reasoning arrives at belief. And we noted that this requires that a ground on which someone may take such-and-such to be something it is right to believe must be the kind of thing to explain why she believes it. In fact, the nexus of theoretical reasoning and belief explanation is tighter than this. A belief explanation, "She believes that p because _____", is true only if the subject thinks, "It is right to believe that

p because ____". If someone believes that p because ____, and this is a belief explanation, then her reasoning that it is right to believe that p because ____ is the causal nexus that the explanation represents. A belief thus explained is its subject's answer to the question what to believe. Hence, in the logically fundamental case, theoretical reasoning *concludes in an act of belief.* We may suppose for the sake of argument that it is possible that someone thinks it is right to believe p without believing it, or while believing it on account of a cause whose causality does not involve her reasoning about what to believe. That was so in the case of Julia, who believed that Justus was in the garden on account of an associative disposition, and also thought it right to believe that Justus was in the garden. Her thinking it right to believe that Justus was in the garden was a distinct reality from her believing it. But if someone's believing something can be given a belief explanation, then it is not per accidens that the ground on which she thinks it is something to believe *is* the cause of her believing it. This identity defines the relevant causality. And then her believing it and her thought that it is something it is right to believe are *the same reality.*

Empiricist Objections to This Account of Belief Explanation

Someone who believes p because she believes q, when this is a belief explanation, thinks that p follows from q. We said that her apprehending the truth connection of p and q is the causality that the explanation represents. Adapting a phrase of Davidson's that we quoted in the preceding chapter, we can say that beliefs cause beliefs *through a course of theoretical reasoning.* It may be hard to resist the temptation to take this to mean that the subject's grasp of the truth connection is a further cause: she believes that p because she believes, first, that q and, secondly, that p follows from q. It is obvious that this is vain. We cannot rule out that the explanation describes the causality of an associative disposition by expanding the content of the explaining belief. And it is useless to require, further, that the subject believe p because she believes q and believes *If q, then p* in a way that involves her recognizing, on such grounds, that it is right to believe p, or, in Korsgaard's words, that she believe p through "her own recognition of the appropriate conceptual connection", and that her belief express "her own mental activity". For, either the activity is a further cause and we are launched on a regress, or it is the causality and then the maneuver is not needed, as it was necessary only because we sought to do without the notion of a causality of thought. In fact, when we give a belief explanation and say someone believes that p because she believes that q, we give the *complete* cause. If we add that she thinks that p follows from q, we do not give a further cause, but specify the kind of causality or, equivalently, the form of our explanation. As the concept of intentional action, so does the concept of belief signify not special causes, but a kind of causality.

Again, our proposal must appear absurd to someone who holds that "thinking" everywhere refers to a mental process. But when we say that someone thinks that p follows from q, or thinks she knows that p through the affection of her senses, we do not contend that such phrases are occurring to her. What we say is not disproved if nothing like that happens. We are not speaking of mental occurrences; indeed, we are not speaking of anything going on, no matter where. That she thinks such thoughts may manifest itself in various ways, one of which is her saying to herself, "q entails p, so . . .". It may be necessary that thinking can appear in this and other ways. But thinking is not identical with any of its appearances.

We say with Davidson that "She believes p because she believes q" gives a cause. For, it not only says that she believes p and q and takes the latter to support the former. It says that q is the ground *on which* she believes that p, which is a causal locution. But Davidson spoils this insight by the way in which he deploys it in arguing for his Anomalous Monism. He arrives at the latter doctrine by conjoining the above insight with the thesis that, although the word "cause" has a sense independent of any form of explanation, a particular form of explanation bears a privileged relation to causality in the sense that terms of a causal nexus necessarily are the object of a true explanation of that form. This privileged form of explanation subsumes events as cause and effect under a strict law of the kind discovered in certain areas of physics. It follows that, as anything joined in a causal nexus, so do the terms of belief explanations fall under such laws, albeit under different concepts, i.e., not as beliefs. However, Davidson's own description of belief explanation gives the lie to this. He says that belief explanations give a cause in the light of which the subject considers what she believes on account of it as something it is right to believe. As is clear from his discussion of "deviant causal chains", he does not think it suffices that cause and ground be identical per accidens. Nor could he, for he wants the condition to capture the idea that the explanation rationalizes what it explains, which it does not do when the identity of cause and ground is accidental. But that the cause is the subject's ground, not per accidens but in virtue of the kind of cause that it is, means that her grasp of the truth connection constitutes the causality of that cause. Then the causal nexus of "She thinks p because she thinks q" cannot be the object of an explanation in terms of, say, laws of chemistry or physics applied to the brain, as neither chemistry nor physics study causal relations that consist in thinking. One cannot conceptually tie causality to explanation by strict laws and yet appreciate that, in belief explanation, as Davidson puts it, "causality is linked to the normative demands of rationality".[17]

Davidson's idea that the terms of belief explanations figure under different concepts in explanations that subsume events under physical laws cannot be made to fit with his own account of belief explanation. But we can independently disprove the idea by attending to the form of temporality of belief. If belief explanations give causes, which surely they do, then it is false that a causal nexus as such links event to event. For, believing that something is the case is a temporally unlimited act. It is no event; events are limited, they have an end. "She believes that p because she believes that q", a causal explanation for sure, does not signify a nexus of events. It does not mention events. Noticing something like this, Davidson suggests that there are events in the offing, namely the "onslaught" of a belief: a transition from not believing that something is the case to believing that it is.[18] And of course there are such transitions. But they are not the terms of belief explanations. "She believes that p because she believes that q" does not say that her coming to believe that p was caused by her coming to believe that q. Suppose I do not know when she came to believe that p, and whether that was before or after she came to believe that q. Then I should be unable to declare with any confidence that she believes that p because she believes that q. In fact I need not inquire into her psychological history in order to give the explanation. My explanation does not rest on historical knowledge because it is not about the past. It is a present tense statement, it speaks of what is now, which "now" is neither that of a state nor that of a movement, but the "now" of a temporally unlimited act. The same holds of "She believes that p because she perceived it", which is a causal explanation. If the explanation is true, then she came to believe that p through

17. "Replies to Essays", p. 246.
18. "Actions, Reasons, Causes", p. 12.

being affected by the object of her thought. But the explanation does not represent an event, a sensory affection, as causing a further event, an onslaught of thinking. It represents the subject's believing that *p* as an act of a power to gain knowledge by means of the senses, which act is temporally unlimited and no event at all.

In the preceding subsection, we left it open for the sake of argument whether the notion of a disposition to believe something (or to come to believe it) whenever one believes something else (or has come to believe it), or suffers certain impressions, is coherent. We now see that it is incoherent if, as we may suppose, a disposition in this context is meant to underlie a causal nexus of events in the following way: when something is disposed to do *A* whenever something else does *B* to it, and now something has done *B* to it, then this was the cause of its doing *A*, if its doing *A* actualized the disposition. We cannot substitute "believe that *p*" for "do *A*" in this schema; believing that something is the case has a different logical form from an act of such a disposition. Thus we must reject what William Alston propounds as a matter of course:

> A given psyche at a given time has a number of relatively fixed dispositions to go from a certain input (beliefs or experiences or a combination thereof) to a belief output with a content that is a more or less determinate function of relevant characteristics of the input. (*The Reliability of Sense Perception*, pp. 4–5)[19]

Nothing could be further from the truth. Believing that something is the case is logically unfit to be the object of dispositions of association, from which we must conclude that beliefs are terms of a different kind of causality. The concept of cause is abstract; in belief explanations, we are dealing with a specific modification of it. The relevant causality consists in a thought of the subject linking its terms.

Belief and Self-Consciousness

Beliefs fall under a form of explanation, belief explanation, such that she whose belief is thus explained takes the believed proposition to be something it is right to believe on the ground of the given cause. We shall argue

19. On these pages, Alston is not arguing for what he claims in the quoted passage. He is introducing his topic, the reliability of "ways (modes, habits, mechanisms . . .) of belief formation" (p. 4). According to our reflections, there is no such topic.

that this entails that she, the believing subject, by being this subject, is equipped to give this explanation. From this it follows that she expresses this explanation of why she believes something by means of a first person pronoun. In giving the explanation, she states knowledge not from observing what she believes, but from ascertaining what to believe, and this way of knowing defines the first person reference of a subject of beliefs. Such is the inner nexus of self-consciousness, belief, and theoretical reasoning.

The First Person Nature of Belief Explanation

When someone believes p because she believes q, and this is a belief explanation, she thinks that p follows from q and therefore is something it is right to believe. Analogously, someone who believes something because she perceived it thinks she knows through the object's affecting her senses how things stand with that object. These thoughts are not causes of her belief, but the causality of its cause. Now consider the subject herself, explaining "I believe that p because ____", and reasoning "It is right to believe that p because ____". The latter thought, her theoretical reasoning, *is* the causal nexus that the former thought, her explanation, *represents*. So it appears that she thinks two thoughts, the one representing her as thinking the other. In fact, her thinking the thought that represents the causality *is* her thinking the thought that is the causality. We can see this from both sides of the equation. (Our argument here is analogous to that by which we established the parallel claim about action explanation.)

Like "Fregean predication", "belief explanation" describes a form, and the normative thought of the believing subject characterizes that form. When we say that the subject thinks this thought, we describe the logical form of the terms of a belief explanation in the same way in which we describe the form of the elements of a Fregean predication when we say it conjoins object and concept. Being an object is being of such a logical nature as to be a subject of Fregean predications. In the same way, the subject's thinking "It is right to believe that p because ____" is that on account of which the terms of that normative thought bear the logical nature to be joined in a belief explanation. Or again, apprehending someone as thinking Fa, we apprehend a to be constituted in such a way as to be thought in this manner; we apprehend it to be an object. Analogously, apprehending someone as thinking "She believes p because she believes q", we apprehend the terms of the explanation as constituted in such a way as to be thought according to that form; and now that is, we apprehend the relevant propositions as joined by the subject in her theoretical reasoning. So the relevant normative thought of that subject is not part of the content of the explanation, not something the explanation asserts exists in addition to the belief and its cause. Rather, it is by virtue of that thought that these have the logical shape to figure in this form of explanation. Now return to the subject herself, thinking "I believe that p because ____" and "It is right to believe that p because ____". Representing her as thinking the former, we represent her as thinking the latter, as her thinking the latter constitutes the logical character of the terms of her former thought. Hence, there is no representing her as thinking "I believe that p because ____" without representing her as thinking "It is right to believe that p because ____", which means that there is but one thought she is represented as thinking.

Conversely, consider someone's thinking that it is right to believe that p because q, when her thinking this is the causality of a true belief explanation. That her thought constitutes the causal nexus of her believing that p and her believing that q does not characterize the content of that thought, nor is it an empirical fact that someone who thinks it is right to believe that p because q can be expected to believe that p because she believes that q. Rather, that she believes that p because she believes that q is a feature of the form of her thought that it is right to think that p because q. It characterizes the manner in which she conjoins p and q in thinking this. But then we cannot distinguish her thinking "I believe that p because I believe that q" from her thinking "It is right to believe that p because q". The former phrase puts into words the form of the latter, the manner in which its elements are conjoined. It stands to it as "a is an object falling under the concept of being F" stands to "Fa". These phrases do not express distinct thoughts.

If the subject's "I believe that p because ____" expresses a true belief explanation, then it expresses the same thought as her "It is right to believe that p because ____". We know from the preceding section that this is a thought the subject thinks if the explanation is true, for it is the causality that the explanation represents. So if a belief has a true explanation of this kind, then its subject is in a position to give this explanation. *The causality of the explanation contains the subject's representation of this very causality.* Therefore, such an explanation, given by the subject, satisfies our formula of first person knowledge: the subject is able to give it *by being its object*. Belief explanations by the believing subject are unmediated first person thoughts. Consider, by contrast, an explanation that represents the causality of an associative disposition. We imagined Julia, who thinks of Justus in the garden whenever she hears her cat purring. On a given day, she thinks of Justus because she heard her cat purring, manifesting this disposition. Julia may know of her disposition, and she may explain her thinking of Justus by it. But she need not be able to give that explanation in order for the causal nexus to hold. The disposition may operate behind her back. Here, subject and object of the explanation are identical only per accidens, wherefore the form of the explanation leaves room for a separate judgment, separate from the explanation, representing the identity. By contrast, if someone gives a belief explanation of why she believes that such-and-such is the case, then the identity of subject and object of the explanation follows from its form. Therefore, there is no space for a separate identity judgment, and the explanation is an unmediated first person thought. For, by nominal definition, a first person thought is a manner of thinking of an object such that the thinking subject is the object of which she thinks. As the form of belief explanation fixes it that it satisfies this description when it is given by the subject, its first person character is a feature of its own form and not extended to it by way of an identity judgment.

The Way of Knowing Actualized in First Person Belief Explanation

We seek to explain the sense of first person reference. In the first chapter, we argued that this requires describing ways of knowing acts of which are unmediated first person thoughts. It is easy to state in the abstract the condition that picks out such ways of knowing: when I know an object in a first person way, I know it by being that object. Acts of thought, practical and theoretical, appear to satisfy this condition: I know that I am doing something intentionally by doing it, and know that I believe something by believing it. Therefore we set out to investigate *how* actions and beliefs contain their subject's knowledge of themselves. It is worthy of note that the difficulty does *not* lie with realizing that the representation of one's own beliefs is first personal or, equivalently, that it is by believing something that one knows that one believes it. Rather, the difficulty is to understand how this is, i.e., on account of what in the nature of belief a subject of beliefs is self-conscious.[20] John Searle, e.g., says that the way in which one knows one's conscious mental states cannot be conceived on the model of sense perception because a conscious state is identical with its subject's consciousness of it.

> Where conscious subjectivity is concerned, there is no distinction between the observation and the thing observed, between the perception and the object perceived. The model of vision works on the presupposition that there is a distinction between the thing seen and the seeing of it. But for "introspection" there is simply no way to make this separation. Any introspection I have of my own conscious state is itself this mental state. (*The Rediscovery of the Mind*, p. 97)

This is good, as a starting point. If we call the power of knowing something in a first person way "introspection", then introspection differs from sense perception in that its acts are identical with their object. This is a negative description of that way of knowing: it is not an act of knowing through sensory affection. As knowing through sense perception is knowing in the way that supports demonstrative reference to the object thus known, this means that the relevant representation is not demonstrative. And indeed, first person reference is not a kind of demonstrative reference. But an account of first person reference must say more than that. It must *explain* the identity of first person knowledge with its object, which is its first person character.

An account of how I know that I believe something when I know it in a way that satisfies the first person knowledge formula, i.e., know that I believe something by believing it, can only come from an inquiry into the nature of belief. And since the concept of belief signifies a form of thought, belief explanation, the account must transpire from a description of this form. So it does. A belief explanation "I believe *p* because ____" gives a cause from which the subject concludes that it is right to believe what she believes on account of it. This is so not per accidens, but rather

---

20. It is sometimes denied that a subject's representation of her own beliefs is first personal, as when it is said to be a meta-representation. But this can be held only out of despair over the task of understanding the idea of a reality that contains its own representation, i.e., the idea of a self-conscious subject.

characterizes the causality of the cause, or the form of the explanation. Now, we found that the conclusion of the subject, "It is right to believe that p", expresses the same thought as the "I believe that p" of her belief explanation. This shows how she knows that she believes p: the cause of her believing it is at the same time, and not per accidens, a ground on which she thinks that she should, or, equivalently, that she does, believe it. So the cause of a belief explanation is, as such, the ratio essendi and the subject's ratio cognoscendi of its effect. Her explanation, being identical with her theoretical reasoning, expresses knowledge that she believes something, and why, that comes not from the senses, but from thought. She knows that she believes p not from observing that she believes this, but from reasoning about what to believe.

In order to explain first person reference of a subject of beliefs, we must describe a way of knowing such that knowing that someone believes something in this way is knowing that one oneself believes it. That way of knowing will not leave room for a separate judgment that one oneself is the object of which one thus knows; first person thoughts about what is known in this way will be identification-free. The way of knowing we described, knowing that one believes something by reasoning about what to believe, satisfies this condition, since it is knowledge one has by being its object. If I know that someone believes something by concluding that it is something it is right to believe, then I know that I believe it; I need not recognize a person. This idea was put forth by Gareth Evans:

> In making a self-ascription of belief, one's eyes are, so to speak, or occasionally literally, directed outward—upon the world. If someone asks me "Do you think there is going to be a third world war?", I must attend, in answering him, to precisely the same outward phenomena as I would attend to if I were answering the question "Will there be a third world war?" I get myself in a position to answer the question whether I believe that p by putting into operation whatever procedure I have for answering the question whether p. (*The Varieties of Reference*, p. 225)

When I know that someone believes that p from ascertaining that p is true, then I know that I believe that p. This way of knowing constitutes the sense of first person reference of a subject of beliefs.

In the preceding chapter, we quoted G. E. M. Anscombe's discontent with the "contemplative conception of knowledge", according to which knowledge, as such, is of an independent object.[21] It is characteristic of the empiricist tradition in epistemology and the philosophy of mind that it thinks it the highest possibility of thought to lay hold of objects that exist independently, as though thought were powerless to be the principle of the existence of its objects. It is impossible to understand first person thought without giving up this conception of knowledge, for unmediated first person knowledge is distinguished by the fact that, here, the thing known is not a reality that is independent of the knowledge of it. Belief, or theoretical thought, is a reality that includes its subject's knowledge of it, which knowledge therefore is unmediated first person knowledge. For, beliefs essentially figure in belief explanations, and it defines this form of explanation that, if a belief can be explained in this way, its subject is in a position thus to explain it. Her knowledge that and why she believes what she does, which she expresses in giving the explanation, is not a separate existence from what it represents. It includes and is included in the reality of which it is knowledge.[22]

21. The attempt to accommodate first person knowledge within a contemplative conception of knowledge inevitably leads to the postulation of queer forms of vision, "a very queer and special sort of seeing eye in the middle of the acting", as G. E. M. Anscombe put it. Dieter Henrich's work on self-consciousness is an example. He writes: "The I must [. . .] in self-consciousness be aware of itself. [. . .] It must [. . .] be capable of asserting with certainty that, in self-consciousness, it is known to itself. [. . .] As is well known, this certainty is infallible, instantaneous and beyond any doubt. [. . .] It [the question, "Who, really, am I?"] presupposes that the question "Is this I, of which I am aware, really my I?", has already been answered." ("Selbstbewußtsein und spekulatives Denken", p. 144.) Henrich speaks of an I of which I am aware. This awareness is like sense perception in that unmediated judgments based on it are *demonstrative:* I refer to the object of my awareness as "*this* I". It follows that I need to identify the object of which I am aware with the subject who is aware of it in order to arrive at a first person thought. I need to ascertain, that is, that the I of which I am aware is my I or, shorter (assuming that I am my I), that I am this I. Now, Henrich observes that it appears that I cannot fail in my recognition of a certain I as myself. I cannot mistake an I that is not mine for my I. My thought that a certain I (the I of which I am aware) is my I is immune to error; it is infallible, beyond any doubt, and surely has many more astounding characteristics. Self-consciousness is an act of a faculty of awareness that is unlike sense perception in that it is not liable to erroneous identification of its object with something it is not. Here is a queer sort of vision.

22. It may again be thought that this must signify that the speech act "I believe *p*" is performative in the sense that saying that I believe something makes it the case that I do. On some views, this would show that the speech act does not express knowledge, a fortiori not knowledge contained in what is known. But it is not true that saying, sincerely, that I believe something makes it the case that I do. There are various ways in which that may fail to be the case. Suppose, e.g., I say "I believe this tomato is ripe". It may be that there is no tomato

The "modern", i.e., empiricist, conception of knowledge is linked up with the notion that a statement of known fact can bear no normative significance. Unmediated first person thoughts, because they express knowledge from reasoning about what to do and believe, have a normative sense; this distinguishes them from thoughts about objects given through the senses, which are contemplative knowledge. When I give a belief explanation why I believe something and say, "I believe that *p* because _____", I determine what it is right to believe. I not only describe myself, but position myself vis-à-vis a normative order. This normative significance of first person thought is irreducible. It cannot be explained by decomposing the thought into a descriptive and an evaluative component. In the following passage, Wittgenstein meditates on this idea:

> "When I say 'I believe . . .', I really describe my own state of mind,—but here, this description indirectly asserts the fact believed." Just as I might describe a photograph in order to describe that of which it is an image.—But then I must be able to say that the photograph is a good image. And hence also: "I believe that it is raining, and my belief is reliable, hence, I am relying on it." (*Philosophische Untersuchungen*, 2:x)

Wittgenstein's interlocutor thinks that a first person judgment "I believe . . ." is composed of two parts. On the one hand, I say that I am in a state that represents or pictures something, as does a photograph. In so describing myself, I do not speak to the question whether things are as I picture them; I merely say how things stand with myself. On the other hand, I claim to believe something it is right to believe, or true. I assert that my belief correctly depicts its object as a faithful photograph does. This reduction of the normative sense of first person thought reduces to absurdity. If the first person representation of beliefs reduced to a descriptive and an evaluative component, then neither would their subject fall under the concept of belief, nor would she have thoughts about what to

---

where I think I see one; then I do not, using the sentence "This tomato is ripe", express a thought. If there is no tomato where I believe I see one, then there is no tomato with respect to which my putative demonstrative thought could be true or false. Hence, there is no such thought. I express nothing using the words "This tomato is ripe" (using them in the way in which they are ordinarily used and in which I intend to use them), and thus believe nothing that would be expressed by these words. Consequently, I do not know that I believe something these words would express.

believe. For, the concept of belief depends on belief explanation: someone falls under this concept only if she figures in explanations of this form. And when she does, she is able to explain why she believes what she does in this way, and then her thought that she believes it has the described normative significance. If first person thoughts could be decomposed into a description of a state of mind and an assessment of this state, then the description could not be true, for the subject would not fall under the concept of belief that allegedly describes her state. Neither could she frame the alleged assessment, for, as she does not possess the concept of belief, she does not think about what to believe. The normative sense of first person thought is irreducible; we cannot isolate its descriptive from its evaluative meaning without dissolving the putative components.[23]

We have uncovered an inner nexus of self-consciousness and belief. Beliefs essentially figure in explanations that, in virtue of their form, she who is the object of the explanation is in a position to give and that she therefore expresses by the first person pronoun. Someone who falls under the concept of belief brings herself under it in first person thought.[24] Acquiring the power of theoretical thought and belief is acquiring the concept of belief and with it the power of first person thought. It has been held that the concept of belief belongs to a folk science, which is bound to be replaced by a scientific theory that will employ more advanced concepts. This idea is sometimes conjoined with the promise that this future theory will deepen our self-knowledge. However, the idea implies that first person thought is a prescientific form of thought that will be abandoned by a more developed culture. Pretending that we can make sense of

23. In *A Study of Concepts,* Christopher Peacocke asks whether the concept of belief is compatible with the "naturalistic world-view", which he defines by the assumption that "any truth is supervenient on purely descriptive truths" (pp. 125–129). It follows from this assumption that unmediated first person thoughts are never knowledge, as they have an irreducibly normative sense. If such a thought is true, its truth does not supervene on purely descriptive truths. Peacocke and the naturalistic worldview assume that first person thought is not objectively valid. But we cannot rest our philosophy on an assumption that excludes ourselves from what is real.

24. Donald Davidson maintains that a believing subject as such possesses the concept of belief ("Thought and Talk", p. 170). He does not pause to meditate on the following consequence of his claim: that the concept of belief essentially figures in first person thought. (Davidson's claim is true of the concept of belief that applies to subjects of theoretical reasoning. It is perfectly irrelevant that the word "belief" may be employed to signify a different, albeit related concept, which applies to nonrational animals, and of which the claim is not true.)

this vision, it would follow that subjects of this culture are logically precluded from referring to themselves first personally and, hence, from possessing self-knowledge. It seems an inadequate response to the difficulties of a self-conscious life to hope for science to liberate us from self-consciousness. First person reference and concept of belief are not part of an empirical theory. They figure in knowledge, not from the senses, but from thought.

4

Reason, Freedom, and True Materialism

The preceding chapters described a parallel structure in the order of action and the order of belief, and in the way in which these underwrite the first person reference of those who are subject to them. In this chapter, we shall abstract this structure and relate it to the notions of reason and freedom.[1] It is the principle thought of German Idealism that self-consciousness, freedom, and reason are one. In our manner of developing it, this thesis is part of a truly materialist theory of self-consciousness.

Self-Consciousness as Reason

It is a venerable idea that self-consciousness and reason are internally related; it is difficult to understand. An account of self-consciousness that treats the concept of reason as independently understood cannot illuminate the nexus of reason and self-consciousness, as it would trace too small a circle. A theory of self-consciousness and reason must reveal their unity by exhibiting their common root. This is a certain kind of order, an order that, in one motion, gives rise to a notion of justification that applies to the acts that it governs and to the power of first person thought of the subjects of these acts.

An intentional action responds to the question what to do; the order that interprets that gerundive is the subject's practical life-form, which thus is internal to her actions. But actions not only fall under a practical life-form. An intentional action subsumes itself under its order. Doing something intentionally is taking it to be something to be done, where

1. A full account of the nexus of self-consciousness and reason includes a description of the manner in which an order of reason sustains mutual knowledge among self-conscious subjects, which we shall give in Chapter 6.

being to be done is being in accord with one's practical life-form. There are not, on the one hand, movements falling under a practical life-form and, on the other hand, thoughts that bring movements under this life-form. A movement falling under a practical life-form *is* a thought that places this very movement under that order. In doing something intentionally, I not only fall under a normative order, and I not only represent myself as conforming to this order; rather, this representation and my action are the same act. With regard to a practical life-form, *falling under it and bringing oneself under it are the same.* We shall call an order of which this holds true *formally represented.* "Formally" is to signify that its being represented characterizes the order with regard to its form, i.e., with regard to the manner in which it relates to what it orders.

Just as actions respond to the question what to do, so do beliefs respond to the question what to believe. The normative order providing the sense of that imperative is, by nominal definition, the truth; substantively characterized, it is the power of receptive knowledge of the believing subject, which is internal to her beliefs. Again, it is not merely that, in believing something, I fall under such a measure. Rather, in believing something, I bring myself under it. I am not confronted with my beliefs as a given reality, which I then assess in the light of the truth.[2] I do not, on the one hand, believe something and, on the other hand, think it something it is right to believe. There is but one act of the intellect, which both these phrases describe. An act that falls under an order of knowledge *is* a thought referring this very act to that order. So in the case of an order of receptive knowledge, too, falling under it and placing oneself under it in thought are one. A power of receptive knowledge is formally represented.

A practical life-form and a power of receptive knowledge are formally represented because they sustain a certain form of explanation, or kind of causality. An explanation of this form gives a cause of an act from which its subject concludes that the act conforms to the relevant order. And it is not per accidens that the cause of the act is identical with its subject's ground for thinking that it is as it should be. Rather, this identity characterizes the form of the explanation, the causality it represents. The explanation represents, as we put it, a *causality of thought.* An order is formally represented if and only if acts that are under it exhibit this kind of causality. For, an act

2. Compare Richard Moran's illuminating discussion of the difference of authority from control, *Authority and Estrangement,* chap. 4.3.

under an order is identical with its subject's thought that it conforms to that order if and only if, not per accidens, but in virtue of the causality of the cause of the act, her ground for thinking that she conforms to the order in performing the act explains why she performs it. Acts of a formally represented order exhibit a causality of thought.

A formally represented order, sustaining a causality of thought, is a source of self-consciousness in subjects falling under it. Acts of such an order are represented by their subjects first personally. For, as we have seen in the preceding chapters, if the subject's thought that A is to be performed because ____ constitutes the causal nexus represented by the explanation that she performs A because ____, then her reasoning that she should perform A because ____ and her explaining that she does perform A because ____ are *one* act of the mind. And then she is in a position to explain the act by expressing a thought that she thinks if the explanation is true. Her explanation satisfies the first person knowledge formula: she is in a position to give it by being its object. Subject and object of the explanation are identical not per accidens, but in virtue of the form of the explanation. It follows that the expression she deploys in stating the explanation is a first person pronoun.

Now, the same character of a normative order that is the source of the first person form of the representation of its acts gives rise to a concept of justification applying to these acts. That character is the order's being formally represented, equivalently, its sustaining a causality of thought. In order to see this, we must first ask what justification is. Provisionally, we can say that a *justification* of something is an account that reveals, or takes a step toward revealing, it to be just, or as it should be; *justifying* is giving such an account; and something *is justified* if and only if it has a true account of this kind. Like an imperative—a "should", a "right", a gerundive—a concept of justification refers to a normative order. "Justification" and its cognates designate a form of concept, and we arrive at a concept when we interpret the above schemata by a determinate order. But not any order will do. A grocer might think that a good apple is shiny. Still, there is no such thing as justifying an apple and no such thing as a justified apple. In Chapter 2, we distinguished internal from external standards. When the grocer thinks his apples ought to be shiny, he assesses his apples by an order that is external to them. He compares them with what he wants in an apple, not with what an apple is. An order defines a concept of justification only if it is internal to what falls under it. But even this does not suffice. The parts and operations of a living being fall under an internal order. When someone is shortsighted, her power of vision is not as it should be. And when someone has caught a cold, her mucous membranes did not operate as they should. The order that defines these imperatives is an order of health, which is internal to its phenomena; when we say what an eye or what mucous is, we describe what each does in the healthy body. Eyes and membranes may act or be, or fail to act or be, as they ought to according to an internal measure. Still, we do not say that someone's eyes or nose are, or fail to be, justified. Catching a cold differs from acting intentionally, and being shortsighted differs from believing something, in this way: catching a cold and assessing one's mucous in the light of its condition of health are distinct realities, and being shortsighted is not a normative thought about this state of one's eyes. Here, falling under the order is one thing; representing it is another. If something is to admit of justification, it is not enough that it should fall under an internal order; it must manifest its subject's consciousness of this order. A phenomenon admits of justification only if it falls under a normative order in a way that includes its subject's representation of this very order. Only an order represented in the acts that it governs provides for a concept of justification.

This yields the following account of justification: justifying something is revealing it, or taking a step toward revealing it, to be just, the sense of "just" being given by a formally represented order. We encountered two orders, or two kinds of order, that are internal to and represented in acts that are subject to them: a power of receptive knowledge, internal to judgment and belief, and a practical life-form, internal to action and intention. Both define a concept of justification. There is *epistemic* justification of belief and *practical* justification of action; justifying an action is revealing it, or taking a step toward revealing it, to conform to one's practical life-form, while justifying a belief is revealing it, or taking a step toward revealing it, to be an act of one's power of receptive knowledge.

We said we comprehend the unity of self-consciousness and reason if we can trace them to the same root. Now it transpires that self-consciousness and reason are features of a formally represented order. Let us say that a rational being is a subject of acts that admit of justification, i.e., of acts that fall under an order that defines a concept of justification; let us call such an order an order of reason. Then we can express our result by saying that *a formally represented order is an order of reason.* Furthermore, an act that falls under a formally represented order is identical with a thought by its subject that places it under this order, which thought therefore is an unmediated first person thought. We may put this by saying that *a formally represented order is an order of self-consciousness.* An order of reason is an order of self-consciousness, and an order of self-consciousness is an order of reason. Or, a rational subject is self-conscious, and a self-conscious subject is rational. Reason and self-consciousness are two sides of a coin; the coin is a normative order internal to and represented by the acts that it governs.[3]

It is the principle thought of Kant and Hegel that self-consciousness and reason are one. And it would not be inept to characterize our efforts as an attempt to articulate that thought, thereby offering a way of reading these authors. But we must note two respects in which our results fall short of recovering the full content of that principle thought. Kant and Hegel conceive of reason as itself an order, which *is* the order of self-consciousness or, simply, self-consciousness. By contrast, in our reflections above, "reason" signifies a *kind* of order, not an order. We employ the notion of *an* order of reason but are not in a position to speak of *the* order of reason. On the one hand, we have not yet shown that there is only one, or the, practical life-form and that there is only one, or the, power of receptive knowledge. But we shall attempt to do this in Chapter 6. On the other hand, we have not shown that the order of the intellect and the order of the will are the same.

---

3. David Velleman, who recognizes that an account of the concept of a reason for acting requires the specification of a measure that is internal to action and practical reasoning (*The Possibility of Practical Reason,* pp. 15–16), holds that this measure is self-knowledge. Thus he explains self-consciousness not as the form of the order of action, but as the content of this order. This is inevitable in the absence of the notion of a causality of thought. Velleman apparently thinks that the idea, or, as he says, the hypothesis that actions are distinguished by their special, mental causes (see "What Happens When Someone Acts?": "One is surely entitled to hypothesize [. . .] that there are mental states and events within an agent whose causal interactions constitute his being influenced by a reason, or his forming and conforming to an intention" [p. 124].) is justified in virtue of being in accord with "our scientific view of the world" (ibid., p. 129). But a sound account of the nature of scientific knowledge does not assign to the sciences the office of providing philosophy with hypothetical foundations. Hegel writes about the manner in which "former metaphysics" treated the concept of mechanical and final causation: "Die vormalige Metaphysik [. . .] hat [. . .] eine Weltvorstellung vorausgesetzt und sich bemüht zu zeigen, daß der eine oder der andere Begriff auf sie passe und der entgegengesetzte mangelhaft sei, weil er sich nicht aus ihm erklären lasse." (*Wissenschaft der Logik,* vol. 2, p. 182.) This is an accurate description of a large part of current philosophy of mind and action.

This means that we lack an account of the unity of theoretical and practical reason and with it of the unity of the subject of action and belief. This gap we shall not be able to fill within this treatise.

Self-Consciousness as Freedom

A certain sort of freedom, the sort also named "autonomy" or "spontaneity", appears to require self-consciousness in the subject of such freedom, and that sort of freedom must have something to do with reason. If this is right, then an account of the unity of self-consciousness and reason will shed light on the idea of freedom, or autonomy, or spontaneity. Our account does that. First, as Kant says, the concept of *freedom* designates a kind of causality. The relevant kind is the one we have described: a causality of thought, sustained by a formally represented, rational and self-conscious, order. This explains the traditional doctrine that freedom is a character not only of acts of the will, but equally of acts of the intellect. The doctrine has been revived recently, but continues to meet with puzzlement.[4] Our reflections allow us to state it in a manner in which it should no longer seem puzzling. Secondly, our account of the nexus of self-consciousness and reason yields an interpretation of Kant's equation of being *autonomous* with being under laws of reason. The equation has seemed incredible to contemporary philosophers who seek to follow Kant in assigning autonomy a central place in their account of reason. They do not see how autonomy can consist in being under laws, as opposed to above them, wherefore they read Kant as claiming that self-conscious, rational subjects institute the norms to which they are bound and in this way ground their authority. But it is hard to see how the authority of a law could spring from an act of imposition, which in turn would have to be lawless and arbitrary. By contrast, we shall expound an account of autonomy according to which, being subject to reason, a self-conscious subject is subject to nothing that is not, in a sense we shall explain, herself. Kant's equation of being subject to one's own laws and being subject to laws of reason is sound. Finally, the nexus of self-consciousness and freedom yields an abstract description of the way of knowing that underlies the first person reference of a rational subject: unmediated first person knowledge of such a subject is knowledge not from receptivity, but from *spontaneity*.

4. For the revival compare, e.g., the work of Wilfrid Sellars, John McDowell, Robert Brandom; for the puzzlement, e.g., David Owens, *Reason without Freedom*.

Freedom as a Kind of Causality—of the Will and of the Intellect

Some authors claim that I am free if my movements are caused by my beliefs and desires, presumably because, in this case, I am doing what I want
to do and am doing it because I want to do it. What else can freedom
be?[5] But I may be doing *A* because I want to do *B* and believe that doing
A is a means of doing *B,* and yet fail to exercise freedom in doing *A.* Remember him who falls ill because he wants to lose weight, develops
symptoms from his depression over his failure, on account of which he
loses weight. His falling ill is not an act of freedom. And he is no freer if,
in addition to his desire to lose weight, there is among the psychic causes
of his decline a belief that he will lose weight on account of this desire.
(Such a belief could quite conceivably deepen his depression and aggra-
vate the symptoms.) Someone who is doing something because ____
manifests freedom not if exalted things follow the "because", but if and
only if the "because" *bears a certain sense.* Freedom is not a matter of
what explains the movement, but a character of the manner in which it is
explained. An action is free if its explanation exhibits a certain form, the
form we described in Chapter 2. When an action can be explained in this
way, then its subject's thought that she is doing something it is good to
do as it brings her closer to a certain finite end, or as circumstances reveal
it to manifest a certain infinite end, is not a further cause, but the
causality. The idea of freedom is the idea of an act that exhibits a causality
of thought.

If the concept of a causality of thought is not available, being free necessarily is misconstrued as being caused to move by certain psychic states
or events, with unlimited space for debate over their kind and content, for
this then is the only alternative to the absurd view that being free is being
not determined by anything.[6] It is undetermined, let us suppose, whether
a rabbit running across a field will pass to the left or to the right of a tree
in its path or whether a rock rolling over a peak rising in its way will be de-
flected to the left or to the right. Neither the rabbit nor the rock manifest
freedom in going right even though, we imagined, it was undetermined
whether they would before they did. The idea of freedom is not the idea
of a lack of determination; it does not signify the arbitrary, absurd, and

---

5. Compare, for example, Peter Bieri, *Das Handwerk der Freiheit,* part 1.
6. The absurdity of the latter view is brought out in ibid., part 2.

null. It is the idea of a kind of determination; it signifies a kind of causality, intelligibility, and reality: a causality of thought, an intelligibility that passes through an order of reason, and a reality that is self-conscious.[7]

As is acting intentionally, so is believing something an act of freedom. Two errors prevent this from being recognized. The first is thinking that if believing something is an act of freedom, then it is an intentional action; the second is construing freedom of action as the freedom to do as one pleases. When these errors combine, the claim that believing something is an act of freedom is heard as the absurd suggestion that one is free to believe what one pleases. We have corrected the second mistake. Being free is being subject to a causality of thought and, hence, is placing oneself under an order of reason. We can correct the first mistake if we realize that the relevant order of reason—the formally represented order of acts of the intellect—is not a practical life-form, but a power of receptive knowledge.[8]

Believing that something is the case is an act of freedom, because a subject of belief as such places herself under an order of reason. This seems puzzling if we overlook what order of reason pertains to acts of the intellect. Peter Bieri writes:

> Applying the concept of justification to beliefs is not without danger. For this concept is originally employed in the context of action and decision: we need to justify what we are doing or have done, and what we have decided to do. Beliefs are not actions. [. . .] When I express my belief, then I assert a sentence. And since asserting is something I decide to do or to refrain from doing, it may seem as if I

---

7. It is therefore a confusion to think that, in order to vindicate the objective validity of the concept of freedom, we must in a prior exercise of speculative metaphysics establish that not everything is determined. The concept of freedom is objectively valid if and only if there are true explanations that represent a causality of thought. Since these explanations represent a causality that is such as to be known in a first person manner by the subject, acts of freedom provide their subject with knowledge of these very acts. The reality of freedom is a self-conscious, or formally represented, reality. Hence, we know that we are free from reflecting on the form of our unmediated first person thoughts. We know that we are free by being free.

8. When Kant calls a judgment an act of the understanding, he does not mean that a judgment is an action. In its primary sense, the word "act" signifies the exercise of a power. In a more narrow sense, it signifies that the power in question is a power of spontaneity (a concept we discuss later in this chapter). The polemic against the notion of an act of the will is based on an analogous misunderstanding.

already performed an action when I "form a belief". [. . .] But this is an illusion. Even where beliefs issue in assertions, they themselves are not actions, but states that come and go. Therefore the application of the concept of justification to beliefs is not straightforward. (*Analytische Philosophie der Erkenntnis*, pp. 40–41)

An assertion is an action, and as such a response to the question what to do. It may or may not be justified in the light of the normative order of this question; it may or may not be *practically* justified. But an assertion is not only an action. It also expresses a belief and may or may not be justified in this capacity. The order that defines the sense in which an assertion may be justified insofar as it expresses a belief is not its subject's practical life-form, but rather her power of receptive knowledge; it may or may not be *epistemically* justified. It is true that the concept of practical justification does not straightforwardly apply to beliefs; it is originally employed in the context of action and intention. Perhaps it is possible in special cases practically to justify a belief in a derivative sense, if it is under the control of the will. By contrast, the concept of epistemic justification directly applies to belief. It is originally employed in this context, for the order of knowledge is internal to acts of the intellect.

Bieri says the application of the concept of justification to belief is not straightforward, because a belief is a state that comes and goes. Indeed, if a belief were a state that comes and goes, it would be unintelligible how a concept of justification could apply to it. But a belief is not a changeable state, it is a temporally unlimited act. There is no difficulty understanding how a concept of justification can directly apply to such an act. My doing something intentionally is not a process that blindly unfolds in me or with me; rather, the source of its progress is my reasoning about what to do. Consequently, I can justify my action in the light of the order to which this question refers. Analogously, my believing that something is the case is not a state that befalls me as an effect of external forces. It is my answer to the question what to believe, to which answer, in virtue of the character of the order that governs it, it is not possible to assign any temporal limit. Hence, my believing something is an act I may justify in the light of this order. Our parallel treatment of action and belief in the preceding chapters reveals the nexus of subject and action to be a species of a genus another species of which is the nexus of subject and belief. It is this nexus that is described when it is said that a subject exercises freedom in passing a judgment in the same way that she does so in acting intentionally.[9] The notion of freedom that applies to action and belief is the notion of an act under a formally represented order. When we say that believing that something is the case is an act of freedom, we describe the kind of order to which it is subject: it is bound to an order of reason and self-consciousness.

Autonomy

Kant teaches that a free will is autonomous. It is autonomous in being subject only to laws that are its own, and that is, Kant maintains, to laws of reason. It has been claimed—and Kant has been interpreted as claiming—that a law is a subject's own law, in the sense in which it must be if being under it is not to compromise her autonomy, only if her acknowledgment of it is the source of its authority over her. This contrasts with the nexus of acknowledgment and authority that, according to our reflections, characterizes an order of reason. An order of reason is formally represented: acts under it include their subject's acknowledgment of it. If being autonomous is being under laws of reason, then it is being under laws whose authority over a subject manifests itself in her acknowledgment of this authority. In the following passage, Robert Brandom distinguishes these two ways in which acknowledgment and authority may be thought to be related in laws of autonomy: as the *ground* of the authority of the law or as the *mode* of its authority.

> Pufendorf's idea that normative statuses are *instituted* by our practical attitudes makes a stronger claim than the idea previously extracted from Kant's demarcation of us as beings who act not only according to rules but according to our conception of rules. For the

9. Tyler Burge says of the nexus of agency and reason: "An instance of this sort of point is commonly associated with a view about moral reasons—the view that reasons that are associated with obligation or with a good must, at least in normal cases and given that the person understands the reasons, be associated with some sort of motivation. [. . .] The point is normally applied to what are commonly called practical reasons. I think that it is embedded in the broader, less restrictive notion of reason, and applies no more to practical reasons and practical agency than to epistemic reasons and epistemic agency. The notions of agency and practice that I am explicating are broader, and I think more fundamental, than the standard notions of action and practical reason" ("Reason and the First Person", pp. 251–252). Burge's broader notion of agency, of which epistemic agency and practical agency are species, is what we call spontaneity.

latter idea requires only that the normative statuses of demarcational interest essentially *involve* the uptake or grasp of such statuses, that is our practical attitudes toward them. But normative statuses could be taken to be unintelligible apart from normative attitudes without thereby being taken to be instituted by and therefore in some sense to supervene on those attitudes. However, Kant does in fact subscribe also to a version of the stronger thesis [. . .]. Kant's practical philosophy [. . .] takes its characteristic shape from his dual commitment to understanding us as *rational* and as *free*. To be rational, for him, means to be bound by rules. But Kant is concerned to reconcile our essential nature as in this way bound by norms with our radical autonomy [. . .] in the thesis that the *authority* of these rules over us derives from our *acknowledgment* of them *as* binding on us. Our dignity as rational beings consists precisely in being bound only by rules we endorse, rules we have freely chosen [. . .] to bind ourselves with. [. . .] If something other than our own attitudes and activity could bind us, we would not be free. Autonomy consists, as the etymology demands, in setting up laws for ourselves. (*Making It Explicit,* p. 50)

According to a thesis Kant inherits from Aristotle, a rational subject acts not only according to a law, but according to a representation of a law.[10] In the terms we have been using: actions and beliefs are explained not only by being subsumed under an order, but are terms of a causality that includes their subject's representation of this causality and thus of the relevant order. Hence, normative statuses of acts under such an order are "unintelligible apart from normative attitudes". Brandom distinguishes from this thesis—the thesis that self-conscious subjects act according to a representation of a law—the thesis that the laws according to a representation of which such subjects act are instituted by their attitudes. He maintains that the latter thesis is stronger; the thesis that acknowledgment is the ground of authority of laws of reason, Brandom says, implies, but is not implied by, the thesis that acknowledgment is the mode of authority of laws of reason. But this misdescribes the relationship of the two theses.

---

10. Compare Aristotle's distinction of "kata ton logon" and "meta tou logou", *Nicomachean Ethics,* Z 13, 1144b. The "meta logou" of this passage is the same as that in "dunamis meta logou", *Metaphysics,* Θ 2, 1046b1–2. "Meta logou" means: formally represented.

The two theses are incompatible. If an act under a law contains an acknowledgment of this law, then the authority of the law does not derive from this acknowledgment. For, the acknowledgment, being contained in acts falling under the law, is subject to the law it acknowledges. But what is under a law is not its source. Conversely, if the authority of a law derives from its acknowledgment, then the acknowledgment is not internal to acts that are governed by the law. Hence, such acts are not performed according to a representation of this law.

A rational subject acts according to a representation of a law. Kant receives this concept of the rational subject from the Aristotelian tradition. Brandom claims that Kant also holds that self-conscious subjects institute the laws of reason to which they are bound, manifesting their "radical autonomy". This is often represented as a distinctly modern idea. As the traditional and the allegedly modern claim are incompatible, the autonomous subject is a paradox if both are true. Robert Pippin and Terry Pinkard, who endorse, and think Kant endorses, both claims accordingly speak of "the Kantian paradox".[11] But before we saddle Kant with a paradox, we should consult his text. There we find no indication that Kant thinks he confronts the task Brandom sets him and that Pippin and Pinkard think is the source of a "Kantian" paradox: reconciling our nature as bound by norms with our autonomy. Instead, Kant thinks it clear, requiring no argument, that the positive concept of freedom designates a causality according to immutable laws.

> Da der Begriff einer Kausalität den von Gesetzen bei sich führt, [. . .] so ist die Freiheit, ob sie zwar nicht eine Eigenschaft des Willens nach Naturgesetzen ist, darum doch nicht gesetzlos, sondern muß vielmehr eine Kausalität nach unwandelbaren Gesetzen, aber von besonderer

11. See, e.g., Terry Pinkard, *German Philosophy, 1760–1860:* "If the will imposes such a 'law' on itself, then it must do so for a reason (or else be lawless); a lawless will, however, cannot be regarded as a free will; hence, the will must impose this law on itself for a reason that then cannot itself be self-imposed (since it is required to impose any other reasons). The 'paradox' is that we seem to be both required not to have an antecedent reason for the legislation of any basic maxim and to have such a reason" (p. 226). Compare also pp. 59–60. And Robert Pippin, "Hegel's Practical Philosophy": "In Kant's case the paradox is even deeper. The idea of a subject, prior to there being a binding law, authoring one and then subjecting itself to it is extremely hard to imagine. It always seems that such a subject could not be imagined doing so unless he were already subject to some sort of law, a law that decreed he ought so to subject himself, making the paradox of this notion of 'self-subjection' all the clearer" (p. 192).

Art, sein; denn sonst wäre ein freier Wille ein Unding. (*Grundlegung zur Metaphysik der Sitten*, p. 446)[12]

A free will not subject to immutable laws would be "ein Unding", a non-thing. If being autonomous were being under laws imposed in what would have to be arbitrary, lawless acts, then autonomy would be a non-reality. If this is right, then there is no need for a concept of autonomy—anyway paradoxical and therefore empty—according to which being autonomous is being under laws one has freely chosen. For then there is no apparent conflict of being free and being under laws, which autonomy so conceived would resolve. This proves that Kant employs a different notion of autonomy from the one Brandom attributes to him.[13] Brandom says the etymology of "autonomy" demands that being autonomous is being under laws whose authority over a subject arises from her having freely chosen to impose these laws upon herself. In fact, the etymology does not demand this interpretation. Being autonomous is being under laws that are one's own. But "one's own" need not signify the origin of the law. It may signify its *logical form*, the kind of law that it is. This is Kant's view, as he says that the immutable laws being under which is being free are of *a special kind*: "von besonderer Art".[14] In what follows, we shall seek to explain the thesis that "autonomy" signifies a form of law.

A law has a general logical subject, a subject of which there may be an unlimited number of instances, for example, a kind of stuff (phosphor) or a life-form (the puma). A law links this generic subject to a state or

12. Since the concept of causality brings with it that of laws [. . .] so freedom, although it is not a property of the will in accordance with natural laws, is not for that reason lawless but must instead be a causality in accordance with immutable laws, but of a special kind; for otherwise a free will would be an absurdity.

13. Robert Pippin and Terry Pinkard maintain that German Idealism in general and Hegel in particular attempt to come to terms with the "Kantian paradox". Compare Robert Pippin, "Hegel's Practical Philosophy," and Terry Pinkard, *German Philosophy, 1760–1860*, pp. 226–227: "It is probably not going too far to say that Hegel viewed the 'Kantian paradox' as *the* basic problem that all post-Kantian philosophies had to solve; and the solution had to be to face up to the paradox and to see how we might make it less lethal to our conception of agency while still holding onto it." If that were true, then German Idealism would be a lost cause. However, if reason and freedom can be understood in a way that allows no paradox to arise, and if this understanding can be found in Kant, then interpretive charity demands that we seek a different account of the concerns of German Idealism.

14. The following two paragraphs are deeply indebted to Michael Thompson's "The Representation of Life". Compare especially pp. 286–287. See also my "Norm und Natur".

movement-form or act by a predication that in turn is general in the sense that it can be exemplified on an unlimited number of occasions: "*N*s (the *N*, an *N*) . . . does *A* (is *F*) . . .", is instantiated by "This *N* . . . is doing *A* (is *F*) . . ." or "This *N* . . . was doing *A* (was *F*) . . .". Now, in the following passage, Kant explains the formal difference of laws of heteronomy from laws of autonomy:

> Die Naturnotwendigkeit war eine Heteronomie der wirkenden Ursachen; denn jede Wirkung war nur nach dem Gesetze möglich, daß etwas anderes die wirkende Ursache zur Kausalität bestimmte. (*Grundlegung zur Metaphysik der Sitten*, p. 446)[15]

A law of heteronomy is one according to which one thing is determined to act by another thing; that is, a law of heteronomy bears the following form: "An *N* does *A*, if an *M* does *B* to it". If, on a given occasion, an *N* is acting according to this law, then something other than it, namely a certain *M*, has solicited its act, which soliciting act of the *M* did not itself accord with a law of the *N*; for we are assuming that *it is not a law of Ns that Ms do B to them.* An explanation of the soliciting act of the *M* will be by a law that does not speak of *N*s and what they are and do. By contrast, if not only "An *N* does *A*, if an *M* does *B* to it" is a law of *N*s, but also "*M*s do *B* to *N*s", then we can say, "An *N* does *A*, when (the time comes and) an *M* does *B* to it." This is no longer a hypothetical, but rather a categorical statement. If an *N* is acting according to such a law, then there is a sense in which the *M*'s having acted on it, soliciting the act of the *N*, manifests the nature of the latter, the *N*, so that the act of the *N* does not depend on anything not explained by its, the *N*'s, own nature. That the *N* is doing *A* then is *completely* explained by itself, viz. by what it is. In this sense, a categorical law is a law of autonomy: the *N*'s own nature, and in this sense the *N* itself, as opposed to something other than it, subjects it to the causality of the cause that acts on it. In Kant's words: Nichts anderes als es selbst bestimmt die auf es wirkende Ursache zur Kausalität.

Laws of the living are laws of autonomy in this sense, while laws of inanimate nature are laws of heteronomy. For, judgments about a kind of stuff and judgments about a life-form relate their generic subject differently to the circumstances that solicit the dispositions and powers they ascribe to

15. Natural necessity was a heteronomy of causes, since every effect was possible only in accordance with the law that something else determines the efficient cause to causality.

it. For example, iron rusts if it is humid, but it is not in the nature of iron
to find itself in a humid environment. Even if all iron were in humid
places, this would be an accident and not a law of iron. Here, what solicits
the disposition is something other than the subject of the solicited disposition. By contrast, laws of a life-form place its instances in circumstances
that solicit the dispositions and powers characteristic of the life-form: pine
trees grow in sandy ground, chimpanzees eat fruit. We need not go beyond the laws of a life-form in order to account for the conditions of ac-
tualizations of its characteristic powers.

A law of autonomy explains acts that exemplify it by the nature of the
subject of this act and by it alone. Laws of a practical life-form satisfy this
description. Kant thinks there is only one, or the, practical life-form (we
discuss this in Chapter 6). If this is right, then the generic subject of its
laws is, simply, *the will*. (On a different view, the relevant generic subject
may be, say, the human will.) The autonomy of the will consists in the fact
that it is its own law, i.e., in the fact that the laws that govern its acts are
laws of autonomy in the sense explained.

> Was kann wohl Freiheit des Willens sonst sein, als Autonomie, d. i.
> die Eigenschaft des Willens, sich selbst Gesetz zu sein? [. . .] Der
> Wille ist in allen Handlungen sich selbst Gesetz. (*Grundlegung zur
> Metaphysik der Sitten,* p. 446)[16]

Kant expresses the same thought when he says that the will *gives* itself the
law.[17] That he speaks of the will "giving" a law has encouraged inter-
preters to find in Kant the claim that the authority of a law of autonomy
over a subject depends on her having imposed it in an act that, as it is the
origin of the authority of the law, is not under it. But Kant says that the
laws of the will are immutable and that thinking otherwise is nihilism in
respect of freedom. In fact, the formula "the will gives itself the law" does
not speak of an act to which belongs a time and a place. The statement has
a generic subject, the will, wherefore its predication, "gives", is atemporal
and does not signify anything happening here and now or there and then.
In the first instance, "autonomous" is said of the *generic* subject of laws
(the will or, more abstractly, a practical life-form), if these are laws of autonomy. In a derivative sense, a *particular* subject is autonomous to the

16. What, then, can freedom of the will be other than autonomy, that is, the will's property of being a law to itself? [. . .] the will is in all its acts a law to itself.
17. See, for example, *Kritik der praktischen Vernunft,* p. 33.

extent that she is under and conforms to laws of autonomy. A law of autonomy is the subject's own law in that it refers to nothing not contained in its own nature.

When Kant says that the will gives itself the law, he means that the law of the will is a law of autonomy in the sense we have explained, and in a further sense. For, laws that are formally represented are one's own in a yet stronger sense. A subject represents acts of hers falling under a formally represented order in unmediated first person thoughts. Her acknowledgment of this order, contained in these acts, is an unmediated first person thought as well. Hence, a formally represented order is one's own in the sense that "one's own", here, is a first person pronoun. As a formally represented order is an order of reason, being autonomous in this stronger sense is being subject to laws of reason.[18] Being under laws of reason, I am subject to nothing other than myself in the sense that these laws spring from, and constitute, the nature of that to which I refer *first personally*.

Knowledge from Spontaneity

We argued that freedom is a character of acts that exhibit a causality of thought. As such, a causality is sustained by formally represented laws; acts of freedom are subject to laws one knows as one's own without mediation. In this way, freedom and first person knowledge are internally related: acts of freedom as such are an object of first person knowledge.

Acts of a formally represented order are the object of unmediated first person thoughts. We can abstractly describe the way of knowing actualized in these thoughts as follows. If I perform an act on account of a cause whose causality is a causality of thought, then my reasoning that the act conforms to the relevant order *is* my explaining why I perform it. In this way, I know that and why I perform the act by reasoning about what act to perform. I know my act and its cause not from the senses but from thinking according to a normative order. Now, when I know an act by reasoning in the light of an order that governs the act, then I know it by being its subject, and my knowledge is an unmediated first person

18. Kant does not distinguish the weak sense of autonomy that characterizes life as such from the strong sense that is peculiar to rational life because he holds that the laws of the living are not objectively valid—a claim that does not concern us here, but which entails that the self-conscious law of reason is the only law of autonomy.

thought. Hence, this way of knowing defines the first person reference in representations of what is known in this way. As the character of acts in virtue of which they are known in this way is their freedom, we can say that first person knowledge of acts of a formally represented order is *knowledge from spontaneity.*

Knowledge from spontaneity bears a special relationship to its object, which distinguishes it from knowledge from receptivity. If an act has an explanation in terms of a causality of thought, then the subject's thought that she performs the act that is part of her explanation is identical with her thought that it is to be performed that is part of her reasoning. And her thinking that thought is the same reality as her performing the act. So her first person representation of her act is not an independent reality of the act that she represents. Rather, her representation includes and is included in the represented act. Knowledge from spontaneity is of a fact that includes its subject's knowledge of this fact. This distinguishes the way of knowing that sustains first person reference from knowledge mediated by the senses, which sustains demonstrative reference. If an object is an independent reality of the subject's knowledge of it, then it must be given to the subject if she is to know it. It must impinge on her and impress itself on her mind. Conversely, she must have the power to suffer this impingement and be capable of receiving, from the object, a representation of it. Hence, if an object enjoys an independent existence of the subject's knowledge, then the subject knows the object through an act of a receptive faculty. Knowledge of an independent object is *knowledge from receptivity.* By contrast, if the subject's knowledge of an object includes and is included in the reality of this object, then the notion of its being given to the subject does not apply. There is no room for a receptive faculty to mediate the subject with what she knows. I know that and why I believe or am doing something by exercising my power of belief and intentional action. There is no room for a *further power* of being aware of my beliefs and actions because acts of the former powers as such are acts of knowing of these acts.

Spontaneous Knowledge of a Material Reality

First person knowledge is spontaneous; it is not an independent reality of its object and therefore does not spring from sensory affection. It is tempting to conclude that the object of first person knowledge can be nothing other than thinking, and in particular that it cannot be a material reality, as a material reality can only be known empirically. In his theses on Feuerbach, Marx contends that this last notion stands in the way of a true materialism.

> Der Hauptmangel alles bisherigen Materialismus (den Feuerbach-schen mit eingerechnet) ist, daß der Gegenstand, die Wirklichkeit, Sinnlichkeit nur unter der Form *des Objekts oder der Anschauung* gefaßt wird; nicht aber als *sinnlich-menschliche Tätigkeit, Praxis,* nicht subjektiv. Daher die *tätige* Seite abstrakt im Gegensatz zu dem Mate-rialismus von dem Idealismus—der natürlich die wirkliche, sinnliche Tätigkeit als solche nicht kennt—entwickelt.[19]

All hitherto existing materialism is flawed by its empiricism: it conceives of material reality exclusively as an object of intuition, or as to be known re-ceptively. Idealism shares this flaw, wherefore it develops spontaneity ("die tätige Seite") in contrast to the material. According to Marx, true materi-alism reveals spontaneity and its knowledge to be of, and thus to be, a ma-terial reality. Our account of self-consciousness aspires to being materialist in this way.[20]

In "The First Person", G. E. M. Anscombe is working toward a true materialism. The essay is known for its seemingly shocking proposition that the first person pronoun is not a referring expression. In fact it argues for two theses: first person thought involves no act of receptive reference; it does not pertain to its object by way of a receptive representation. And, first person thought exhibits a form of predication that leaves no room for an act of reference contrasting with and complementing the act of predi-

---

19. The chief defect of all hitherto existing materialism (that of Feuerbach included), is that the thing, reality, sensuousness, is conceived only in the form of *the object or of contem-plation,* but not as *sensuous-human activity, practice,* not subjectively. Hence, the *active* side was developed abstractly in opposition to materialism by idealism—which of course does not know real, sensuous activity as such.

20. Kant states that, insofar as we are under the causality of freedom, we know ourselves not as appearances, but as things in themselves. He means that, as subjects of intentional ac-tion, we do not know ourselves receptively; our knowledge in this case does not depend on a faculty of sensibility that mediates between ourselves and the objects we know. Since "ap-pearance" refers to an object known by means of a *receptive* faculty, our knowledge of our-selves as agents is not knowledge of appearances. The power of this insight has been under-estimated. Kant's claim that, in practical thought, we know ourselves as noumena can only be rejected by a truly materialist account of spontaneous knowledge, an account that ex-plains how there can be nonempirical knowledge of a material reality.

cation. This paves the way for a true materialism, for it shows that in order to understand how the first person thought of a man relates to that man, we must comprehend how there can be nonreceptive knowledge of a material substance, and it shows that this comprehension must come from an analysis of the form of predication that characterizes first person thought. We recapitulate Anscombe's argument and then describe how our theory of self-consciousness follows its materialist ambition.

Anscombe's "The First Person"

The content of Anscombe's thesis that the first person pronoun is not a referring expression transpires from the manner in which she establishes it.

> Our questions were a combined reductio ad absurdum of the idea of "I" as a word whose role is to 'make a singular reference'. I mean the questions how one is guaranteed to get the object right, whether one may safely assume no unnoticed substitution, whether one could refer to oneself 'in absence', and so on. The suggestion of getting the object right collapses into absurdity when we work it out and try to describe how getting hold of the wrong object may be excluded. [. . .] Getting hold of the wrong object *is* excluded, and that makes us think that getting hold of the right object is guaranteed. But the reason is that there is no getting hold of an object at all. [. . .] "I" is neither a name nor another kind of expression whose logical role is to make a reference, *at all*. ("The First Person", pp. 31–32)

Anscombe reduces to absurdity the idea that "I" is a referring expression by showing it to be absurd to conceive of first person thought as *getting hold of the right object*. She discusses three ways in which one may get the object wrong. Referring to an object by name, one may misidentify a given object as the bearer of that name. Referring demonstratively, one may erroneously identify the given object with one encountered earlier. And thinking demonstratively of what appears to be the same object for a stretch of time, one may fail to notice that the object has been replaced. If first person thought referred to an object in a manner that allowed for its description as getting the object right, then it would be guaranteed to get it right in these three ways: I cannot mistake someone else for him whom I call "I"; I cannot go wrong in identifying the object of my first person thought with an object of which I previously thought in the same way;

and it is impossible that, while I am thinking of an object in this way, it is replaced by another object without my noticing it.

Anscombe's claim that there is no first person reference deploys a concept of reference according to which referring to an object is relating to it in a way that gives application to the notion of getting the object right. This is *receptive reference,* reference mediated by an act of receptivity. In the fundamental case, receptive reference depends on a perceptual relationship with the object. Such a relationship may obtain between a subject and a manifold of objects, time being a dimension of this manifold, a form of receptivity, as Kant puts it: I may perceive different objects at different times. Thus when my receptive link to an object has been broken and reestablished, the nature of that link as an act of a receptive faculty whose form is time does not fix it that it is the same object from which I receive representations on both occasions. Hence, there are two acts of reference, and the identity of their object is the content of a separate judgment. Furthermore, a continuous perceptual relationship with an object enables continuous demonstrative thinking of it in the same way. But again, since a perceptual nexus is a relationship I may bear to a manifold of objects, it does not follow from the nature of this relationship that, when I bear it to an object for a stretch of time, I remain connected with the same object throughout. There is space for erroneously thinking that the object has, or has not, been replaced. So I am liable to be confused about an object of receptive reference in these ways: I may be under the illusion of enjoying a continuous receptive relationship with one and the same object, and I may erroneously identify objects I have perceived at different times.

First person knowledge has no room for these forms of error. For, the relationship to an object that is the source of first person knowledge is not *sensory affection by,* but *identity with,* the object. First person knowledge is knowledge I have of an object by being that object. It follows that, here, a temporal difference does not give rise to distinct acts of reference. No temporal determination attaches to first person reference because identity does not obtain at a time. This also explains why there is no such thing as unnoticed replacement: there is no room for replacement of the object I know in a first person manner because identity is a relation I do not bear to a manifold of objects. Anscombe equates referring to an object with laying hold of it in a manner such that the notion of getting the object right applies. She thus defines reference as receptive reference; "I" expresses no reference mediated by an act of receptivity.

This is not an arbitrary restriction of the concept of reference. Reference is commonly represented as an act that contrasts with and complements an act of predication: in order to predicate a concept of an object, it is necessary, in an act distinct from the predication, to single out from a manifold of objects the one that must satisfy the concept if the thought is to be true.[21] But first person thought, because it contains no act of receptive reference, does not contain an act of reference distinct from the predication. This is the point of the positive account of the function of "I" that Anscombe sketches on the last pages of her essay. She argues that the first person pronoun indicates that the thoughts expressed by its means are "unmediated agent-or-patient conceptions of actions, happenings and states". "I"-thoughts represent movements and states in a certain manner, and as these are determinations, a manner of representing them is a form of predication. "I", then, signifies a form of predication. Anscombe calls such predications unmediated. While we have called any singular thought that does not depend on an identity judgment unmediated, in her use "unmediated" designates the special character of "I"-thoughts:

> It was that his thought of the happening, falling out of the carriage, was one for which he looked for a subject, his grasp of it one that required a subject. [...] He did not have what I call 'unmediated agent-or-patient conceptions of actions, happenings and states'. ("The First Person", p. 36)

The idea of a predicative thought the thinking of which does not require looking for a subject may appear contradictory. It may seem that any act of predication requires looking for a subject, for, as a predicate is general, a use of it must be joined with an act of specifying the object to which it is applied. However, that a predicate is general does not imply that there cannot be a form of predication that leaves no room for a separate act of reference. We described the forms of predication associated with demonstrative reference and first person reference as follows: I know demonstratively that something is F by perceiving that it is F. And I know first personally that something is F by being F. Now, as perception is a relation I may bear to a manifold of objects, this manner of knowing an object leaves open which object I thus know. The object must be specified, which is the office of the act of reference complementing a perceptual predica-

---

21. Compare, e.g., P. F. Strawson, "Singular Terms and Predication".

tion. By contrast, as identity is a relation I bear only to myself, in this case the manner of knowing settles which object I know in this manner. Here the form of predication leaves no room for a separate act of specifying an object. Applying the concept, I settle to whom it pertains, not in a separate act of reference, but by virtue of the form of my predication. (The difference manifests itself in our formulae in this way: the description of how I know what I know demonstratively contains a referential expression, "by perceiving that *it* is *F*", while the description of how I know what I know first personally needs only the predicative material "by being *F*".)

We have been arguing that self-consciousness is a form of reference, to be understood through a form of predication. It would be a mistake to think that thereby we disagree with Anscombe. One can articulate the difference of the forms of predication associated with demonstrative thought and first person thought respectively by saying that the latter does not require an act of reference, or by saying that it contains an act of reference, which therefore is no separate act. "I"-thoughts contain no act of reference distinct from the act of predication, in contrast to demonstrative thoughts, which join a perceptual predication with a reference, to which the notion of getting the object right applies, as it singles out an object from a manifold.

The First Person Material Substance Concept

Here Anscombe's essay leaves us. It leaves us knowing what we must do to comprehend how first person thought can represent a material substance: we must describe the first person form of predication as a manner of knowing a material substance. The illusion is widespread that there is an easier path to comprehending how "I"-thoughts can represent a material substance: through observing that first person thoughts bear, and are known by their subject to bear, a truth-value link to third person thoughts about that subject, which third person thoughts unquestionably represent a material substance. Anscombe refutes this idea in her discussion of the "logician". The logician takes himself to be able to explain reference in terms of an inferential order: a thought refers to an object if it is part of a suitable totality of thoughts whose inferential relations are represented by the predicate calculus. This, the logician's, concept of reference applies to first person thoughts: from "I am *F*" follows "Someone is *F*"; I can contradict someone who says "Everyone is *F*" by saying "I am not"; and "I am this one" and "This one is *F*" together entail "I am *F*". Anscombe did not fail to realize this:

> Of course we must accept the rule "If *X* asserts something with 'I' as subject, his assertion will be true if and only if what he asserts is true of *X*." ("The First Person", p. 32)

This ensures that whatever follows from, and whatever entails, a free-standing deployment of "*X* is *F*" follows from, and entails, a free-standing deployment of "I am *F*" by *X*. Hence, if the logician's concept fits third person thought about a given subject, then it fits the first person thought of that subject. However, the logician's concept of reference is of little interest in the present context. We want to understand how "I"-thoughts can be of a man, a temporal and spatial, perishable and divisible substance, and the logician can give no account of how a thought relates to a material substance. For, thought about such a substance includes application to it of a principle of temporal and spatial unity; it includes application of a *material substance concept.* Possession of material substance concepts constitutes a power to represent something as a bearer of changeable states and as a subject of movements, and since this power cannot be reduced to a capacity to draw inferences according to rules, the logician is not equipped to give an account of material substance concepts and therewith of thought about material substances.[22]

First person thoughts are not about a substance by virtue of a receptive relationship that the subject bears to that substance. We need another account of how they may pertain to a material substance. A description of the inferential behavior of first person thoughts is not such an account. It does not show how representation of a material substance may be accomplished otherwise than through sensory affection.[23] Rather, we must explain how a material substance concept can be applied in a way that does not rest on a receptive

---

22. Compare my *Kategorien des Zeitlichen*, chap. 3.

23. Edward Harcourt, in "The First Person: Problems of Sense and Reference", observes that Anscombe employs a concept of reference that cannot be defined in terms of inferential relations, but he misidentifies the relevant concept as the concept of reference by way of a "conception" of the object. In Anscombe's text, a "conception" is a material substance concept (see "The First Person", pp. 26–27). So Harcourt credits Anscombe with having established that the first person pronoun refers to a material substance in a manner that does not include the application of a material substance concept. But no one can have established this, for it is a contradiction. An inference from "no conception" to "no reference", if it were Anscombe's, would be sound.

representation of the substance to which it is applied. In other words, and here we are returning to Marx, we need a true materialism, which conceives of material reality not merely as an object of intuition, but as spontaneity.[24]

Demonstrative thought is mediated by a receptive relationship, which I may bear to a manifold of objects spread out in time: I may be affected by an object at one time and cease to be so at a later time. Thus there is, as we may put it, present tense and past tense demonstrative reference, and I may mistakenly identify the object of the one with the object of the other. Furthermore, as I can enter into a receptive relationship with a manifold of objects, it is possible that a different object surreptitiously replaces the object that affects my senses. By contrast, my "I"-reference figures in knowledge I have of an object by being that object. Thus there is no present tense or past tense first person reference, as identity does not hold at a time. There is no multiplicity of acts of first person reference of a given subject. So in first person thought, I do not apply criteria of identity in identifying the object I refer to now with an object I referred to earlier in the same way, nor do I bring these criteria to bear in keeping track of an object. That is, I do not apply these criteria *by way of a receptive representation* of the object.

24. P. F. Strawson fails to appreciate this. He writes: "'I' can be used without criteria of subject-identity and yet refer to a subject [. . .] because—perhaps—it [. . .] is used by a person who would acknowledge the applicability of those criteria in settling questions as to whether he, the very man who now ascribes to himself this experience, was or was not the person who, say, performed such-and-such an action in the past. 'I' can be used without criteria of subject-identity and yet refer to a subject because, even in such a use, the links with those criteria are not in practice severed" (*Bounds of Sense*, p. 165). A thought does not represent a material substance unless it applies a material substance concept, a principle of temporal unity. It looks as though first person thoughts do not bring their object under such a concept, since "I" is, as Strawson puts it, "used without criteria of subject-identity". It is used without such criteria in the sense that, using "I", one does not apply criteria of identity *in the way one does in getting the object right*: identifying a given object with one encountered earlier, retaining one's hold on the same object for a stretch of time. As these are ways in which criteria of identity necessarily are involved in thought that depends on receptivity, this proves that "I" expresses no receptive reference. And "yet", Strawson says, it "refer[s] [. . .] because . . .". After the "because", we expect an account of how first person thoughts represent a material substance; we expect a description of how a nonreceptive representation of a material substance may be achieved. We expect the germs of a true materialism. The expectation is disappointed. Strawson merely reminds us of the truth-value link of "I"-thoughts and third person thoughts, and of the fact that the subject understands this link. This allows us to apply the logician's concept of reference to first person thought. It provides no understanding of how such a thought can be of a material substance. It is useless to locate a material substance concept in first person thought by way of its truth-value link with third person thought. We must find the material substance concept in the form of predication that constitutes self-consciousness.

Often this point is made by saying, simpliciter, that first person thoughts do not apply criteria of identity.[25] This is misleading. Criteria of identity are applied to an object as it is brought under a material substance concept. If it were true simpliciter that first person thought did not subsume its object under a material substance concept, it would be true simpliciter that it does not represent a material substance. If first person thoughts represent a material substance, then there is a material substance concept I am in a position to apply in a first person manner, that is, not by being affected by something falling under it, but by falling under it. A material substance that is the object of a first person thought is of such a kind that being a substance of this kind *is* bringing it under its principle of temporal unity.[26]

"I"-thoughts represent a material substance only if they include the application of a material substance concept and thus of criteria of identity. And so they do. The criteria are not applied in identity judgments. But identity judgments anyway are a secondary occasion for the application of criteria of identity. In the primary instance, criteria of identity are applied in *predicative judgments*.[27] A predicative judgment contains a principle of unity of its object, for unless the object is subsumed under such a principle, no conditions are fixed under which the predicate applies, and no judgment is made. That first person thought does not span time by time-spanning identity

25. P. F. Strawson conflates applying criteria with applying criteria in *experience:* "When 'I' is thus used, without any need or any possibility of its use being justified by empirical criteria of subject-identity, it does not, however lose its role of referring to a subject. 'I' can be used without criteria of subject-identity and yet refer to a subject" (*The Bounds of Sense,* p. 165). Empirical criteria are criteria applied empirically (compare ibid., p. 164: "empirically applicable criteria"). But a self-conscious subject may apply the criteria of its own identity in another way. In fact the principle of temporal unity of a self-conscious subject is *not empirical* in that its primary application to an object does not rest on sensory experience. Strawson's conflation is an example of the mistake Marx finds in all hitherto existing materialism; the conflation puts true materialism out of reach.

26. In "What Is It to Wrong Someone?" Michael Thompson argues that an order of justice presupposes a kind or form as instances of which subjects enter into relations of justice, and notes that such a form must be capable of being known "from the inside", in our terms, from spontaneity. He thinks this raises an epistemological difficulty for the view that the human form is the source of an order of justice, since according to his general principle this entails that men have nonempirical knowledge of man. A solution to this difficulty is needed not only for an account of justice on which any man can do, or fail to do, justice to any man, but already for an account of self-consciousness according to which first person thought is of a man.

27. Gareth Evans argues this in "Identity and Predication". He charges W. V. O. Quine with the mistake of trying to anchor the sense of material substance concepts in identity judgments. Perhaps this mistake stands behind the monotonous repetition in the literature of the unqualified assertion that first person thoughts do not apply criteria of identity to their object.

judgments is no indication that it does not apply criteria of temporal identity. If we want to see the substance concept in first person thought, we must not look to identity judgments. We must attend to *the forms of predication* of first person thoughts. With regard to *temporal* identity, two forms are pertinent: thoughts that join changeable states to the same object under different tenses, "*x* was *F* and is *G*",[28] and thoughts predicating movement-forms under different aspects, "*x* is doing *A*", "*x* did *A*". (The latter form contains the former, for something that has moved was in contrary states at different times.) A thought of the first form represents an object as being now in this and then in that state, wherefore such a thought contains a principle of temporal unity of its object. A thought of the second form depicts something as moving and thus brings its object under a principle of temporal unity, which holds the moving object together through its movement. It follows that these forms of thought apply a material substance concept. Thinking that *x* is (or was) *F* or is doing *A* is thinking that *x, an N*, is doing *A*, or is (was) *F*, *N* being a material substance concept.

First person thoughts of an acting subject bear the form "I * do *A*", one of whose guises is "I am doing *A*". So our result, that judging that *x* is doing *A* is judging that *x*, an *N*, is doing *A*, applies: thinking "I am doing *A*" is thinking "I, an *N*, am doing *A*". That the expression of first person thoughts usually does not contain a word that designates the relevant substance concept has no tendency to show that no such concept is deployed in thinking these thoughts.[29] It has been noticed that the logical subject of demonstrative thoughts is articulated, "this such-and-such". For the reason just given, this holds true more generally of thought about movement and changeable states. It holds of demonstrative thought because and insofar as it is of moving substances. It equally applies to the first person thoughts of a moving substance. Their logical subject is articulated, "I such-and-such". I do not simply think, "This is walking down the stairs", but, say, "This man is walking down the stairs". In the same way, thinking "I am walking down the stairs", I think "I man am walking down the stairs".

Thinking first person thoughts representing movement, "I am doing

28. Compare Gareth Evans, "Identity and Predication", p. 44.

29. Compare Evans, "Identity and Predication", p. 37: "We have considered how we might be able to explain the truth conditions of compound sentences of the form (*F G*) and (not-*F G*), given their manifest sensitivity to the identity conditions of rabbits, by suggesting that the sentences involve predicates of rabbits. (It is interesting to observe that we might be forced to this conclusion even though there was no explicit *G* term of divided reference with whose significance we were concerned.)"

A", I apply a material substance concept to myself. In the fundamental case—the one without which there would be no first person thought of a moving substance—I know from spontaneity that and why I am doing something. We have uncovered the source of this nonempirical knowledge of movement: the unity of action explanation and practical reasoning. It turns out that thereby we have explained how I represent a material substance otherwise than through a receptive relationship with it. I have spontaneous knowledge of the kind of substance I am, the kind of substance that the concept designates that is contained in my first person thoughts that represent my intentional actions. I know that I fall under this concept not by perceiving a substance that falls under it, but by being a substance that falls under it, or, shorter, by falling under it. An acting subject is a material substance of a kind such that she knows what kind of substance she is by being a substance of that kind.[30] This follows from our account of self-consciousness, which thus transpires to underwrite a true materialism, which conceives material reality not only as an object of intuition, but as human spontaneity.

30. In "Reductionism and the First Person", John McDowell argues as follows against the view that "consciousness" is not awareness of a material substance: "We can say: continuous 'consciousness' is intelligible (even 'from within') only as a subjective angle on something that has more to it than the subjective angle reveals, namely the career of an objective continuant with which the subject of the continuous 'consciousness' identifies itself" (ibid., p. 363). This is a difficult passage. It appears to say that, from the subjective angle, that on which it is an angle is not revealed to be an objective continuant. It transpires from the context that what the subjective angle reveals is what is represented in unmediated first person thought, while an "objective continuant" is a material substance. On the one hand, then, unmediated first person thought is said not to reveal its object to be a material substance. But the passage also says that the subjective angle is conceived to be an angle on a material substance "from within", and "from within" can only mean: in unmediated first person thought. On the other hand, then, unmediated first person thought is said to represent its object as a material substance. This seems to be a contradiction. Our account of self-consciousness avoids the contradiction by rejecting its first side: The subjective angle is an angle on something that is essentially what and only what the subjective angle reveals it to be. First person thought represents an object whose essence is such as to be represented in first person thought. (For this reason, the metaphor of an angle is a poor fit for first person knowledge, which is identical with its object. It fits receptive knowledge, which is a distinct reality from, and thus an angle on, its object.) Only someone committed to the empiricism of all hitherto existing materialism will suppose that this, Descartes', insight entails that the object of self-consciousness is immaterial. A true materialism lets us see that we need not (anyway impossibly) have recourse to something outside the subjective angle in order to recognize that on which it is an angle as a material substance.

5

Receptive Knowledge

In the preceding chapter, we described an inner nexus of self-consciousness and reason: a self-conscious order is an order of reason and an order of reason is self-conscious because justification and first person reference are two sides of a coin, a formally represented order. Beliefs are subject to the self-conscious and rational order of knowledge; believing something, I not only fall under, I subsume myself under this order. Therefore beliefs figure in unmediated first person thought and admit of justification. In this chapter, we shall further develop the conception of epistemic justification and receptive knowledge contained in this account of self-consciousness.

The empiricism of all hitherto existing materialism not only makes it impossible to comprehend how there may be first person thought of a man. It stands in the way of a sound theory of receptive knowledge as well. I know an object that exists independently of my knowing it in virtue of its affecting my senses. This sensory relationship with an object joins material substances and joins them as material. Contemporary epistemology, sharing in the empiricism of all hitherto existing materialism, presupposes that the sensory nexus to an object by which I know how things stand with it is something to be known in turn only empirically, or through the senses. On this empiricist doctrine depends the opposition of internalism and externalism, which is widely held to provide a valid classification of theories of knowledge, as well as the so-called fallibilist conception of knowledge, according to which it can always turn out that things are not as I believed they were because the grounds on which I rest my beliefs never exclude that possibility. We shall depart from this empiricism and develop a truly materialist account of receptive knowledge. According to it, the sensory relationship with an object by which it is known from receptivity is itself known from spontaneity. It is a material, yet self-conscious reality.

The materialist account of receptive knowledge that we shall develop will say the following. Knowing from receptivity that something is the case is *an act of a self-conscious power,* a power whose acts are known by their subject from spontaneity. Since the contemporary literature does not develop the theory of knowledge as part of the theory of self-consciousness, the concepts central to our account are foreign to it: the concept of spontaneous knowledge, the concept of a power, in particular the concept of a power of knowledge, and the concept of a self-conscious power. We shall trace its shortcomings to its conceptual poverty.

In the first section, we shall introduce the idea of spontaneous knowledge of receptive knowledge by asking whether she who knows something from receptivity as such knows that she does. This question gives rise to an antinomy when, in "she knows that she knows", both occurrences of "know" are taken to designate the same form of knowledge. A critical solution to this antinomy distinguishes receptive knowledge from spontaneous knowledge. She who receptively knows something knows that she does, not from receptivity, but from spontaneity. In the second section, we shall argue that the misnamed fallibilist account of knowledge provides no understanding of fallibility. For, *the concept of fallibility follows the concept of a power,* which fallibilist authors eschew. I am liable wrongly to think I know not because, as fallibilism has it, my grounds do not exclude that things are otherwise than I think, but because, in giving grounds that *do* exclude this, I exercise a fallible power. Our materialist and fallibilist account of receptive knowledge has consequences regarding the nature of epistemology and *its* knowledge, which the third and final section of this chapter expounds. Epistemology is split into a naturalist and a normativist camp: the former seeks to describe knowledge as a natural phenomenon in the life of a certain kind of animal, while the latter insists on the normative significance of attributions of knowledge, accusing the opposing camp of a naturalist fallacy. Both parties to the dispute fail to see that the concepts of epistemology are *not empirical* concepts, as their primary deployment is in *spontaneous* knowledge. The concept of receptive knowledge describes a material form of life, but one that is self-conscious and, that is, is such as to bring itself under its own order. The opposition of naturalism and normativism reflects the empiricism of all hitherto existing materialism. If we are to comprehend ourselves, material self-conscious subjects that we are, we must rid ourselves of it.

The Self-Consciousness of Receptive Knowledge

Internalism and externalism are poles of an antinomy. We first expound the antinomy, then its critical solution.

The Antinomy of Knowledge

The antinomy arises when we ask whether someone who knows something as such knows that she does. Externalist theories of knowledge do not require that the facts by which someone knows something be in turn known by her, while internalist theories demand that, if someone is to know something, she must know the relevant facts or, as it is sometimes put, she must be aware of them, or they must be available to her. As externalism is a negative claim, an argument for it must show that internalism is false. A way to do this is to reduce internalism to absurdity, as follows. It is clear that grounds on account of which a subject knows how things stand with an object, if the object exists independently of her knowledge, must include a material, sensory relation that she bears to this object; for, unless the object in some way affects her, it will be an accident if she represents it correctly. Internalism requires that this sensory relation be available to the subject; she must know that it obtains, if she is to know something through it. And this is absurd. For the requirement applies again: in order to know that she bears the relevant relation to the object, it does not suffice that she be materially related to this fact in a suitable way; rather, she must again know that she is. It transpires that internalism says that, in order to know one thing, I must know another thing. There can be no concept of knowledge that satisfies this condition.

Externalism is true, for internalism is absurd. In the same way, we can show that internalism is true: by showing that externalism is absurd. We start again from the fact that knowing something about an independently existing object involves being affected by it. Externalism maintains that, in order to know how things stand with an object through this relationship with it, the subject need not know that the relationship obtains; she may know this, but this is not a condition of her knowing what she knows through the relationship. And this is absurd. In order to see this, suppose that she in fact bears a sensory nexus to the object in virtue of which it is no accident that the object is as she believes it is. Now, if she does not know that she does, then she cannot revert to that fact in determining what to believe. The nexus does not place her in a position to establish that it is right to think that the object is as she thinks it is. This does not change if she knows, as she may, *in the same externalist sense,* that she bears the relevant relationship to the object. For, she knows that she bears this relationship to the object in virtue of being suitably connected to *that* fact. But since, again, she does not know that she is so connected (or if she does, then in a further act, of which we must say the same), this does not enable her to establish that it is right to think that she bears the relevant receptive relationship to the object. Her second-order knowledge does not advance her quest for something by which she can ascertain whether she is right in believing about that object what she believes about it. I may in the externalist sense know something, know that I do, know that I know that I do, and so on, to no matter how high a level, while having, on reflection, no clue whether things are as my original belief represents them as being. No hierarchy of externalist knowledge recovers the position of her who can justify her belief.[1] But a theory that cannot represent the position of being equipped to answer the question whether or not to believe such-and-such does not treat of the concept of knowledge that applies to subjects who confront this question.

We asked: Is it a condition of knowing something that one knows that one does? The question gives rise to an antinomy: externalism is true, because internalism is false, and internalism is true, because externalism is false. The antinomy arises if it is assumed that I would, if I could, or if I did, know that I receptively know that *p in the same manner* in which I know that *p*: from receptivity. On the one hand, the refutation of internalism assumes that internalism holds that, in order to know something through a sensory relationship with an object, I must know in the same way, i.e., by a sensory nexus, that this relationship obtains. And this is absurd. On the other hand, the refutation of externalism trades on the fact that, if I do not know through a sensory nexus that I know that *p*, then I do not know that I know that *p*. And this is equally absurd. We infer from the antinomy its critical solution: she who knows that *p* through sensory affection knows that she does, but in a manner different from that in which she knows that *p*, i.e., not through sensory affection.

It is not that the literature knows of nothing of which one may know otherwise than by its affecting one's senses. On the contrary, it is routinely

---

1. This is well brought out by William Alston on the first pages of his *The Reliability of Sense Perception*.

assumed that beliefs and sensory impressions are materials from which one could attempt to construct grounds of knowledge that would satisfy an internalist requirement. But it is never contemplated that these materials might include the sensory relationship with an object by which one gains knowledge of it. Donald Davidson, for example, explains that "nothing can count as a reason for holding a belief except another belief", since "we can't get outside our skins to find out what is causing the internal happenings of which we are aware".[2] We are said to know (be aware of) "internal happenings", which knowledge must be of a different kind from that of which Davidson, in the essay we are quoting, gives a coherence theory: we are aware of internal happenings, but not by having a reason to believe they occur. Davidson does not say how we are aware of them, but it is reasonable to suppose that he thinks such awareness is an act of a faculty of inner sense. As this faculty does not reach all the way to the objects causing our sensory impressions, we would need to "get outside our skins" to find out what affects our senses. Or compare William Alston:

> We engage in a variety of doxastic (belief-forming) practices that are ineluctably rooted in our lives. A prominent member of this group is the practice of going from sense experience (together, sometimes, with relevant background beliefs) to beliefs about things [. . .]. Thus I have an experience that I would be disposed to describe as something in front of me looking like a birch tree, and on that basis I believe that there is a birch tree before me. [. . .] Leaving background beliefs out of the picture, we can say that a common type of function here is one that goes from "looks P" to "is P". (*The Reliability of Sense Perception*, pp. 7–8)

Alston does not say how he knows that it is his practice to go from "looks P" to "is P", but presumably he thinks he is aware of it by inner sense. As he cannot know in this way whether, on a given occasion of exercising this practice, an object is affecting his senses in such a way that he represents it to be as it is, he is not in a position to tell whether this practice yields true beliefs.[3]

2. "A Coherence Theory of Truth and Knowledge", pp. 426 and 429.

3. Since it disregards self-consciousness, reliabilism, the doctrine that a belief is justified if it springs from a habit of forming beliefs such that beliefs issuing from this habit can be relied upon to be true, cannot account for the applicability of the concept of justification to belief. If reliabilism were true, its topic would not exist, for the concept of justification applies only to acts of a formally represented order, and habits are not formally represented.

Davidson and Alston presuppose that grounds on which I know how things stand with an independent object, if they are to satisfy an internalist requirement (i.e., if I am to know them in a manner not to be explained in the same way), cannot include a sensory relation to this object, but, at best, impressions and beliefs resulting from impressions. Behind this stands the notion that beliefs and impressions belong with a spiritual world of a subject to which she has immediate access, while a sensory nexus to an object is part of the material world, to be known only empirically, by mediation of the senses. So the thesis underlying the antinomy of knowledge is this: there is *no nonempirical knowledge of a material relationship with an object*. This is an application of the dogma of all hitherto existing materialism, that material reality is an object only of experience. Our account of receptive knowledge, which critically solves the antinomy, will reveal the material nexus to an object by which one gains knowledge of it to be *such as to be known from spontaneity*.

Spontaneous Knowledge of Receptive Knowledge

Let us recall some of the things we said in the previous chapter. A justification of an act is an account that reveals it to conform to a formally represented order, an order under which this act subsumes itself. An act is justified if and only if it has a true account of this kind. A reason is what serves as cause in such an account. Beliefs admit of justification because they are subject to a formally represented order, which defines a notion of justification, epistemic justification. Justifying a belief in this sense is revealing it, or taking a step toward revealing it, to be true; a reason for believing something establishes, or contributes to establishing, that it is true.

Suppose I think, "I am doing *A* because I want to do *B*", which I believe manifests my disposition to do one thing whenever I want to do a certain other thing. And suppose I further think that doing *A* will take me some way toward doing *B*. I might be pleased to find myself disposed to respond to a desire with an act that helps to satisfy the desire. I might thank my creator, or evolution, for this beneficial arrangement. But not only do I not justify my doing *A;* I do not apprehend it as a proper object of justification. I bring it under a form of description that does not represent it as something that admits of justification. Or suppose I think, "I believe that *p* because I believe that *q*", subsuming my beliefs under a habit to believe one thing whenever I believe another. I may further think that *p* follows from *q*, and think myself blessed with this habit. Again, thankful contemplation of evolution, which rooted out those with less advantageous mental manners, may be in order. But so long as I think of my belief in this way alone, I do not conceive of it as something to which a concept of justification applies.

We also said that beliefs attract a certain question "why?"; they fall under a certain form of explanation, or are subject to a certain kind of causality. Now, when I explain in this way why I believe something, I conceive of what I believe as something it is right to believe on the strength of the cause that I give. I take myself to trace my belief to a cause that establishes its truth. That is, I conceive of my explanation as a justification and of its cause as a reason. A justification is a *causal* account; she who justifies her belief gives its cause. Its causal sense links justification to knowledge. I not only believe, but know if things are as I believe, and this is no accident. A justified belief has a cause that reveals it to be true; its justification cites a cause in the light of which it can be seen to conform to the truth. Then it is no accident if it is true; it must be, given its cause. Thus, as I represent my explanation as a justification, I conceive of the belief I explain as being knowledge in virtue of having this explanation.[4]

When I explain why I believe something, giving a belief explanation, then this is how I represent the cause that I give: it establishes that my belief is true. Of course, it may be that this is not how things stand. I may think that the cause of my belief establishes its truth, while in fact it does not, or even while my belief is false. So when I explain why I believe that *p*, giving a belief explanation, I take myself to know that *p*, but it may be that I only think I know, while in fact I do not. However, it may also be that things are as I think, and I indeed know that *p*. Now we ask, when things are this way, when I know that *p* as my believing it has a cause that establishes that *p* is the case, *how do I know, if I do, that things are this way?* It will transpire that I know it from spontaneity. My knowledge satisfies the formula of first person knowledge: when I know that *p* in virtue of my believing it having the relevant kind of cause, then I know that I know that *p by knowing that p*. My knowing that *p* includes and is included in my knowing that I know it, which latter knowledge therefore is unmediated first person knowledge.

Consider this abstractly. I think that *X*. It may be that I am wrong and *X* is not the case. It may also be that *X* is the case. Now we ask, supposing

4. If an explanation "I believe that *p* because ____" does not give the cause, but only, as one might want to put it, the reason, then this reason why I believe that *p*, which reveals *p* to be true, leaves it open whether I believe that *p*, while the cause, in virtue of which it is no accident that I believe it, leaves it open whether it is true. It is a commonplace that, in order to be justified in doing something, it is not enough that I can give reasons for doing it. The reasons must have power and explain why I am doing it. The concept of acting from duty has a causal sense. The same holds of belief and epistemic justification.

that X is the case, how do I know that it is, if I do? The answer depends on the nature of X. X may be such as to be known from spontaneity, i.e., a self-conscious act, which includes and is included in its subject's representation of it. Then I know that X is the case in virtue of its being the case; its being the case is the same reality as my knowing it to be the case. Our X is this: I know that p, believing that p on account of a cause that reveals p to be true. We must consider the nature of this X in order to determine whether it is a proper object of spontaneous knowledge.

We said that knowledge was nonaccidentally true belief. Necessity comes from causality, and kinds of causality, or senses of "why?" give rise to kinds of necessity, or senses of "no accident". The causality of belief explanation defines a sense in which it is no accident if a belief thus caused is true, and this is the sense of "no accident" that belongs to the concept of knowledge, for it is the one that applies to beliefs as such. So belief is knowledge if and only if it has a true belief explanation, or equivalently, if and only if it is justified. More precisely, this defines receptive knowledge. By contrast, since an object known from spontaneity is identical with the subject's thought representing it, there is in this case neither need nor room for something other than this object, a mediating term, to show that things are as the subject thinks. The notion of justification does not apply. If someone says, "I am cooking partridges", which she knows from spontaneity, it makes no sense to ask, "Why do you think you are cooking partridges?" She already said why she thinks this: she is cooking partridges. Her cooking partridges *is* her thinking that she is cooking partridges, and this, the practicality of her thought, makes it no accident that things are as she thinks. So a thought is nonaccidentally true either on account of itself, when it is identical with its object, or, when its object has an independent existence, on account of its cause, which binds it to its object. With regard to thought about an independent object, being nonaccidentally true *is* being justified; the causality of justification defines the relevant sense of "no accident". Hence, while the first definition of knowledge defines it as nonaccidentally true belief, its definition as justified belief explains what this comes to for *receptive* knowledge, knowledge that is a distinct reality from its object.

Now the X of which we inquire whether it is an object of spontaneous knowledge is this: I know that p from receptivity. We can develop this content further by reverting to what we said in Chapter 3. There we found that an act of receptive knowledge is represented by its subject as an *act of a power*. "Act of a power" contrasts with "act of a habit". A power is the cause of the existence of its acts in such a way as to be, at the same time, the cause of their conforming to a normative measure, which thus is internal to these acts. A habit, by contrast, does not bring its acts under a standard. For example, a virtue is a power: it is analytic that actions that spring from a virtue are good. Whether acting in a certain way manifests a virtue therefore is not independent of whether the subject is acting well in so acting. The concept of a power of knowledge stands to the true as the concept of a virtue stands to the good: it is analytic that a belief that springs from a power of knowledge is true, so that whether a belief manifests such a power is not independent of whether it is true. This distinguishes a virtue from a habit to do things of a certain description, and a power of knowledge from a habit of forming beliefs. (We are ignoring for the sake of argument that the concept of such a habit is incoherent on account of the logical, or temporal, incongruity of an act of believing that something is the case with what can be the object of a habit.)

A belief explanation establishes that the belief it explains is true, representing it as an act of a power of knowledge. In saying this, we are developing the content of a first person thought. We are not supposing that such a thought cannot be false. We are supposing that it can be true, and we ask how it can be known to be true when it is. Before we can answer this, we must remember another result of Chapter 3: that the normative significance of a first person belief explanation is irreducible and cannot be explained by supposing that she who gives it performs two speech acts, an explanation why she believes what she does that does not speak to the question whether it is true, and an assessment of the belief as true in virtue of its cause. For, this means that the concept of a power of knowledge is fundamental; it is prior to the concept of a habit of forming beliefs (or would be, if there were such a concept).

Consider the first form of belief explanation of Chapter 3: inference. Gottlob Frege says an inference proceeds from true premises.[5] This is curious. Cannot one draw conclusions from false propositions? But Frege's thought is that, fundamentally, inferring a proposition is a way of establishing that it is true and, hence, of coming to know it. And I cannot acquire knowledge in this way unless I proceed from true premises (indeed,

5. See, e.g., "Gedankengefüge", p. 47; "Logik in der Mathematik", *Nachgelassene Schriften*, pp. 263–267.

unless I proceed from premises I know to be true). If this is Frege's meaning, he will further think it impossible to infer p from q, if p does not follow from q. So his concept of inference seems to be this: an inference proceeds from propositions known to be true in conformity to the order of what follows from what. Someone who believes that p because she believes that q manifests a power to draw inferences only if q is (known by her to be) true and entails p. The power to draw inferences, so understood, is a power of knowledge; a belief cannot manifest it and yet be false. Whether a belief springs from this power is not independent of whether it is true. By contrast, let us explain *moving to a belief* in this way: I move from believing that q to believing that p, when I believe that p because I believe that q, but neither does q need to be true, nor does p need to follow from it. Moving to a belief is not an act of a power of knowledge. Perhaps it is an act of a habit. Now, someone might try to define inferring as moving that satisfies certain conditions: I infer p from q if and only if I move from believing that q to believing that p and q is true and implies p. But this definition is unsound, for in first person thought Frege's concept of inference is prior to the concept of moving. In giving a belief explanation "I believe p because q", I do not conjoin a nonnormative report that I moved from q to p with the normative claim that, since q is true and entails p, I thereby have come to believe something true. If the explanation could be decomposed in this manner, its components would be empty. I explain why I believe what I do not by a habit of believing or a belief-forming mechanism, acts of which, as acts of this habit or mechanism, may be true or false, but by a *power* to infer, whose acts, as such, cannot fail to be true.

According to the second form of belief explanation we considered, I explain why I believe something not by something else I believe, but by the fact that I perceive or have perceived what I believe. Now, I perceive something only if, through my sensory impressions, I am in a position to tell how things stand with the object that affects my senses. The power to tell how things are through sensory affection is a power of knowledge: its acts as such are true beliefs. In contrast to perceiving that p, let us define *being appeared to as if p* as a sensory affection that involves the proposition p in a way that is neutral as to whether p is true. If I believe p on account of having been appeared to as if p, then my believing p does not manifest a power of knowledge. (It may manifest a habit.) Now, one might try and define perception in terms of appearance: I perceive that p if and only if I am appeared to as if p, which appearance is explained by the fact that p.

This is inadequate; it is easy to think up situations in which the fact that p enters into the explanation of why someone is appeared to as if p without the appearance amounting to perception. (We only must see to it that the content of the appearance and what explains it are identical only per accidens.) But we need not consider attempts to mend the definition by adding conditions, for the mistake lies in conceiving of a perception that something is the case as an appearance that satisfies further conditions. In first person thought, the concept of perception is fundamental; it is prior to the concept of appearance. When I give a belief explanation and say "I believe that p because I perceive that this is how things stand", I do not conjoin a non-normative explanation that I believe that p because I have been appeared to as if p—which does not speak to the question whether p is true—with an assurance that p must be, or is likely to be, true given that I have been appeared to in this way. When the normative sense of the explanation is reduced in this manner, its components dissolve. A first person belief explanation does not subsume its object under a habit. It represents it as an act of a power to gain receptive knowledge.[6]

The X of which we are asking how it may be known is this: I know that p, exercising a power of receptive knowledge. This shows how X, when it is the case, is known to be the case. Since belief explanations describe a causality of thought, a subject of a belief so caused is, as such, in a position to explain it. Hence, she who possesses a power of receptive knowledge knows the acts of her power and knows them *as* acts of this power. In other words, a power to gain receptive knowledge is formally represented, or self-conscious. Its subject's knowledge of acts of this power is not a distinct reality from these acts; it is knowledge from spontaneity. I know it from spontaneity when I know something by inferring it from something else that I know. And I know it from spontaneity when I know that something is the case because I perceive or perceived it. If someone's beliefs are related in such a way that the one is knowledge in virtue of the other's being that, then she knows that her beliefs are so related, and knows it by virtue of their being so related. And if someone bears a receptive nexus to an object by which she is in a position to gain sensory knowledge of it,

---

6. Compare Andrea Kern, *Quellen des Wissens*: "The concept of a sensory impression, as it applies to a subject of empirical judgment, acquires its sense from its employment in the description of a rational power of knowledge. [. . .] This means that the case of a sensory impression that is not a case of perceiving [. . .] is logically derivative from the case of an impression that is a case of perceiving" (p. 297).

then she knows that she does, and knows it by bearing this nexus to the object.

In Chapter 3, we considered the suggestion that the answer to the question what to believe "I believe that p is the case because I perceive that it is" bears the same form as "I believe that p because q": it gives, as the ground on which I believe something, something else I believe, of which I can and must be asked on what grounds I believe it. But when I explain that I believe something because I perceive it, this answer does not reattract the question "why?" that it answers. I know *what I perceive* from receptivity, *by virtue of a receptive nexus with the object* I thus know; but I know *that I perceive* what I do from spontaneity, *by virtue of the object* of my knowledge. We said previously that, when someone says, "I am cooking partridges", something she knows from spontaneity, then it makes no sense to ask her, "Why do you think you are cooking partridges?" She already said why she thinks this: she is cooking partridges. The same holds true here. When someone says, "I believe that p because I perceive it", it makes no sense to repeat the question and ask, "How do you know that you perceive it?" For, she already said how she knows this: she perceives that p. This is how she knows that she perceives it.

In a well-known article, William Alston claimed that the epistemological tradition confused being justified in believing something with being justified in believing that one is justified and, consequently, or in parallel, knowing something with knowing that one knows it. He called this a "level confusion".[7] But the confusion is Alston's. It resides in thinking that there are levels of justification and knowledge, which one might confuse. There are such levels if justification and receptive knowledge are such as to be known from receptivity, for it follows from the definition of receptive knowledge as of an independent object that knowing something is not the same as receptively knowing that one knows it. Conversely, if justification and receptive knowledge are objects of spontaneous knowledge, then receptively knowing something is knowing that one knows it, and there are no levels to climb. If the tradition identifies being justified with knowing that one is, and knowing something with knowing that one does, then this shows that it takes justification and knowledge to be essentially represented in first person thought, i.e., such as to be known from spontaneity. Our reflections vindicate the tradition.

7. See "Level Confusions in Epistemology".

It is essential to realize that we do not simply say that knowing something entails knowing that one knows it. A calculus of epistemic logic that licenses inferences exemplifying the schema "$Kp \supset KKp$" is incapable of representing our claim. It suggests that "Kp" is known in the same manner as "p", as it employs the same letter to signify the nexus one bears to both these propositions. Thus, on the one hand, when p is known receptively, the calculus suggests that the fact that one receptively knows something is something one knows from receptivity, which is absurd. On the other hand, when p is known spontaneously, the calculus suggests that "$Kp \supset KKp$" has content, while in truth it is of the form "$p \supset p$". As the object of an act of receptive knowledge differs from the object of an act of spontaneous knowledge of this act, it is a nonempty statement to say about it that one not only knows, but knows that one knows. But the object of spontaneous knowledge is the same reality as the knowledge, wherefore it is a tautology that who knows the former knows the latter.

The X we are discussing, "I know that p, exercising my power of receptive knowledge", is such as to be known from spontaneity. Of course such a thought may be false; I may erroneously think I know that p in an act of my power of receptive knowledge, while in truth I do not. But if my first person thought is true, then I know that it is true from spontaneity. When I know that p, exercising my power of receptive knowledge, my receptively knowing that p and my knowing that I receptively know it are one reality. An act of receptive knowledge is an act of a self-conscious power and as such an object of spontaneous knowledge. When we distinguish spontaneous knowledge, which is identical with its object and is of oneself as oneself, from receptive knowledge, which is of an independent object and is of something as other, then the antinomy of internalism and externalism dissolves. This critical solution of the antinomy is out of reach of an epistemology that defines its topic by the phrase "knowing that p", not inquiring into the logical form of "p", in particular ignoring whether it represents its object first personally or demonstratively. Thus our account cannot be placed on a map of positions whose layout can be described without drawing this distinction. It cannot be classified as externalist or internalist, for it removes the error that is the source of that opposition. Without the notion of spontaneous knowledge of the material nexus to an object by which one gains receptive knowledge of it, epistemology remains stuck in the antinomy of internalism and externalism. This is a fair price for isolating the theory of knowledge from the theory of self-consciousness.

Fallibility

She who knows something from receptivity knows from spontaneity that she does. We derived this from the more fundamental fact that receptively knowing something is an act of a self-conscious power. In the contemporary epistemological literature, the place of the concept of a power of knowledge is often assumed by the concept of a reliable habit, or mechanism, of belief formation, a habit such that beliefs issuing from it can be relied upon to be true. But it is impossible to comprehend fallibility without distinguishing power from habit. For, fallibility is a characteristic of powers.[8] As advocates of fallibilism attempt to do without the concept of a power of knowledge, they are unable to articulate the notion of a fallible subject of knowledge. In this section, we first show how fallibilism, as expounded by Michael Williams and Robert Fogelin, fails as an account of knowledge. Then we develop the notion of fallibility from the concept of a power.

Fallibilism

We said receptive knowledge is justified belief; we can also say that it is justified true belief, for what is known is true. But the truth-condition is redundant, as the justification required for knowledge secures truth. Of course, I may be justified in believing that something is the case even when my grounds do not establish, but perhaps only render it likely, that things are as I believe that they are. But the theory of knowledge is concerned only with the kind of justification on which knowledge rests, and if I cannot exclude, on the strength of my grounds, that things are otherwise than I think, then I do *not* know. Consider: I judge that p on the ground that q, which is something I know. If p may be false even while q is true, then this is not a way of coming to know that p. For, even as I know that q, it may not be the case that p. Thus, for all I know, it may not be the case that p.[9] And this means that I do not know whether p.[10]

8. It is the principle point of John McDowell's "Criteria, Defeasibility, and Knowledge" that fallibility characterizes a capacity, not its acts.

9. I am echoing a formulation of John McDowell's in "Criteria, Defeasibility, and Knowledge", p. 371.

10. An extensive literature devotes itself to the discussion of cases, introduced by Edmund Gettier in his "Is Justified True Belief Knowledge?", in which justified true beliefs fail to be knowledge because they are true by chance. As a justified belief can be true by chance only if the grounds that justify it do not establish its truth, Gettier's thesis, that justified true belief need

Yet it is widely held that, whenever I believe something concerning an independent object, I cannot in principle give grounds that establish the truth of my belief.[11] No matter how good my grounds are, there are circumstances that my grounds do not rule out and that are such that, if they obtained, I would not be in a position to exclude, on the strength of my grounds, that I am mistaken. Suppose, for example, I think there is a container of milk in the refrigerator because I looked in the refrigerator and, so I think, saw it there. Now, what if my roommate emptied the container and filled it with white paint? All the same, I would think there is a container of milk, although in fact the container holds no milk. I would be fooled because things look just as they would if there were a container of milk. This shows that the ground on which I think that there is a container of milk, namely the visual appearance presented by the inside of the refrigerator, does not rule out that my roommate emptied the container and filled it with paint. Hence, they do not rule out that I am wrong in thinking that there is a container of milk.

A line of reasoning of this shape can be constructed whenever I ostensibly know something with regard to which I might have been fooled. For, when I am fooled, I do not recognize that I am (otherwise I would not be fooled); when I am fooled, things appear to be as they are when I am not fooled. Hence, even when I am not fooled, I cannot rule out certain circumstances that are such that, if they obtained, I would be fooled. Since I am never in a position to rule out, on the strength of my grounds, that I am fooled, I am never in a position to establish, through my grounds, that things are as I believe.

If this argument, the argument from illusion, were sound, it would show that there is no knowledge of things with regard to which we are liable to be fooled. When the argument is presented as an account of such knowledge, we must expect contortions. Consider the following passage from Williams's *Problems of Knowledge*:

---

not be knowledge, deploys a concept of justification that allows a justified belief to be false. This renders the thesis uninteresting. For, a belief whose justification leaves it open whether things are as believed is anyway not justified in the way necessary for knowledge. So the obvious conclusion is not that knowledge cannot be defined as justified true belief, but that this definition deploys a concept of justification according to which justified beliefs cannot fail to be true.

11. A notable exception is John McDowell. Compare, e.g., "Knowledge and the Internal". It would be apt to describe our objective in this chapter as that of articulating the account of self-consciousness and spontaneous knowledge contained in McDowell's epistemological writings.

> While we certainly take ourselves to know all sorts of things, [. . .]
> we recognize that the possibility of error can never be logically ex-
> cluded.—In claiming knowledge [. . .] we are issuing a particularly
> strong and open-ended guarantee of the correctness of what we be-
> lieve. We are betting that there is no non-misleading counter-
> evidence to our belief. (pp. 41 and 54)

Williams says we *take* ourselves to know many things. He is not prepared
to say, not here, that we *do* know them. For he is calling attention to the
fact that the things we take ourselves to know may fail to be the case, in
which case we do not know them. Williams explains that, when we claim
to know something, we issue a guarantee that it is true. But how can we
guarantee that, if we have no way of establishing it?[12] Williams corrects
himself and says we *bet* that it is true. But why then do we say "I know"
and not "I bet"? Williams lacks the resources to distinguish knowing that
something is the case from betting that it is. My grounds at best put me in
a position to play an advantageous lottery, and even this is saying too
much, for there is no way of knowing that the lottery is advantageous, as
there is no finding out that I won, only betting that I did—a bet on whose
success I can only bet.[13]

Similar tensions are helpfully explicit in Fogelin's *Pyrrhonian Reflections*. He writes:

> It seems natural to ask how grounds can establish the truth of some-
> thing when at the same time there are undercutting possibilities that
> have not been eliminated. The answer to this [. . .] is that this is how
> we employ epistemic terms. We assert something, thus committing
> ourselves to it without reservation, while at the same time leaving
> eliminable refuting possibilities uneliminated. This is a fact—a fact
> about how we employ knowledge claims. [. . .]—We have thus ar-
> rived at two factual claims. The first concerns what we mean when we

---

12. One may "issue a guarantee" that something is the case in the sense of agreeing to
pay a penalty if it is not the case. This is not knowing that it is the case. There is a tendency
to conceive of knowledge claims on this model: she who claims to know something lays herself open to sanctions should it turn out to be otherwise. Even if this were true, it would not
explain how it is possible to know something, and it would not show that the alleged practice of sanctioning is a practice of reason.

13. Compare David Lewis, "Elusive Knowledge", p. 222.

say that *S* knows that *p:* "*S* knows that *p*" means "*S* justifiably believes that *p* on grounds that establish the truth of *p*". The second describes how people actually employ and actually understand knowledge claims: When people claim to know things, they do not do so in the belief that they have eliminated all eliminable refuting possibilities, nor do their auditors suppose that they believe this. (pp. 94–95)

Clearly, it is not possible to explain how grounds can establish truth while failing to exclude falsity—a question Fogelin rightly finds it natural to ask—by considering how we employ epistemic terms. On that topic, Fogelin claims to have observed two facts. First, we do not take someone who says "I know that *p*" to take herself to be in a position, on the strength of her grounds, to exclude that she is mistaken. Secondly, when we say, "I know that *p*", we mean, "I am in a position to establish, on the strength of my grounds, that *p* is true". If this is how we employ epistemic terms, then we employ them in this way: when we claim to know something, we do not take ourselves to know it.

When skepticism is put forth as a theory of knowledge, this indicates an unrecognized difficulty. Williams thinks of himself as taking the measure of our fallibility as seekers of knowledge; he calls the doctrine that knowledge rests on grounds that fall short of establishing the truth of what one thus knows a "fallibilist conception of knowledge".

> In most interesting cases of empirical knowledge, we want to use empirical evidence to justify conclusions that are logically stronger than the conjunction of the premises. [. . .] The link between premises and conclusions is not deductive but inductive. And because the conclusion of an inductive inference is logically stronger than its premises, such an inference never guarantees its conclusion's truth. [. . .] The modern conception of knowledge is *fallibilist*. [. . .] What I mean by this is that [. . .] we recognize the possibility of error can never be logically excluded. It can always turn out that we only *thought* we knew. (*Problems of Knowledge*, p. 41)

We are fallible in our empirical judgments in that it may befall us that we erroneously think we know something when in fact we do not. Williams suggests that this shows that this grounds of our empirical beliefs are "inductive", i.e., do not rule out that one believes something false on their basis.[14] He must think, then, that we would not be, or are not, vulnerable to error, if we could, or where we can, rest a claim on grounds that exclude its falsity. He does not say why he thinks this, but presumably he follows the argument from illusion: Even as I think I know something, I recognize that I might have been fooled. Had I been fooled, I would not have known that I was; I would not have been able to distinguish my situation from one in which I am not fooled. So whenever I think I know something, I cannot rule out certain states of affairs such that I would be fooled if they obtained. If such a state of affairs obtains, it can turn out that it does. If that turns out, it turns out that my belief is false, or true only by accident. And then it turns out that I was wrong in thinking I knew. Conversely, if I could rule out all states of affairs such that I would be fooled if they obtained, then I would know that I am not fooled. And if I knew that I was not fooled, then it could not turn out that I was, hence it could not turn out that I erroneously thought I knew.

If I believe that p on "inductive" grounds, i.e., on grounds that do not establish the truth of what I believe on their basis, then this explains how it may happen that, while I believe that p, this is not the case or, given my grounds, only accidentally so, so that I would be wrong if I thought I knew that p. But it explains it in a way that makes it a mystery why I would think I know that p in the first place. Let p and q be propositions with independent truth values. Suppose I know that p. If on this basis I believe that $p \wedge q$, it may turn out that I am wrong. Should I think I know that $p \wedge q$, it may turn out that I falsely thought I knew this. But I have no business thinking I know that $p \wedge q$, if my grounds for believing this reach no further than my knowledge of p. However, according to Williams and Fogelin, whenever I claim to know something, I am in the position of someone who holds that $p \wedge q$ on the basis of p: let q be the proposition that is true if and only if none of the circumstances obtains that p does not exclude and that are such that, if they obtained, I would be fooled.[15] Fogelin says, correctly given his view: "In

14. The claim that singular empirical beliefs rest on inductive inferences was proposed by Alfred Ayer, and there based on the logical distance of sense data, on which empirical beliefs allegedly rest, from the material substance they purport to represent (see *The Foundations of Empirical Knowledge*). Since then, the claim has come loose from its phenomenalist origin and simply expresses the notion that grounds of empirical judgments are inferentially weaker than the beliefs they justify. Compare Robert Fogelin, *Pyrrhonian Reflections*, pp. 21–22.

15. Michael Williams describes inductive inference as a matter of "us[ing] empirical evidence to justify conclusions that are logically stronger than the conjunction of the premises."

making knowledge claims, we always (or almost always) assert more than we have a right to assert."[16]

Fallible Powers

The fallibilist conception of knowledge provides no comprehension of fallibility. It explains our liability erroneously to think we know in a way that entails that we never think we know, not when we think clearly. The cause of the failure of fallibilism is its lack of the concept of a power of knowledge. For, fallibility is a character of a power: a fallible power is one whose exercise is liable to be thwarted by unfavorable circumstances. Here, the relevant power is a self-conscious power of receptive knowledge, a power to explain why one believes something by a cause that excludes that one goes wrong in believing it.

Consider first a practical power such as the ability to juggle five balls. Someone who is able to juggle five balls may still on a given occasion fail to keep the balls in the air if there is, say, strong wind. Shall we say, then, that she does not possess the power to juggle five balls, but rather the power to: juggle five balls, if the wind is not too strong? This is nonsense because, on the one hand, there is no end to the list of circumstances that may be unfavorable to juggling. If we made it our principle to include circumstances unfavorable to its exercise in the description of the object of a power so as to render it immune to being frustrated by unfavorable circumstances, we would never arrive at a description of a power. On the other hand, circumstances unfavorable to juggling cannot be specified ex-

---

If this is induction, then induction is not a way of gaining knowledge. Williams defends it in this way: "Such inference takes place against a background of reasonable presuppositions: for example, that a sample used to gauge the incidence of a particular trait is representative of the target population" (*Problems of Knowledge,* p. 46). The content of the "reasonable presupposition" is nothing other than that it is correct to infer judgments about the population from judgments about the sample. It is as reasonable as this inference. If there are doubts whether such an "inference" yields knowledge, the "reasonable presupposition" will not lay them to rest. (David Hume was right not to be impressed by John Locke's assurance that inductive inference takes place against the background of the reasonable presupposition that the future will resemble the past.) This does not mean that there is no such thing as knowing a kind through its instances or, if this is our name for this way of gaining knowledge, inductive inference. It means that the difference of induction from deduction is profounder than its depiction by Williams as defective deduction allows. See my *Kategorien des Zeitlichen,* chap. 6.

16. *Pyrrhonian Reflections,* p. 94.

cept as circumstances unfavorable to juggling. For example, it is not possible to determine the relevant strength of wind independently of what juggling is. The only way correctly to specify it is as the strength of wind that makes juggling balls impossible. We do not first have a conception of an action-form, juggling balls, which then is limited by the condition that certain impediments be absent, e.g., that there not be too much wind. Rather, the conception of the action-form already excludes the impediment, which therefore must not be added to the description of the power.[17] The two points connect as follows. It would be sensible to include unfavorable circumstances in the description of a power (seeking to make it infallible by limiting its object) only if, in this way, we arrived at an action concept that no longer included the idea of circumstances that prevent its instantiation. Its instances would be *logically* exempt from being prevented by circumstances from being brought to completion. They would not admit the notion of interruption. In other words, they would always already be complete. But with the contrast of progress and completion falls the contrast of a power and its actualization. If we abstract from fallibility, we do not arrive at the idea of a subject of infallible powers of action—there is no such thing—but at the idea of a divine subject who is, in traditional terminology, pure act.

Let us apply these reflections to the power to gain knowledge by means of the senses. It is a fallible power; its exercise is liable to be thwarted by unfavorable circumstances such as, notoriously, falsifying light, misleading mirrors, and the like. Shall we say, then, that we do not possess the power to tell how things are by means of the sense of vision, but rather the power: to tell how things are by means of the sense of vision, if (to make a start) there are no misleading mirrors? No. First, there is no end to the list of circumstances that might prevent one from taking in how things are by means of the senses. Secondly, the notion of such a circumstance in each case depends on the notion of sensory knowledge; it is the notion of a circumstance unfavorable to the acquisition of knowledge by means of the senses, or a certain sense: the mirrors are *misleading,* the light is *falsifying.*

17. This almost quotes Aristotle, *Metaphysics* Θ 5, 1048a16–21. Aristotle makes only our second point, not the first, because, as we are about to see, the second point, properly understood, contains and is the ground of the first. Compare the interpretation of this passage by Jon Moline in "Provided Nothing External Interferes" and Andrea Kern's discussion of "favorable and unfavorable circumstances" in *Quellen des Wissens,* pp. 284–295.

The two points connect as above. If we could exhaust the circumstances and arrive at a description of a power whose acts then no longer would be liable to be frustrated by unfavorable circumstances, then acts of this power would not depend on anything not provided by their subject in and through these acts. Hence, these acts would not be acts of receptivity, which depend on their object, but acts of what Kant calls original intuition, which is the origin of its object. Original intuition is not the object of a power, but pure act; the contrast of power and act does not apply to it. So again, if we abstract from fallibility, we arrive not at the idea of a subject of infallible powers of receptive knowledge—there is no such thing—but at the idea of a divine subject of original intuition, who is pure act. Fallibility is not a limitation of a power of receptive knowledge. It is not an empirical fact that our power of receptive knowledge is fallible. It is a logical or metaphysical fact. The notion of a power—upon which the idea of fallibility follows—is contained in the notion of a material subject of action and knowledge.

Lacking the concept of a power, one is bound to misrepresent the fallibility of a power to gain knowledge as the less than perfect reliability of a habit or mechanism of forming beliefs. In fact, no difference could be greater than that of a fallible power from a reliable habit. Consider again a practical power. A power to do A is, first, a source of acts of doing A, and, secondly, if "do A" is an action verb, the source of its subject's knowledge of these acts. If someone is able to do something, then there is a sense in which this explains why, on a given occasion, she succeeds in doing it. For example, if someone can juggle, then it is not an accident if she manages to keep the balls in the air, whereas this would be a miracle in someone who cannot juggle. In this sense, a power provides an account of its acts. A power also figures in the explanation of its corrupted or impeded acts, but, adopting Aristotle's happy phrase, "by negation and subtraction".[18] A failed exercise of a power must be explained by un-

---

18. Compare *Metaphysics*, Θ 2, 1046b14–15. Aristotle's point there is different, however. He says an account of what it is to do something reveals both what it is to do that thing and what it is to fail in doing it, the former in itself, the latter by negation and subtraction. The topics connect where the description of what it is to do A is a description of how it is done, or how one does it, so that recognizing given proceedings as a case of doing A, successful or aborted, is tracing them to a capacity to do it, as such or by negation and subtraction.

favorable circumstances, which have prevented the proper exercise of the power. One may be tempted to think that, in parallel, a successful exercise of a power is explained not by the power alone, but by the power together with the absence of unfavorable circumstances. But no content is indeterminately specified by the phrase "no unfavorable circumstances obtain". That no such circumstances obtained means that circumstances were such that the power was properly exercised, and adds nothing to the explanation why it was properly exercised. A power does not bear the same explanatory relation to its failed acts as it does to its successful acts. Its successful act is explained by the power *alone,* its failed act by the power through negation and subtraction, that is, by circumstances unfavorable to its exercise.

A power to do something explains actions that manifest it. This modal character of a power underlies its subject's spontaneous knowledge of its acts. If I have the power to do *A*, then the action explanation "I am doing *A* because I want to do *B*" expresses spontaneous knowledge that I am doing *A*. For, since I can do *A*, it is no accident if I am in fact doing it. One may object that, in order to know that I am doing *A*, it is not sufficient that I be capable of doing *A*; in addition, I need to know that circumstances are not unfavorable to the exercise of this power. But again, "circumstances are not unfavorable" does not indeterminately signify a content, nothing I could, or could fail to, know. Since a power alone accounts for its acts, it alone, when it is self-conscious, accounts for its subject's knowledge of its acts.[19]

This applies to a power of receptive knowledge. First, it is no accident if someone with the power to gain knowledge by means of the senses on a given occasion gains knowledge in this way. When she comes to believe

---

19. There is a complication. It may happen that I have the capacity to do *A*, am doing *A* upon having determined that it is to be done, and yet do not know that I am doing it, because, although circumstances are not unfavorable, I have reason to think that they are. Andrea Kern calls this situation one of *reflectively unfavorable* circumstances (see her *Quellen des Wissens*, pp. 332–333). Reflectively unfavorable circumstances frustrate the exercise of my capacity to do *A*, not by preventing me from doing *A*, but by preventing me from doing it in such a way that my doing includes my knowledge that I am doing it. In this way, they prevent the proper exercise of my capacity, for in its proper exercise, a self-conscious capacity is a source of knowledge of its acts. Capacities are liable to be frustrated by unfavorable circumstances. Self-conscious capacities enjoy the privilege of being liable to be frustrated by reflectively unfavorable circumstances.

something false, this is to be explained by the power "through negation and subtraction", i.e., by circumstances unfavorable to the exercise of the power. We must not conclude that, therefore, successful acts of the power are explained not by the power alone, but by it and the absence of unfavorable circumstances. For, no content is specified by the phrase "unfavorable circumstances are absent". Thus there is an asymmetry: successful acts of a power are explained by the power alone, failed acts by the power by negation and subtraction, i.e., by circumstances unfavorable to its exercise. Moreover, a power of knowledge, in particular the power to gain sensory knowledge, is self-conscious. For, acts of a power of knowledge essentially figure in explanations that describe a causality of thought. If I am capable of gaining knowledge by means of the senses, then, unless circumstances are unfavorable, my explanation "I believe that p because I perceive it" expresses spontaneous knowledge that I know, by means of the senses, that p. One may think that, in order to know that I perceive and thus receptively know that p, it is not sufficient that I be capable of gaining knowledge in this way. In addition, I must know that circumstances are not unfavorable to the exercise of my power. Again, the phrase signifies nothing, a fortiori nothing I could, or could fail to, know.[20] A power of sensory knowledge alone accounts for its acts, and therefore alone accounts for its subject's knowledge of its acts.[21]

We are fallible in that we are liable erroneously to think we know when we do not. Williams thinks that this is so because, or when, the grounds on which our beliefs are based do not exclude that we are wrong. But this does not explain why we are vulnerable to falsely

20. Andrea Kern notes that this is impossible to comprehend on the supposition that inference is the only mode of justification: "As long as one attempts to reconstruct an act of knowledge from a basis that is not conceived as an actualization of a rational power, but as a premise from which the truth of the belief must be inferred [. . .] one will construe the description of favorable circumstances for gaining knowledge as the description of something that is external to that basis. Favorable circumstances then have the status of *further premises*, which must be *added* to that premise, and must be valid if we are to derive from the original premise how things are" (*Quellen des Wissens*, p. 298).

21. Again, there is the complication noted in note 19. It may happen that I perceive something and do not know that I perceive it because I have reason to think that circumstances are unfavorable. Circumstances may be reflectively unfavorable to the exercise of a power to gain receptive knowledge, as this is a self-conscious power.

thinking we know. While it explains adequately why we would be wrong if we thought we knew, it does not explain why we would think that. In fact, we routinely give grounds that rule out the possibility of error. For example, when I believe something because I perceived it, my belief cannot be wrong. It is true that empirical knowledge cannot in general rest on deductive inference; I cannot in general establish empirical propositions by inferring them from other empirical propositions. Williams concludes that, "in most interesting cases", empirical justification is a matter of inductive inference. But inferring a belief from another belief is not the only manner of justifying beliefs. "I believe that *p* because I perceive it" is not a deductive inference, but it is not for that reason an inductive inference. It is *no inference*. In justifying my belief in this way, I do not give another proposition to which I bear the same relation as I bear to the proposition in question. Rather, I redescribe my nexus to this same proposition. I invoke a receptive nexus to the object of my belief and represent my believing about it what I do as an act of a power of knowledge. Since this power is a self-conscious power, I not only gain receptive knowledge as I exercise it, I also know that I do from spontaneity.

This explains what the so-called fallibilism leaves incomprehensible, namely how I may falsely think I know. For, a power of receptive knowledge is fallible; unfavorable circumstances may thwart its exercise. When they do, I do not come to know that *p*, but merely, and perhaps falsely, believe that *p*. By the same token, I do not come to know that I know that *p*, but merely, and indeed falsely, think that I know it. My power to know spontaneously that I have gained sensory knowledge is *as fallible as* my power to gain sensory knowledge *because it is the same power*. When I bear a receptive nexus to an object in virtue of which I am in a position to gain knowledge of this object, then I know that I do and thus know that I know. This does not make me infallible. If I know that I know that *p*, then I know that *p*. And if I know, it cannot turn out that I erroneously thought I knew. But that it cannot turn out that I erroneously think I know, when I know, leaves open the possibility that, when I do not know (because unfavorable circumstances have thwarted the exercise of my power of knowledge), I falsely think I know, and that this comes out. Circumstances that prevent me from gaining knowledge by means of the senses prevent me from knowing that I am so prevented.[22] As Heidegger put it, "Das Verbergen verbirgt sich."[23]

The mistake of the argument from illusion is now obvious. The argument is: Whenever I seem to know something, I might have been fooled. Had I been fooled, I would not have known that I was. I would not have been able to tell my situation apart from one in which I am not fooled. This shows that my grounds do not place me in a position to exclude that I am in such a situation. They do not enable me to exclude that I am fooled.— The argument supposes that, had I been fooled, I would have believed the proposition in question *on the same grounds* on which I believe it now that I am not fooled. This straightforwardly entails that these grounds do not establish the truth of what I believe and therefore do not provide me with knowledge. But when I know something on the ground that, say, I perceive it to be the case, then I would not, had I been fooled, have believed it on this ground, for, had I been fooled, I would not have perceived it to be the case. Hence, when I am not fooled, my grounds exclude that I am fooled: when I perceive how things are, I am not fooled with regard to how they are. One might object that this grants me grounds that rule out error at the price of making it impossible for me to know whether my belief is based on such grounds. For, when I am fooled, I do not know that I am fooled. So I can never know whether I am not

22. Reflection on unfavorable, or reflectively unfavorable, circumstances has led some authors to distinguish two concepts of justification. In one sense, I am justified in believing something if I have discharged my epistemic responsibilities, in another sense, I am justified if my belief is based on grounds that establish its truth. (Compare Robert Fogelin, *Pyrrhonian Reflections*, pp. 26–27.) The distinction is motivated by cases in which I come to believe something through an ostensible exercise of a power to gain receptive knowledge in circumstances that are unfavorable to the exercise of this power, having no reason to suspect they are unfavorable, and by cases in which I come to believe something through an ostensible exercise of a power of knowledge in circumstances that I have reason to suppose unfavorable although they are not, i.e., in reflectively unfavorable circumstances. If we distinguish two senses of justification, we will say about the first kind of case that I have discharged my epistemic responsibilities, but have failed to establish the truth of my belief. If we employ a unified notion of justification, we will say that I have failed to discharge my epistemic responsibilities, which require that I establish the truth of my belief, through no fault of my own. About the second kind of case we can say that I have established that my belief is true, but failed to discharge my epistemic responsibilities; or we say that I have failed to establish that my belief is true, for I do not know that my belief cannot fail to be true. Nothing hangs on what we say.

23. "Der Ursprung des Kunstwerks", p. 40.

fooled and my beliefs are based on grounds that establish their truth, or whether I am fooled and such grounds are unavailable to me. This objection repeats the mistake: from the fact that, when I am fooled, I do not know that I am, it does not follow that, when I am not fooled, I do not know that I am not. When I know that p as I perceive it to be the case, then I know that I perceive that p. Thus I am in a position to distinguish my situation from any possible situation in which I would be fooled, for, in any such situation, I would not perceive that p, while in the given situation I do.

It is easy enough to see that a refutation of the argument from illusion must take this form. But we shall not comprehend how this refutation could possibly describe our condition, until we recognize that, in the fundamental case, justifying a belief about an independent object is representing it as an act of a fallible self-conscious power of receptive knowledge.

The Nature of Epistemology

Receptive knowledge is an object of spontaneous knowledge. This has consequences for the nature of epistemology, the inquiry into what knowledge is and whether we have any. We shall discuss two consequences: first, that the question after the concept of knowledge and the question after the reality of knowledge cannot be separated; second, that epistemology itself articulates first person knowledge, knowledge from spontaneity.

The Concept and the Reality of Knowledge

We said that I know from spontaneity that I know from receptivity, as receptive knowledge springs from a self-conscious power to gain receptive knowledge. But how do I know that I have this power? Could I not falsely think that I have it, while in truth I do not, but must instead make do with reliable habits? No. A self-conscious power is not only a source of its acts, and not only a source of its subject's knowledge of its acts. It is the source of its subject's knowledge of the power and her possession of it. For, I acquire the concept of a power to gain knowledge by reflecting on the content of my first person belief explanations. That is, I acquire the concept of the power by reflecting on my exercise of this power. As I acquire the concept in this way, I know that I instantiate it. As a self-conscious power provides a subject possessing it with knowledge that she possesses it, knowledge that one has the power to gain knowledge by means of the senses satisfies the formula of first person knowledge: one knows that one has that power by having it. A power of knowledge has always already answered any doubt—concerning its acts, concerning knowledge of its acts, concerning knowledge of itself.

This is how it must be. Michael Williams correctly notes that skepticism is unavoidable as soon as we ask for a criterion that distinguishes knowledge from mere belief, a criterion whose satisfaction by a belief can be ascertained without prejudging the belief's claim to knowledge.[24] And indeed, if knowing that I know something were finding that my believing it satisfies a criterion, I could never know that I know. For, recognition that a belief satisfies the criterion would be a further belief, which would not in the same act be known to satisfy the criterion. It follows that, if I know myself to know things, then knowledge itself provides for its distinction from error. A theory of knowledge does not give a criterion of knowledge. It explains how knowledge can be what it must be: *its own criterion*. The principle of knowledge cannot leave room for doubt concerning itself. That is, it must be a self-conscious power.

Contemporary epistemology routinely presupposes that there are two distinct questions: the first asks what it is to know something and is after the concept of knowledge, while the second inquires whether we know something and is after the reality of knowledge. Treating the first question, one begins with the idea that knowledge is justified true belief, then adds or replaces some clauses. As it is assumed that one thus defines

---

24. *Problems of Knowledge*, pp. 61–63. Michael Williams writes: "The Aristotelian solution to this problem is that knowledge depends on self-evidence [. . .]. The skeptical counter move is to inquire why something's striking us as self-evident should be a guarantee of its correctness." *The "skeptical counter move"* describes an act of reason as an instance of a psychic habit and thus gives no argument for, but *expresses a skepticism already in place*. No Aristotelian ever thought that what strikes me as self-evident cannot fail to be true. If I am enough of an idiot, the most errant nonsense may strike me as self-evident. Descartes does *not* think I know something if it strikes me as though I perceived it clearly and distinctly. He thinks I know something if I perceive it clearly and distinctly. And he notes that, "because of a habit to believe them", he had been taking himself to perceive things clearly and distinctly that he did not so perceive: "Aliud autem quiddam erat, quod affirmabam quodque etiam ob consuetudinem credendi clare me percipere arbitrabar, quod tamen revera non perciebam [. . .]." (*Meditationes de prima philosophia*, 3:3.) It is difficult to develop and maintain the power to perceive things clearly and distinctly, but she who possesses this power acquires knowledge in its acts.

knowledge in terms intelligible independently of the concept they define, the definition leaves it open that there may be no knowledge; belief and truth and whatever else is thought to be needed may never come together. The concept of knowledge *does not include* its reality. But this is not all. We saw just now that I cannot know that I know something, if knowledge is belief with certain properties. Hence, a definition that defines knowledge as belief with certain properties not only makes room for skepticism, it entails skepticism. The concept of knowledge *excludes* its reality. We find that a definition of knowledge entails skepticism unless it shows that and how the concept of knowledge includes its reality.[25] Our definition, at which we arrived by reflecting on the self-conscious nature of knowledge, is this: Someone believing that *p* knows that *p* if and only if, believing it, she manifests a power of knowledge. This answer to the question after the concept does not leave open a separate question after the reality. For, given what we said about the origin of the concept of a power of knowledge, this account of the concept is given by a subject who, as she gives this account, possesses and exercises a power of knowledge. The concept of knowledge cannot be severed from the reality of knowledge because applying the concept of knowledge is, in the fundamental case, recognizing the reality of knowledge in oneself.

If it is objected that our account of knowledge is circular, then we must answer that, in one sense, it is not, while in another sense, a sound account of knowledge must be circular. The account is not circular, for a power of knowledge is something completely different from an act of knowledge, as different as a concept is from an object that falls under it. It is not empty to explain something as the act of a corresponding power. The account is circular in the sense that it does not define knowledge in terms that do not include and depend upon the concept they define. But this can be no objection, for the demand that the definition of knowledge not be circular in this sense entails skepticism, and we cannot make skepticism a methodological premise of epistemology.

The idea that the concepts of belief and truth, which specify conditions of knowledge, are independent of the concept of knowledge manifests a conception of conceptual analysis according to which explaining a concept is giving necessary and sufficient conditions for its correct application. An

---

25. In Hegel's terminology, a definition of knowledge must show that and how the concept of knowledge is an *idea*. See *Wissenschaft der Logik*, 2:3.

analysis of this kind discovers analytic relations in Kant's sense; it discovers that one concept contains another. Neither the concept of belief nor the concept of truth contains the concept of knowledge; beliefs may be unjustified and truths unknown. If we attend only to analytic relations, we see no dependence of belief and truth on knowledge. But the concepts that interest philosophy are formal concepts, categories, as Kant defines them: concepts that contain nothing but a form of a thought of an object. Such concepts cannot be explained by giving conditions of application, but only by describing the relevant form.[26] The dependence of the concepts of truth and belief on the concept of knowledge does not reflect analytic relations, but springs from the form of explanation on which these concepts depend, the form we described in Chapter 3. It is not analytic that belief is knowledge; beliefs may be justified or not. But these cases are not on a par. Justified belief is fundamental, for the concept of belief would be empty if it did not figure in belief explanations, which justify the explained beliefs. Neither is it analytic that a truth is known; a truth may be known or not. Again, the cases are not on a par. "Truth" is the name of a formally represented order, and a subject of acts falling under this order explains them by a cause in virtue of which she recognizes them as conforming to this order. Only someone who engages in this manner of explanation possesses the concept of truth. Thus the notion of truth is understood through thoughts that represent their subject as capable of gaining knowledge. In this way, the unity of belief and truth in knowledge precedes and is the source of the elements that it unifies.

Epistemological Realism

We said one acquires the concept of a power to gain knowledge by reflecting on one's exercise of this power. This sheds light on the following passage from Wilfrid Sellars:

> In characterizing an episode or a state as that of knowing, we are not giving an empirical description of that episode or state; we are placing it in the logical space of reasons, of justifying and being able to justify what one says. (*Empiricism and the Philosophy of Mind*, p. 76)

26. Ernst Tugendhat makes this observation, but wrongly takes the definition of knowledge as justified true belief to indicate that the concept of knowledge is an exception. ("Überlegungen zur Methode der Philosophie", pp. 268–269.)

Followers of Sellars have interpreted this in a particular manner. They have understood "not giving an empirical description" to mean not giving a description, and have taken placing something in the space of reasons to stand opposed to giving the cause of its existence. Thus Robert Fogelin maintains that someone who seeks to explain how grounds establish truth commits a naturalistic fallacy, for when we say that someone's grounds establish the truth of her belief we do not describe her grounds, but endorse her reasoning.[27] Williams argues that there can be no theory of knowledge that traces knowledge to its sources, for such a theory would construe knowledge as an object of a descriptive science and thus fail to appreciate the normative significance of attributions of knowledge; whether someone knows something is not a question of fact, but a question of norms of "justificatory practices".[28] The metaphysical dogma that opposes description and norm in this way is a manifestation of the empiricism that, according to Marx, incapacitates all hitherto existing materialism. It has been the objective of this chapter to show that we cannot understand the concept and the reality of knowledge unless we rid ourselves of this empiricism. The concept of knowledge essentially figures in first person thoughts, which bear an irreducibly normative significance. They do not for this reason fail to be knowledge of material fact. They represent a material reality, the reality of a self-conscious subject of receptive knowledge.

We distinguished knowledge from receptivity, which is of an independent object, from knowledge from spontaneity, which includes and is included in its object. Let us introduce a parallel distinction of empirical concepts and concepts of reflection. An empirical concept essentially figures in thoughts that articulate receptive knowledge, while a concept of reflection is primarily deployed in the articulation of spontaneous knowledge. Empirical concepts spring from experience, concepts of reflection spring from spontaneity. The concept of knowledge is implicit in first person belief explanations, which express knowledge from spontaneity, and so it is not an empirical concept. The same holds for the concept of a power of knowledge. This concept, as well, is implicit in acts of spontaneous knowledge. Finally, the concept of sense perception that applies to subjects of thought is not empirical. Its primary application is in explanations that state knowl-

27. *Pyrrhonian Reflections*, pp. 28–29.

28. See Michael Williams, *Problems of Knowledge*, pp. 170–172. Robert Fogelin thinks it would be a question of fact if there were a "justificatory framework" or a "justificatory procedure" that was "final" or "ultimate", and maintains that there is none (*Pyrrhonian Reflections*, pp. 98 and 195).

edge from spontaneity.[29] The nature of our faculty of sensory experience is revealed not by empirical inquiry, but by reflection on what we know from spontaneity, a reflection of which the present treatise gives an example. Of course it is possible empirically to investigate the physiology and psychology of perception in the human species. But such investigations presuppose, and do not provide, knowledge of what human perception is.

Williams is right in thinking that there can be no empirical concept of a source of knowledge. He is wrong to conclude that the concept of a source of knowledge is not the first and principal concept of the theory of knowledge. His inference rests on the empiricist dogma that a concept that does not spring from sense experience does not describe a material reality and is not used to express factual knowledge. The concept of a power to gain knowledge describes a reality that is such as to be known from spontaneity. In his book *Unnatural Doubts,* Michael Williams observes that there is such a thing as a theory of knowledge only if the ostensible object of this theory has the appropriate unity. He quotes David Hume, who finds this unity in the "powers and faculties" of man, and conceives of the theory of knowledge as part of the "science of man".[30] Williams calls the view that knowledge is an object of theory in this sense "epistemological realism". Now, we claim that a belief is knowledge if and only if it springs from a power of knowledge. This is epistemological realism, if anything is. It is perfectly immune to Williams's objections against this position.[31] The problem is not epistemological realism, but the empiricist

29. A philosophy of perception that abstracts from the question how perceiving something is a manner of coming to know it is misguided if it pretends to speak about human perception. There is no philosophy of human perception that is not epistemology.

30. *Unnatural Doubts,* pp. 104–105. The quotation is from David Hume, *A Treatise of Human Nature,* Introduction. Compare Immanuel Kant, according to whom the question "what can *I* know?" is contained in the question "what is *man?*" (*Logik,* p. 25). David Hume, after his exhilarating pronouncement that "there is no question of importance, whose decision is not comprised in the science of man", disappointingly falls into the error of supposing that "the only solid foundation we can give to this science [the science of man; S.R.] must be laid on experience and observation" (p. 5), failing to appreciate something implicit in Kant, namely that when I embark on the science of man, my thought turns upon myself.

31. In particular, it does not ignore the "normative character of justification". It is an error to think that appreciating the normative character of justification consists in holding that "epistemic norms are standards we set" (*Problems of Knowledge,* p. 170). Such a conception of the normative falls victim to the "Kantian paradox", which we discussed in Chapter 4. Neither does our doctrine have any truck with the idea of "pass[ing] judgment on [our evolving views of the world and our place in it] from a standpoint outside them", an idea Williams thinks is internal to epistemological realism (p. 197).

conception of material reality, through which Williams interprets it and which has impeded the development of a true materialism. Williams forgets a peculiarity of the nature of man that affects the way in which we know it: the nature of man is *our* nature. If we inquire into the nature of knowledge, we inquire into our own nature. And knowledge of ourselves must, in the case that is fundamental in the sense that only in virtue of it do we know ourselves, be unmediated first person knowledge. Such knowledge is not based on observation. The science of man, of which the theory of knowledge forms a part, is not an empirical science. It is pursued not by observing men and drawing inferences from these data but by articulating what we know of man by being men.[32]

32. Michael Thompson discusses the implications of this form of knowing man for ethical theory in "Apprehending Human Form."

6

The Second Person

We have given an account of self-consciousness in terms of a certain form of predication. Thoughts that exhibit this form articulate knowledge from spontaneity, i.e., from reasoning under a formally represented order. Predicated in this way are concepts of thought, practical and theoretical. We have not yet touched on how these concepts are applied to someone else. And it may seem that we can leave this question alone, for it is clear that the way in which I know that someone else is doing something intentionally or believes that something is the case is different from the way in which I know these things of myself. Having distinguished the manner of knowing that sustains first person reference, it seems we have finished our task.

In fact we have not. It is often said that certain concepts, e.g., concepts of experience and action concepts, are self-ascribed in a special manner, different from the way in which they are ascribed to someone else. Equally frequently is it added that, yet, the same concepts are ascribed in these different ways. It is not obvious how both can be true. If ways of predicating what seems to be one concept are simply different, then we must conclude that the corresponding expression is ambiguous.[1] It does not help to insist that the expression must bear a uniform sense in its first person and its second person use.[2] We seek to understand how it can, which we do only if we recognize the first person use and the second person use of the expression as guises of one form of predication. Therefore, an account of self-consciousness that only says how action concepts and concepts of experience are applied to oneself is incomplete. We do not

1. Compare Donald Davidson, "First Person Authority", pp. 7–8.
2. This is as far as P. F. Strawson's argument in the chapter "Persons" of *Individuals* takes us. See pp. 99–101.

comprehend first person predication until we see that and how it is one side of a form that has two sides, the other side being the manner in which the same concepts are predicated of someone else. In this chapter, we describe the application of concepts of thought to someone else in a way that reveals its unity with the first person use of these concepts.

We shall proceed as follows. In the first section, we inquire into the form of explanation of someone else's actions and beliefs, equivalently, into the kind of causality such explanations represent. As in the case of first person reference, the form of knowledge that sustains reference to a second person transpires from the way in which her self-conscious acts are explained. In the preceding chapters we argued that, in first person explanation, explaining the act *is* judging it to conform to an order of reason in virtue of its cause. It may seem that this is not true of second person explanation. Perhaps the cause must *appear to the acting subject* to be something that reveals her act to conform to the relevant order. But as she may have skewed ideas of this order, representing the causality cannot *be* representing her to conform to this order. Yet, this view of second person explanation cannot be true, for it excludes that the same concepts figure in first person and in second person thought. In fact, explanations of the form on which action concepts and the concepts of belief and experience applied to someone else depend explain self-conscious acts in terms of their subject's *knowledge* of the relevant order of reason and, therefore, in terms of *the order itself*. In the second section, we shall consider what this means for the way in which I know another self-conscious subject. There is a sense, which we shall explain, in which I know a second person *from spontaneity*. Second person knowledge is not receptive, but spontaneous; it is not from the senses, but from thought. In the third section, we describe how this form of knowledge underwrites a distinct form of reference, the linguistic expression of which is the *second person pronoun*, "you". Anticipating this result, we speak throughout the chapter of the other subject as a second person. As the words indicate, the third person comes after the second person.

Second Person Explanation

Since first person thoughts about actions and beliefs essentially are terms of explanations of a certain form, the kind of predication they exhibit and the kind of knowledge they articulate transpires from this form of explanation. In the same way, we arrive at an account of the form of predication, or form of knowledge, that constitutes second person thought by inquiring into the form of explanation of someone else's actions and beliefs.

Causality of Thought and Causality of Reason

Actions and beliefs are terms of explanations such that she whose acts are explained in this way concludes on the ground of the given cause that she believes something it is right to believe or is doing something it is good to do. The explanation represents a *causality of thought*, a causal nexus that involves the subject's thinking that her act conforms to an order of reason in virtue of its cause. Hence, when she herself gives the explanation, she thinks of it as showing that she is doing or believes something that she should do or believe; she thinks her act conforms to the relevant order in virtue of the cause that she gives. For her, the explanation, representing a causality of thought, represents, as we may put it, a *causality of reason:* a causal nexus sustained by the relevant order of reason.

Let us dwell for a moment on the notion of a causality of reason, as it may seem strange. In fact, it is perfectly familiar. John McDowell expounds it in a passage we quoted in Chapter 3:

> The concepts of propositional attitudes have their proper home in explanations of a special sort: explanations in which things are made intelligible by being revealed to be, or to approximate to being, as they rationally ought to be. This is to be contrasted with a style of explanation in which one makes things intelligible by representing their coming into being as a particular instance of how things generally tend to happen. ("Functionalism and Anomalous Monism", p. 328)

McDowell contrasts revealing something to conform to an order of reason with representing it as an instance of how things generally tend to happen. However, an order of reason is general, too; there is no limit to the number of acts that may exemplify, and to the number of subjects whose acts may be explained by, such an order. So the first style of explanation, as well, explains what it does by subsuming it under something general. The styles differ not in that one invokes something general while the other does not. They differ in respect of the general item each invokes: an order of reason in contrast to a law of the kind described by the natural sciences. Now, in explanations of the latter style, in one sense an event is explained by a preceding event; in another sense, it is explained by the law it exemplifies. Gilbert Ryle gives this example: we say, "The glass broke because *the stone hit it*", and also, "The glass broke when the stone hit it, because *it was brittle*".[3] Here, the explanation refers to a disposition; it can also appeal to a law. Indeed, it is more fitting to say, "The glass broke when the stone hit it, because *glass is brittle*". Since a law is a "because", we may call it a cause. It is a cause of events that are explained by being shown to instantiate it. Some think that a causal nexus of events as such exemplifies a law,[4] and if this is so, then there is a sense in which the ultimate cause of events is always a law, for then a law always underlies the causality of an event. By contrast, when we explain in the first of McDowell's styles, the general item underlying the causal nexus is an order of reason; the act is explained by being shown to exemplify—not a law of the natural sciences, but—an order of reason. In a parallel manner of speaking, we call this order the ultimate cause of the act.

We said action explanations and belief explanations represent a causality of thought, which is conceived by the subject as a causality of reason. As we noted above, McDowell makes an apparently stronger claim. He says the causality of second person explanations not only is conceived by the second person to be, but *is* a causality of reason. In the logically fundamental case, I explain why someone is doing or believes something by revealing her to *conform* to an order of reason. Now, even if we agree that this is how I conceive of the explanation of my own acts, must we not, precisely for that reason, say that I explain why someone else acts as she does by showing her act to *seem to her to conform* to the relevant order? This is what Donald Davidson suggests.

> There is a certain irreducible—though somewhat anaemic—sense in which every rationalization justifies: from the agent's point of view, there was, when he acted, something to be said for the action. ("Actions, Reasons, Causes", p. 9)

A self-conscious subject thinks of first person explanations of her own acts as representing a causality of reason. But this view of things is a distortion inflicted by the lens of the first person. In truth, her act is explained by a cause in the light of which it appears to her to conform to an order of

---

3. *The Concept of Mind*, p. 50.
4. Compare, e.g., Donald Davidson, "Laws and Cause".

reason. It is irrelevant to the causality of the cause whether the act indeed conforms to this order. She cannot help but think it does; she necessarily thinks good and true what appears to her so. Therefore she sees her thought that depicts her act as conforming to the relevant order of reason as reflecting, and thus as itself accounted for by, this order. However, what explains her act is not this order, but rather her idea of it. Robert Brandom and Richard Moran articulate this view in the following passages.

> Norms (in the sense of normative statuses) are not objects in the causal order. [...] Normative statuses are domesticated by being understood in terms of normative attitudes, which *are* in the causal order. What is causally efficacious is our practically taking or treating ourselves and each other as having commitments. (Brandom, *Making It Explicit*, p. 626)

> The reasons that explain an action are states of mind of the agent, which may themselves be either veridical or mistaken. When a belief that is an explanatory reason is a false belief, this need not affect its explanatory validity in the slightest. (Moran, *Authority and Estrangement*, p. 128)

Moran maintains that a false belief provides as good an explanation as a true one; its truth or falsity is irrelevant to its explanatory power. This must be an instance of a principle other instances of which are: misleading sensory impressions explain why someone believes what she does as well as veridical ones; that someone believes that p explains why she believes that q given that she believes that p entails q whether or not it does entail it. The relevant principle is that second person explanations describe a causal nexus that does not depend on the fact that the act conforms to the relevant order of reason in virtue of its cause so long as it appears to do so to its subject.

We have come upon two opposing descriptions of the form of explanation of someone else's actions and beliefs. According to McDowell, I explain why someone else is doing something by revealing her to conform to an order of reason; this order is the ultimate cause of her act. According to Brandom, I explain her act by revealing her to conform to what she takes to be required by the relevant order—not a rational order or normative statuses, but her ideas of the order or her normative attitudes are the ultimate cause of her act. "Ultimate" is crucial here: since a causality of reason essentially passes through a representation, normative attitudes figure essentially in the explanation of self-conscious acts on any account. The issue is whether they are the ultimate cause or whether they are in turn to be traced to the order they represent.

In the next subsection, we shall reject Brandom's account because it undermines the unity of first person and second person thought. In the following subsection, we argue that McDowell's account is true. In fact, this account is contained in what we said about action explanation and belief explanation; it follows from the fact that these represent a causality of thought. For, not only is a causality of thought conceived by the subject of the thought to be a causality of reason; in the fundamental case, it *is* a causality of reason.

Normative Attitudes as Ultimate Causes

Let us begin by recognizing that people often act and judge on the basis of false beliefs. Consider an example of G. E. M. Anscombe's: A man is pumping water to replenish the water supply while the pipes are broken and the water is running into the ground. He erroneously thinks that pumping is a way to fill the tank and good to do on that account. Yet we refer to his thinking this to explain why he is pumping. Such cases are common, and irrelevant. The claim we are discussing is that second person explanation by the subject's knowledge of, and thus by, an order of reason is fundamental in the sense that reference to a second person and the application of concepts of practical and theoretical thought to someone else depend on—in McDowell's words, "have their proper home in"—this form of explanation. If this is right, then explanation by knowledge of the order, and thus by the order itself, is constitutive of the concepts deployed in explanation by false belief, which thus is logically, or metaphysically, secondary.

Brandom does not rest his claim that normative attitudes are the ultimate causes of action and belief on the fact that people act on false beliefs, draw conclusions from false premises, and base beliefs on misleading impressions. He propounds a metaphysical thesis (for which this fact would provide no basis): explanations of self-conscious acts refer to the subject's representation of an order of reason, to normative attitudes, and not to the order she represents, or normative statuses, because the latter are not the kind of thing that may be the cause of anything. This may seem only sane. Must we not reject the extravagant notion that reason is the ultimate cause of thought and action in favor of a causality of "normative attitudes" and "states of mind"? But here we forget ourselves, and what we know ourselves to be. I think of another subject only if I deploy concepts under which I bring myself in first person thought. And the seemingly sane view entails that thoughts ostensibly about someone else's actions and beliefs do not employ the same concepts as corresponding first person thoughts do. If there is no causality of reason, then there is no second person thought.

Second person explanations may bear a normative sense, when I say, e.g., "She believes that p because she inferred it from q" or "She believes that p because she saw it". If they do not describe a causality of reason, then this normative significance is reducible. Explaining, e.g., "She believes that p because she inferred it from q", I make two speech acts with one form of words: I explain that she moved from believing that q to believing that p, and I assert that q is true and entails p (I endorse her move). In the same way, with "She believes that p because she saw it" I explain that she formed a belief because she suffered certain impressions, and contend that these were veridical (I endorse the belief she acquired on account of these impressions). As applied to someone else, then, the concept of moving is prior to the concept of inferring, and the concept of being appeared to is prior to the concept of perceiving; an inference is a moving, and a perception an appearance, that satisfies further conditions. If this is the true account of second person explanation, then the normative sense of a first person explanation disappears when it is transposed into the second person. The irreducibility of its normative sense is not a feature of the explanation, which is given in the first person, but an illusion effected by its being given in the first person.

Thus we explain the illusory appearance of a causality of reason as the distorted conception of a causality of normative attitudes by the subject of these attitudes.[5] Now, who embraces this doctrine? *A self-conscious subject rejects it.* She rejects it in the unmediated first person representation of her self-conscious acts. Explaining why she believes something by representing it as right to believe, or why she is doing something by repre-

5. Peter Bieri's account of freedom in *Das Handwerk der Freiheit* represents my unmediated conception of the cause of my own acts as necessarily illusory in this way. Given what we said in Chapter 4, this entails that Bieri fails to make contact with his announced topic, the concept of freedom, which designates the character of an act of whose causes its subject has spontaneous knowledge.

senting it as good to do, she denies Brandom's account of the cause of her acts. She denies it *in giving these explanations,* which cite a normative order as the ultimate cause, not a normative attitude.

A self-conscious subject rejects Brandom's teaching in her unmediated first person thought. But will not she be sufficiently enlightened to frame a disengaged view of herself and see herself as others do? If she cannot embrace the doctrine in identification-free first person thought, she should be able to apply it to herself via an identity judgment, reasoning as follows:

When I say, "She believes that *p* because ____", my statement can be decomposed into an explanation why she believes that *p* and an assessment that *p* is, or is likely to be, true. If she says the same about me, her statement can be decomposed in like manner. But she thus explains what I explain saying, "I believe that *p* because ____". So although this is not how I see things when I think of myself without mediation, I recognize that the true cause of my belief is not a normative order, but a normative attitude.

But this line of reasoning is invalid. Its first premise, that someone else's thought about me, "She believes that *p* because ____", conjoins explanation and assessment as independent elements, entails that the second premise, that, in thinking this, she brings me under the same concept under which I bring myself thinking "I believe that *p* because ____", is false. If her speech act "She believes that *p* because ____" reduces to a nonnormative explanation conjoined with an act of endorsement, then she does *not* explain what I explain using these same words. She does not employ the concept of belief I apply to myself, for *that* concept is posterior to the concept of knowledge, which is not true of the concept she applies to me. It is perfectly useless to insist, now, that it must be the same concept. This is true, but we cannot revert to this truth to defend an account that contradicts it.

The doctrine that mental states and normative attitudes as opposed to an order of reason are the ultimate cause of self-conscious acts ignores a condition under which I apprehend someone else as a subject of states of mind and normative attitudes. One misses this condition if one fails to attend to the way in which self-consciousness is implicated in the apprehension of another subject. A second person thought represents its object as *the kind of subject one knows oneself to be.* And self-knowledge is, fundamentally, articulated in unmediated first person thoughts; something is self-knowledge only if it is knowledge of the object of such thoughts. Therefore, first person knowledge (not of the causes in the particular case, but) of the nature of the causes of action and belief cannot be challenged from the allegedly superior point of view of a second or third person; such a challenge only proves that its allegedly superior point of view provides no view upon action and belief and self-conscious subjects. *Self-consciousness is sovereign in respect of the nature of acts of self-consciousness.* We self-conscious subjects know that Brandom misrepresents the cause of our acts. If someone is to apprehend us as the self-conscious subjects that we are, her thought must bear a different form. And so must ours if we are to think about her.

An Order of Reason as Ultimate Cause

A first person explanation of action and belief, representing a causality of thought, is taken by her who gives it to represent a causality of reason. That the relevant thought of the subject may be false does not show that this does not hold of second person explanation, as well; it does not disprove that here, too, in the fundamental case, explaining the act *is* representing it to conform to an order of reason. Indeed, this is how it must be. For, we know about our own self-conscious acts—know it spontaneously, by being their subject—that they exhibit a causality of reason. And since our own acts cannot bear a different metaphysical nature from those of someone else, it follows that what in Chapters 2 and 3 came into view as a causality of thought must be a causality of reason.

In order to see why a causality of thought, in the fundamental case, is a causality of reason, or, in other words, why the subject's normative thought that constitutes the causality of her self-conscious act is, fundamentally, not a mere thought, but knowledge, we must reflect anew on the notion of a causality of thought. We shall restrict our discussion to intentional action. The abstract structure shared by practical and theoretical thought makes the application of our considerations to the latter straightforward.

In Chapter 2, we found that a thought of the subject linking her movement and its cause in such a way as to reveal the former to be good is the causality in virtue of which her movement is an intentional action. Kant captures this in the formula that intentional action is action according to a representation of a law. Both finite ends and infinite ends are laws in the relevant sense. A finite end unites potentially infinitely many actions that serve it and that a subject pursuing it may derive from it by instrumental reasoning. An infinite end unites potentially infinitely many actions that manifest it, any of which a subject adhering to this end may derive from it, representing the action as manifesting this end and thus her practical life-form. Now, when someone is acting according to a representation of an end, finite or infinite, then the representation of the end is the cause of her action. But this does not suffice. It is not sufficient that the representation cause the action in any old way in order for the subject to be acting *according to* the representation. The causality must be such that the action accords with the end not per accidens, but in virtue of being caused by the representation of the end. And the causality is a source of accord and thus the causality of a representation according to which someone acts only if the representation of the end causes the action *by way of the subject's deriving the action from the end*. Hence, as Kant puts it, the will is practical reason: "Da zur Ableitung der Handlungen von Gesetzen Vernunft erfodert wird, so ist der Wille nichts anders, als praktische Vernunft."[6] We expressed the same idea by saying that intentional action is subject to a causality of thought.

An end represented in unmediated first person thought—that is, an end self-consciously sought or, for short, a *self-conscious end*[7]—is the object of a representation with this kind of causality: a representation that is such as to figure as cause in explanations describing a causality of thought. In other words, a representation of a self-conscious end is the kind of representation according to which its subject may act. Of course, a representation may cause actions without them being in accord with it in virtue of being caused by it. We imagined someone who is falling ill because he wants to lose weight. His falling ill is caused by his representation of the end, and it accords with the end (as he will lose weight by falling ill), but *causation and accord have come together per accidens*. As the causality of the representation in respect of the action is not the source of the action's accord with the end, it is not on account of its power to cause actions in this way that a representation is of an end. A representation is of an end in virtue of being fit to cause actions in a way that ensures accord with the end. For example, something is an act of wanting to make coffee in virtue of its power to cause actions that, as so caused, serve the end of making

---

6. *Grundlegung zur Metaphysik der Sitten*, p. 412. Since reason is required for the derivation of actions from laws, the will is nothing other than practical reason.

7. A self-conscious end is not only represented; it is represented as an end. Compare Thomas Aquinas, *Summa Theologica*, IaIIae, qu. 6, art. 2.

coffee. And something is an act of wanting, for example, justice, in virtue of its power to cause actions, which, as this is their cause, are just. Of course, the representation of an end may be prevented from actualizing this power in many ways. The point is that, if we abstract from this power, we lose the concept of a representation of an end.

Now, if someone's wanting to make coffee in this way explains why she is doing what she is doing, then she is making coffee. And if someone's love of justice thus explains why she is acting as she is, then she is acting justly. *Acting on account of wanting to do A,* in the manner constitutive of the concept of wanting to do something, is *doing A.* And *acting from an infinite end X,* in the manner constitutive of the concept of adhering to an infinite end, is *acting so as to manifest X.* A representation of an end is such as to cause the reality of the end in an action. It is the nature of a representation of an end to be productive—not of any old thing, but—of its object. And when it does produce its object, the subject's thought, which is the causal nexus of representation and action, is *true.* Moreover, since its truth is a constituent of the proper causality of the representation, it is no accident that a subject of representations of ends has suitable true thoughts. So when such thoughts are true, they are nonaccidentally true, or knowledge.

It might seem that we have not addressed the objection, which says that a causality of thought is not a causality of reason because the thought that represents the action as in accord with the relevant order of reason may be false. For, we considered a case where the representation of an end causes a movement without mediation by a thought of the subject, while the cases we ought to consider are those in which, on account of ignorance or stupidity, the subject's thought deriving the action from the end is false, so that the action does not accord with the end, or only per accidens. Instead of discussing the man who is falling ill because he wants to lose weight, we must discuss the man who is pumping water because he wants to replenish the water supply, though he is not replenishing the water supply, as the pipes are broken. Here, the representation of the end does not cause the reality of the end; the representation is not productive of its object. However, it is clear how such cases are to be understood: as cases in which unfavorable circumstances interfere with the causality that is proper to the representation.

In the preceding chapter, we discussed receptive knowledge, a representation that nonaccidentally conforms to its object because it is *receptive of its object.* It may happen that I take a representation to be receptive of its object when it is not. An argument from illusion concludes that therefore the first concept of a theory of knowledge must be that of a representation that is caused by whatever it is caused, which may or may not be its object, and which is knowledge if it satisfies further conditions. But this undermines the very idea of a material subject of theoretical knowledge. We must begin with the concept of an act of a power of receptive knowledge, a power to represent an object by being affected by it. Then we can understand a sensory representation that merely seems to be receptive in terms of the same power, by negation and subtraction: it results from unfavorable circumstances, circumstances that impede the proper exercise of the power.[8] We must treat the concept of a representation that is *productive of its object* in the same way. It may happen that I take a representation to be productive of its object when it is not, as when I am pumping water into broken pipes. An argument from illusion would claim that, therefore, the principle concept of a theory of the will, of action theory, must be that of a representation of an end that causes whatever it causes, which may or may not realize the end. Then an explanation why the end was realized must appeal to circumstances external to the representation. But this destroys the idea of a representation that causes actions so as to accord with it, which is the idea of a self-conscious end. Instead, we must proceed from the concept of an act of a power to represent ends in a way that is productive of their reality. A representation that merely seems to be productive (as his representation of replenishing the water supply seems to him who is pumping water into broken pipes) is to be explained in terms of the same power, by negation and subtraction: it results from unfavorable circumstances, from circumstances thwarting the proper exercise of the power.

It is impossible to recognize that a subject's thought of her action as serving or manifesting an end is, fundamentally, knowledge, if one thinks of the representation of an end and the thought of an action as suitable for it as joint causes of the action, the causality being of the same kind as the causality that governs the movements of nonrational or even inanimate substances. According to this view, being caused by the representation of the end and being in accord with the end are in principle only externally related. Then, of course, a true thought is as good a cause as a false one: while with true belief there is accord and with false belief there is not, accord is in any case not internal to the power of the representation to cause

---

8. Compare the discussion of fallible powers in Chapter 5.

the action. By contrast, if the relevant thought of the subject is not a further cause, additional to the representation of the end, but the causality of this representation, then such thoughts cannot in general be mere thoughts. If an action progresses toward a finite end through a thought that puts means to this end, then this thought is knowledge. And if an action gives an example of an infinite end through a thought that subsumes it under this end, then, again, this thought is knowledge. In action according to a representation, the representation of the end and its reality in the action are inseparable.[9] Action and representation depend on their unity, on the nexus of accord. Therefore, the thought that is the accord is knowledge and constitutes the subject's grasp of the relevant order of reason. Causality of thought is causality of reason.

Second Person Knowledge

Actions and beliefs are subject to explanations that explain an act by revealing it to conform to an order of reason. Action concepts as well as the concepts of belief and experience depend on this form of explanation; the representation of a second person as acting intentionally or as believing that something is the case essentially is a term of explanations of this kind. We shall now argue that this entails that knowledge of another subject is not receptive knowledge. In a sense we shall explain, second person knowledge is from spontaneity.

Knowledge of Self-Conscious Acts Mediated by Spontaneous General Knowledge

We are claiming that knowledge of someone else's beliefs and actions is spontaneous. This may seem obviously wrong. Cannot we see that someone is doing something intentionally, and cannot we hear her say what she thinks? And are not seeing and hearing modes of sensory representation? G. E. M. Anscombe writes:

> The greater number of the things which you would say straight off a man did or was doing will be things he intends. [. . .] I am sitting in

---

9. Kant's definition of an end entails this: "Zweck [ist] der Gegenstand eines Begriffs, sofern dieser als die Ursache von jenem (der reale Grund seiner Möglichkeit) angesehen wird" [An end is the object of a concept insofar as the latter is regarded as the cause of the former (the real ground of its possibility)]. (*Kritik der Urteilskraft*, §10, p. 220.)

a chair writing, and anyone grown to the age of reason in the same world would know this as soon as he saw me, and in general it would be the first account of what I was doing. (*Intention*, §4, p. 8)

And John McDowell:

There can be facts that are overtly available (so that conviction that they obtain need not be a matter of speculation as to something hidden behind what is overtly available), but awareness of which is an exercise of a perceptual power that is not necessarily universally shared. Command of a language is partly constituted by just such a perceptual capacity. [. . .] I mean the idea of a perceptual capacity to be taken seriously. Some may think that it can amount to no more than this: in learning a language, one learns to put a certain theoretical construction on the facts that one "really" perceives to obtain [. . .]. But this is not what I mean. [. . .] I mean to be offering a more radical alternative: one that rejects the assumption [. . .] that our genuine perceptual intake can be exhaustively described in terms that do not beg the question of the status, as knowledge, of what we ascribe to people when we say they understand utterances. ("Anti-Realism and the Epistemology of Understanding", pp. 331–332)

Saying that we perceive thought, theoretical and practical, has a negative point. It is to reject the idea of a realm of phenomena that can be apprehended without being recognized as manifestations of thought and yet exhaust our evidence for the existence of thought in someone else. In the fundamental case, I apprehend the sensible reality of someone else's act of thinking, an intentional action or a speech act, without passing through the observation of something that does not involve recognition of it as an act of thinking. Thus McDowell contrasts perception with theoretical construction and Anscombe calls the relevant awareness of what someone is doing "straight off". As this negative claim rejects but does not give an account of the form of knowledge of someone else's self-conscious acts, it does not touch our thesis that such knowledge formally differs from knowledge of a nonrational reality in being spontaneous.[10]

---

10. It will transpire that we have no sympathy for the view McDowell attacks. According to this view, someone else's thoughts are further away from us than states and events of which we know by observation. On the view we shall propound, thoughts of another subject are nearer to us than anything we know from receptivity.

When we hear someone speaking and understand what she is saying, then, McDowell says, we perceive her thinking. Now, in perceiving thinking—we say "perceiving" to emphasize the negative point—spontaneity is involved in a way in which it is not in perceiving nonrational operations. For, the representation of self-conscious acts essentially involves subsuming them under an order of reason, and this affects the way in which such acts are known. In order to see this, it will be helpful to remember how, in general, knowledge of laws underlies the apprehension of substances. For, the character of the knowledge of self-conscious acts reflects the character of the laws by which they are governed and through which they are apprehended.

David Hume held that the senses deliver impressions that in themselves bear no connections among them. If they appear connected, then this reflects subjective habits to associate them in certain ways. In particular, the unity of a substance, which holds together changeable states, and the unity of a movement, which joins a state from which with a state to which, cannot be found in what is given to the senses. It is a construction put on impressions that on their part do not depend on these forms of unity. Kant argues that we must abandon this conception of sensibility. Our sensibility delivers intuitions that necessarily exhibit the forms of unity described by the pure concept of a changing substance, for it is only by exhibiting this unity that intuitions represent its object as in time. It is incoherent to maintain, as Hume did, that the unity of a changing substance is a projection of habits acquired by the repeated experience of the succession of certain impressions. For, an experience of temporal succession is an experience whose object falls under the category of substance. Kant further claims that, if the unity of a substance is not constructed from impressions devoid of this unity, but is always already contained in receptive intuitions, then an intuition of a given substance and its changes presupposes knowledge of general laws. Substances are apprehended through their kind, which contains the principle of their temporal unity as it is the logical subject of general statements that describe the laws according to which substances of this kind change.[11] Hume insists that, if he is right, then there is no such thing as gaining general knowledge from observation. And in this, he is right: given his notion of sensibility, the assertion of a law on the basis of experience can only be the expression of a

11. I develop and defend this reading of the Analogies of Experience in *Kategorien des Zeitlichen*.

habit. By contrast, if we appreciate Kant's critique, we see how knowledge of general laws can, as it must, be based on experience. For we now recognize that experience is always already fraught with (perhaps implicit and inarticulate) general knowledge. Hume saw that it is not possible to acquire general knowledge from confrontation with particulars the apprehension of which does not include the application of general knowledge. Knowledge of particular substances and knowledge of laws according to which they move and change come on the scene together. There is no possessing the one without the other.

These, Kant's, reflections are perfectly general; they hold of any material substance and its movements, in particular of movements of such a substance that are intentional actions and speech acts. We found in Chapter 2 that most if not all verbs that on occasion describe intentional actions are action verbs, i.e., they depend for their sense on explanations by a causality of thought, which is, as we have seen now, a causality of reason. Anscombe makes a corresponding point about speech acts.

> The tree waves in the wind; the movements of its leaves are just as minute as the movement of my hand when I write on a blackboard, but we have no description of a picked-out set of movements or a picked-out appearance of the tree remotely resembling "She wrote 'I am a fool' on the blackboard." (*Intention,* p. 83)

The unity of an act of writing depends on the thought it expresses, which therefore is not attached to an independently apprehended reality. The same holds for oral speech acts. When a tree waves in the wind, subtle sounds can be heard, but we have no description of them remotely resembling "She said 'I am a fool'". If the unity of an act depends on a thought of which, therefore, it is the sensible reality, then it depends on an order by being subsumed under which the act is conceived as an act of thinking. Such an order is an order of reason—a power of receptive knowledge or a practical life-form.

Perceiving nonrational substances and their movements includes subsuming them under a general order. Therefore we can, as we must, acquire knowledge of such an order from receptivity. When the substance is a self-conscious subject and her operations self-conscious acts, then, too, we apprehend the subject and her acts through a general order. But here we may know the order *as the order that governs our own acts.* Then we know it not from receptivity, but from spontaneity, not by observing what people do and believe, but by reflecting on what to do and believe. If we apprehend someone's acts through an order we know from self-consciousness, our knowledge of her acts is not based on observation alone, but depends on spontaneous knowledge, knowledge articulated in unmediated first person thought.

The Impossibility of Receptive Knowledge of an Order of Reason

When the order of reason through which I explain someone else's acts is my own, then I know this order, and thus her acts, from spontaneity. Now, Kant writes:

> Nun kann ich von einem denkenden Wesen durch keine äußere Erfahrung, sondern bloß durch das Selbstbewußtsein die mindeste Vorstellung haben. (*Kritik der reinen Vernunft*, A 347/B 405)[12]

Kant says the representation of a thinking subject cannot arise from experience, but only through self-consciousness. He does not mean that the representation of a thinking subject does not involve experience, but rather that experience alone is not the source of the representation of a thinking subject. When I abstract from everything I know from spontaneity, I shall not find a thinking subject in anything given to me by the senses. So Kant not only says that a self-conscious subject can be known through self-consciousness; he says, a self-conscious subject can be known *only* in this way. This is true if and only if an order of reason, through which alone a self-conscious subject is apprehended, cannot be known otherwise than from spontaneity. If the order of her acts is not the same as the order under which I know myself to be, and yet I know her self-conscious acts, then I must know this order of reason from receptivity, and my representation of her acts must rest on experience alone. Ruling this out, Kant rules out receptive knowledge of an order of reason.

At the end of Chapter 2, and again at the end of Chapter 3, we left open a question we promised to take up in the present chapter: whether the concept of an order of theoretical reason, or the concept of an order of practical reason, signifies a form, which contains the idea of a manifold of instances, or a content, so that we can speak of *the* order of reason,

---

12. Now I cannot have any representation whatsoever of a thinking being through any outer experience, but only through self-consciousness.

practical or theoretical. Philippa Foot and Michael Thompson maintain that there is no such thing as *the* practical life-form. That concept, they think, signifies a kind of order, of which there may be indefinitely many instances. And Kant maintains that there is no such thing as *the* power of receptive knowledge; any such power owes its specific character to the nature of the receptive faculty on which it depends, and the concept of such a faculty is the concept of a kind of which there may be indefinitely many instances. Now, Kant's claim that a self-conscious subject can be represented only through self-consciousness entails that there is no such thing as *knowing* that a subject exists who falls and brings herself under an order of reason different from ours. There is no representing an order different from ours as *actual*.

We shall argue that this is right: there is no knowledge of an order of reason, and of acts falling under it, from receptivity. For, in order to be able to represent an act of thinking, I must be able to represent its object. And I cannot represent the object of a theoretical thought that is an act of a power of receptive knowledge different from mine. Nor can I represent the object of a practical thought that is an act of a practical life-form different from mine.

With regard to theoretical thought, the argument is straightforward. Powers of receptive knowledge differ on account of the nature of the receptive faculty on which they depend. But if my receptive faculty bears a different form from yours, then I do not receptively represent the objects that you receptively represent. For example, if my receptive faculty is such that its objects are spatial and temporal, and yours is such that its objects are not spatial and temporal, but of a different form, then there is no community of receptively represented objects between us. But if I can have no receptive knowledge of the objects of which you do, then I cannot know that you have receptive knowledge of these objects. I cannot represent you as a subject of receptive knowledge.

There is no such thing as knowing that someone thinks theoretical thoughts that manifest a different power of knowledge from my own, because I do not *receptively represent* objects represented in such thoughts. Something analogous holds with regard to practical thought: I do not *productively represent* the objects productively represented in a thought that manifests a different practical life-form from my own. A practical life-form is a unity of infinite ends. And the representation of infinite ends is productive in that it is such as to cause actions that accord with the represented end. Someone's representation of justice, say, is the cause of her acting justly, and this is no accident, for the causality of her representation is mediated by a thought deriving her action from this end. Thus her knowledge that she is acting as justice requires is spontaneous; it includes and is included in its object. Now, if you bear a different practical life-form from mine, then I do not represent the infinite ends that constitute your practical life-form. More precisely, I do not represent them as ends; my representation does not have the causal power just described, by virtue of which it would be of an end. Hence, I do not have spontaneous knowledge of actions that accord with your infinite ends; I do not productively represent anything that manifests your practical life-form.

Clearly, if I do not receptively represent objects represented in acts of a power of receptive knowledge different from mine, then I do not represent them at all. By contrast, it may seem that, if I do not productively represent the objects productively represented in acts of a practical life-form different from mine, I may still represent them receptively. Let us imagine an infinite end X, an element of your practical life-form, which we imagine to be different from mine. We are supposing that, in spite of the fact that I do not represent X as an end, I may know from receptivity that you are acting so as to manifest X. "X" is a term like "justice". We shall give no example of such a term, as we gave no example of a form of receptivity different from ours. Our question is whether we could understand it and apply the concept it designates to movements, given that we deploy it only in acts of receptive knowledge.

Your acting as X requires includes your representation of yourself as conforming to the demands of X. Hence, in order to apprehend you as *acting so as to manifest X*, I must apprehend you as *thinking that you are acting in this way*. More precisely, apprehending the one must *be* apprehending the other. Now, if I am to apprehend you as thinking of yourself as acting in accordance with X, I must think what you think; the same concept that you deploy in thinking of your action must figure in my thinking. I must possess the concept you possess in order to represent instances of that concept, which are instances of its spontaneous application by you. But this is impossible. Since for me the concept is receptive, an explanation how I come to possess it must make reference to instances of the concept that affect my senses. However, we just said that I receptively represent an instance of the concept only if I apprehend you as applying this very concept. Therefore we cannot appeal to the fact that I receptively represent something as an instance of *X* in explaining how it is that I apprehend your thinking of it as such an instance. If I am to acquire a concept from receptivity, i.e., from its instances, and the concept is one you apply spontaneously, that is, instances of it are acts of your applying it, then my possessing the concept is a condition under which alone I can acquire it. That is, there is no acquiring such a concept from receptivity.

I do not productively represent the objects productively represented in a thought that manifests a different practical life-form from mine. Since there is no acquiring the relevant concepts from receptivity alone, I do not represent these objects at all. Thus I cannot know anyone to represent these objects and, hence, to be a bearer of this practical life-form.

Thompson and Foot may agree that there is no receptive knowledge of acts of a practical life-form, as Kant agrees that there is no receptive knowledge of acts of a power of receptive knowledge. While they may agree that, therefore, there is no such thing as *knowing* acts of an order of reason under which I do not bring myself, they may hold we can nevertheless *entertain the idea* of such acts. We need not decide whether this is coherent. (Surely, the idea of a concept essentially unfit for deployment in knowledge is difficult.) For, we are interested in the way in which I *know* someone else as a subject of self-conscious acts, which way of knowing underwrites second person *reference*.

The Nexus of Second Person Knowledge and Its Object

In Chapter 4, we distinguished receptive knowledge from spontaneous knowledge as follows. My receptively knowing an object is a distinct reality from the object I thus know, wherefore the object must be given to me and I must receive it. By contrast, my spontaneously knowing an object is the same reality as the object I know; there is neither need nor room for mediation by a receptive faculty. Now, there is a sense in which second person knowledge is spontaneous: I apprehend acts of a second person through an order of reason under which I fall and that I know from spontaneity. It follows that there must be a sense in which the object of second person knowledge does not exist independently of second person knowledge of it. Of course, my knowing that you are doing or believe something is not your doing or believing it; you may do or believe something without my knowing it. And yet, my knowledge of your self-conscious acts is not as external to its object as my knowledge of the states and movements of a nonrational substance. Second person knowledge and its object are internally related in that they have *the same ultimate cause.*

Consider second person knowledge of theoretical thought. In the fundamental case, I know that someone believes something by explaining why she believes it in a way that reveals her to believe something it is right to believe in the sense defined by a power of knowledge. In thus explaining why someone believes such-and-such, I not only represent her as manifesting a power of knowledge; I manifest the same power. For example, when I explain why you believe something by showing that you conform to the order of valid inference, I exercise my grasp of this very order and thus manifest the same power to draw inferences that I recognize in you. And if I know that you believe that p because you perceived it, then I know that you perceived that p, and thus know that p. As knowledge from the senses is the fundamental form of receptive knowledge, my knowing what I know you to know through your power to gain knowledge from the senses is, in the fundamental case, an act of the same power. So the same power of receptive knowledge accounts for my explanation why, and thus for my knowledge that, you believe what you do, and accounts for your believing it. The power whose presence in you accounts for your belief is the same as the power whose presence in me accounts for my knowledge of your belief. Second person knowledge of belief is not identical with its object, but it has the same ultimate cause: a shared power of receptive knowledge.

This inner nexus of second person knowledge and its object did not go unnoticed, but the awareness of it has been distorted by the lack of the concept of a causality of reason. It has been claimed to be an artifact of the necessary method of interpretation that, for the most part, I find myself agreeing with her whom I interpret. If I am to understand someone else at all, I largely have to read my opinions into her, especially very dear opinions like the truths of my logic. Now, it is true that I will for the most part agree with someone whom I understand. But this agreement is not the fundamental phenomenon; it has a cause, and this cause, not the agreement, is the source of understanding. Our agreement manifests the presence of the same order of reason in both of us; we agree because our thoughts have this common cause. Were it not for this common cause, our agreement would be either an accident or the product of my projecting my opinions onto you. In neither case would agreement be connected to understanding.

Second person knowledge of action, too, has the same ultimate cause as its object. In the fundamental case, I know that someone is doing something intentionally by explaining why she is doing it in a way that reveals it to be good to do in the sense defined by our practical life-form. (We can now say "our", as we have excluded that I bring someone under a practical life-form that is not mine.) A practical life-form is articulated into infinite ends, which in turn are the principle of unity of finite ends. Suppose I explain your action by an infinite end and think, "She is doing A because she is (wants to be) X". As an action manifests an infinite end only if it manifests the practical life-form of which it is an element, it follows that, if my explanation is true, then I know that your doing A manifests this practical life-form. This means that my explanation, if it is true, manifests my knowledge of this form. But my knowledge of this practical life-form is spontaneous and a manifestation of this very life-form. So in explaining your action by an infinite end, I manifest the practical life-form that you, according to the explanation, manifest in the action I explain. The same holds of explanations by a finite end, "She is doing A because she wants to do B". I trace your action to the order of what is a means to what, which is, according to the results of Chapter 2, an aspect of our practical life-form. In explaining your action by reference to this order, I manifest knowledge of it, and since the order is formally represented and known from spontaneity, my knowledge of the order manifests its actuality in me. Again, the same order manifests itself in your action and my knowledge of your action. A shared practical life-form is the ultimate cause of second person knowledge and its object.

Second Person Reference

Demonstrative thought depends on an act of receptivity; it has an object in virtue of a receptive representation of this object, a representation that is of this object by being effected by it. Demonstrative reference is *perceptual*. First person thought, by contrast, does not depend on an act of receptivity; it is a spontaneous representation and is of an object in virtue of being identical with it. First person reference is *intellectual*. Since there is a sense in which second person knowledge is spontaneous and, in consequence, not of an independent object, it follows that there is a sense in which second person reference is not perceptual, but intellectual, not mediated by a sensory nexus, but by a nexus of thought. We shall now explicate this sense.

Thought for Two

We have been calling a thought of a subject like oneself a *second person* thought, anticipating a claim we shall now defend, that, fundamentally, a thought about another self-conscious subject is a thought whose linguistic expression requires the use of a second person pronoun. In what follows, we shall mean by "second person thought" a thought expressed by a second person pronoun, in contradistinction to a third person pronoun. One might suppose that a second person thought is a third person thought satisfying certain conditions that pertain to the context of its expression, but do not affect the thought expressed. Richard Heck thinks this is a matter of course:

> Consider the indexical "you". As a matter of its standing meaning, an utterance of "you" refers to the person addressed in that utterance. But in the sense that there is such a thing as a self-conscious, first-person belief, there is no such thing as a second-person belief, or so it seems to me. Of course, I can identify someone descriptively, as the person to whom I am now speaking, and may have beliefs whose content involves that descriptive identification. But that is not what I mean to deny: I mean to deny that there is any such thing as an essentially indexical second-person belief. The phenomenon of the second-person is a linguistic one, bound up with the fact that utterances, as we make them, are typically directed to people, not just made to the cosmos. [. . .] The word "you" has no correlate at the level of thought [. . .] I don't really know how to argue for this claim: it just seems right to me, even obviously so.—"You", on this view, acts as if it were a special kind of demonstrative, one that always refers to the addressee. So if you want an analysis of "you", try "That person to whom I am speaking". ("Do Demonstratives Have Senses?", pp. 12 and 15n)

Thinking, as such, Heck believes, is to the cosmos. It is accidental to thought that we find occasion to address our thoughts to other people. This seems right to Heck, even obviously so. But obvious it is not. John McDowell writes:

> Suppose someone says to me, "You have mud on your face". If I am to understand him, I must think an "I"-thought, thinking something to this effect: "I have mud on my face: that is what he is saying."

> Frege's strategy for keeping the special and primitive way in which I am presented to myself out of communication suggests nothing better than the following: the "I"-sense involved here is the sense of "he who is being addressed". But this would not do. I can entertain the thought that he who is being addressed has mud on his face, as what is being said, and not understand the remark; I may not know that *I* am he who is being addressed. ("*De Re* Senses", p. 222)

In the first chapter, we encountered an attempt to explain first person reference as reference to her who is uttering "I". Although this specifies the referent of a given use of the first person pronoun, it does not specify its sense, for I might fail to recognize that I am uttering "I"; "I am uttering 'I'" is not a tautology. Analogously, second person reference cannot be explained as reference to her who is being addressed; this specifies the referent, but not the sense of a given use of the second person pronoun. "I am addressing you" is not a tautology, but something that she who is being addressed may fail to realize, and which she realizes if and only if she thinks, "He is addressing *me*". This proves that "you" cannot be explained as "that person to whom I am speaking".

In order to understand your saying "This *S* is *F*", I must perceive, with you, the object to which you refer; I must share in your perceptual relationship with the object. Now, since an object perceived is not as such the subject perceiving it, so that an object perceived is apprehended as other, understanding a demonstrative never includes recognition that I am its object. I can understand your assertion about myself, "This man is *F*", while failing to recognize that I am this man. If I acquire knowledge by testimony from these words, it is knowledge that this man is *F*. I come to know that I am *F*, if indeed I do, by way of an identity judgment not contained in the assertion. By contrast, I understand your assertion "You are *F*" addressed at me only if I recognize that I am its referent. I acquire first person knowledge from these words without mediation by an identity judgment. This proves that second person reference is not a kind of demonstrative reference. It is not perceptual. Second person reference does not reach its object through a receptive representation of this object. If it did, I would grasp a second person thought about myself by sharing in this relationship, which I do not. Second person reference must be intellectual.

This does not mean that perception of the subject referred to plays no role in second person thought. It means that its role is subordinate to an intellectual relationship and can only be understood through it.[13] For example, I may recognize that you are addressing me by noticing that you are looking at me. But noticing that you are looking at me is not noticing, on the one hand, that you perceive a certain man and, on the other hand, that I am this man. Rather, it is noticing without mediation, "She is looking at *me*". This mode of perception presupposes and cannot explain second person reference. And so it is with any sensory nexus that may be deemed essential to second person reference. Such a sensory nexus will be of a peculiar kind, an account of which will depend on an account of second person thought.

When you say "This *S* is *F*", I understand you by perceiving, as you do, the object to which you refer. When I am this object, then this is so per accidens. Since I understand a second person thought addressed to me by framing a first person thought, your nexus to me by which you refer to me second personally is not perceptual. The relevant nexus must differ from perception in that my recognition that you bear this nexus to an object must be, when I am this object, an *immediate* recognition that you bear this nexus to *me*. This means that my knowledge of this nexus, when I am its term, is spontaneous, and that is, that your nexus to me by which you think second personally about me is such as to provide me with knowledge of this very nexus. But then the nexus is a self-conscious act on my part. It is my thinking a certain thought.

What thought joins me to you in such a way as to enable you to think second personally about me? If my thinking this thought is to join me and you, it must be a thought about you. But how does it represent you? Thinking this thought, I know without mediation that you are addressing me. Hence, it is not enough that I be thinking of you as the man who perceives me, for this thought would depend on an identity judgment that I am the one whom you perceive (as it is not in virtue of being perceived by you that I know that I am perceived by you). It equally will not do to say that I am thinking of you as the man who is addressing me, although this will be true. For, an account of what it is to address someone presupposes a specification of the thought we are seeking. Now, my thought about you must represent you as thinking about me; that is, it must, by virtue of its form, represent you as a self-conscious subject like myself. This fixes its form: it is a thought of the very kind we are in the process of elucidating, a second person thought. It is by thinking second personally about you

---

13. Here I was greatly helped by a conversation with Michael Thompson.

that I am positioned to take up your second person thought addressed to me in an unmediated first person thought.

So our result is this: your nexus to me by which I am the object of your second person thought consists in my thinking a second person thought about you. Your second person thought reaches me through my thinking back at you in the same way, second personally.

But what if a second person thought is not taken up? I may fail to recognize that you are addressing me. And this does not seem to mean that there is no one you have addressed, or that you do not know whom you have addressed. So I do not need to think back in order for your thought to have me for its object. But how is it that you know whom you address? You do not know this by perceiving me. If that were the case, I would understand your thought by sharing in this perception, which I do not. If you know that you are addressing me, then this is because you are anticipating my thought returning to you. It is by apprehending my power to think about you as you think about me that you think about me second personally. This apprehension is not of a property you attach to an object to which you refer independently. It is internal to the way in which you refer to me. But then there is a sense in which your thought comes to fruition only as my power to return it is actualized. Without my response, your second person reference to me is ungrounded in the way in which your attempted demonstrative reference is ungrounded when there is no object where you take yourself to perceive one. As the perceived object completes your demonstrative reference and makes it possible as the reference to that object that it is, so my second person reference to you completes your second person reference to me and makes it possible as the reference to me that it is.

We said the nexus to me by which your second person thought refers to me consists in my thinking a second person thought about you. Since the relation is symmetric and my second person thought reaches you through yours, we can say that second person thought is thought for two. It takes two to think one. Compare Aristotle's claim that one and the same act is the act of a passive capacity of one thing and the act of an active capacity of another thing; for example, the statements "the fire is heating the water" and "the water is being heated by the fire" describe one act. Analogously, one and the same act is an act of your active power to think second personally about me and an act of my active power to think second personally about you. The same act manifests the power in both of us to refer to the other. Indeed, we are defining second person reference as the form of reference of which this holds true.

Since there is a sense in which knowledge of someone else's self-conscious acts is spontaneous, reference to another subject must be intellectual. Now, second person reference, reference whose linguistic expression is the second person pronoun, is intellectual, which suggests that it is the fundamental form of reference to a self-conscious subject.[14] Demonstrative thought is sustained, in general, by a faculty of receptivity and, in particular, by an act of this faculty. First person thought is sustained, in general, by a power of spontaneity and, in particular, by an act of such a power. In the preceding section, we found that thought about another subject is sustained, in general, by a shared order of reason. Hence, what sustains it in particular will be an act that manifests an order of reason, and manifests it as shared. Since the presence of an order of reason in a subject is a power of spontaneity, and since an act of spontaneity is a thought, reference to a self-conscious subject is an act that manifests the same spontaneous power in the thinker and in her of whom she thinks. It is an act of thinking by two. This is second person reference as we described it, which thus emerges as the fundamental manner of referring to another subject.

We could have concluded already from the last section of Chapter 4 that reference to a self-conscious subject is not demonstrative. Reference to a material substance includes application to it of a material substance concept, which specifies the principle of its unity. In the case of nonrational substances, this concept is empirical. It is received from its instances, and its fundamental application is in thoughts that depend on receptivity, demonstrative thoughts "This N . . .". By contrast, the concept that specifies the unity of a self-conscious subject is a reflective concept. As it is not received from its instances, its first application is in acts of sponta-

14. Jürgen Habermas seems to argue that second person thought is fundamental because it enables cooperation, which he maintains is the function of language: "Erst der Imperativ der gesellschaftlichen Integration — die Nötigung zur Koordination der Handlungspläne unabhängig entscheidender Interaktionsteilnehmer — erklärt die Pointe sprachlicher Verständigung." ("Von Kant zu Hegel. Zu Robert Brandoms Sprachpragmatik", pp. 175–176.) This argument confronts a dilemma. Either acting together is thinking (practical) second person thoughts or it is not. If it is not, as Brandom maintains ("Facts, Norms, and Normative Facts", pp. 362–363), then nothing about the second person follows from a proof that cooperation is the function of language. If it is, then a proof that language is essentially a power of joint action will have to take the form of a proof that it is essentially a power of second person thought. It will provide no independent basis for that claim.

neous knowledge, "I, an *N*, . . .". Now, the same concept must be capable of *spontaneous* application to someone else if it is to be applied to someone else at all. Hence, there must be a manner of thinking about someone else through this concept that is not demonstrative and does not rest on an act of receptivity. And indeed there is. A material substance concept applied in first person thought is applied spontaneously to another subject in a second person thought, "You, fellow *N*, . . .".

Thought of the Self-Conscious

Second person thought requires and includes first person thought, for I apprehend a self-conscious subject through an order under which I subsume my own acts and that I represent first personally. We will now see that it is equally true that first person thought requires and includes second person thought. The same power is exercised in both ways of thinking.

Second person thought is thought for two. If it is essential to self-consciousness, then self-consciousness is a manner of being for two: it essentially manifests itself in mutual recognition of self-conscious subjects as self-conscious. The slogan that self-consciousness is recognition has no content on its own; its meaning derives from the argument it encodes. One argument propounds recognition as a way to manage the "Kantian paradox".[15] We discussed this paradox in Chapter 4. It bears on the conditions of self-consciousness as follows. It is a condition of my self-consciousness that I conceive of my acts as being subject to an order of reason. Since autonomy requires that I be the source of the authority of any order to which I am subject, I must have instituted this order. However, instituting the order must be a self-conscious act. But then this act depends on that of which it is to be the origin: an order of reason. A self-conscious subject must be, and yet cannot be, the source her own self-consciousness; she must be, and yet cannot be, the source of the order being under which she is self-conscious. The solution of this paradox in terms of recognition, put blandly, maintains that, what one cannot do alone, two can do together, if each does for the other what none can do for herself. If I give you your law and you give me mine, then every law is

---

15. Compare Robert Brandom, "Some Pragmatist Themes in Hegel's Idealism", pp. 216–222.

instituted in a self-conscious act, and every self-conscious act is under a law.

If there is a paradox, then this does not solve it. If "p because p" does not give grounds for thinking that p, then neither does "p because q; q because p". A larger circle may be more difficult to discern, but it is no less a circle. In the same manner, if it is incoherent to represent a self-conscious act of A as the source of A's self-consciousness, then it is equally incoherent to represent a self-conscious act of A as the source of B's self-consciousness, whose self-conscious act is to be the source of A's self-consciousness. In Chapter 4, we distinguished two ways in which acknowledgment and authority may be thought to be linked in laws of autonomy: acknowledgment may be the source of a law's authority or the manner in which its authority manifests itself. The first idea is paradoxical and therefore does not explicate any notion of autonomy; the second idea follows from our account of first person knowledge. We can draw a parallel distinction of ways in which mutual recognition and a shared order or reason may be linked: mutual recognition may be the source of, or it may manifest a shared order. Again, the first notion is empty, while the second follows from our account of second person thought.

It is clear that an order of reason may manifest itself in mutual recognition of subjects who fall under it. But now we are asking whether it must, that is, if being self-conscious is a manner of being for two. We shall now give an argument for this claim, which rests on the results of the present chapter. In general, a thought about a particular substance and its movements subsumes its referent under a concept that designates a general order that is the principle of unity of the substance. The thought represents its referent as an element of a manifold, the manifold of instances of the order that constitutes the unity of its object. The idea of this manifold is contained in any thought about any of its elements, and a power to think about a particular material substance is a power to think about an indefinite number of substances that exhibit the same principle of unity and fall under the same order. For example, someone thinks a thought about a particular tree only if she has it in her to think about other trees, which she distinguishes from that one. Of course, it may be that only one tree is left upon the earth or that she will ever encounter only one. Then she lacks occasion to exercise her power to think about other trees than this one. Still, her thinking about this tree is an act of a power other acts of which, were there occasion for them, would be thoughts about, not this, but other trees. Now, this equally holds of first person thought. A first person thought represents an act as manifesting an order of reason. An order of reason is general; it induces a manifold, the manifold of those whose acts can be explained by being subsumed under it. An unmediated first person thought contains an idea of this manifold and places its referent among its members. In first person thought, I represent myself as one of a kind, which means that, thinking first person thoughts, I deploy the general idea of a subject of that kind, and thereby have the idea of other subjects of the order that governs my actions and beliefs. Of course, I may be the last man, or stranded on a lonely island, in which case I will have no occasion to exercise my power to think about other subjects. But even then my first person thinking would be an act of a power other acts of which, if there were any, will be thoughts about other self conscious subjects. Now, we argued above that the fundamental mode of referring to another subject is second personally. Hence, as the power of first person thought is a power to think about other subjects, it is a power of second person thought. A self-conscious subject is a subject of second person thought, which manifests the same self-conscious order operating in both thinkers, who thus recognize each other as united under this order.

In the first chapter, we explained self-consciousness as a power of knowing a subject in a way that sustains unmediated first person thoughts. In this last chapter, we find that the same power is a source of second person knowledge. So mutual knowledge of self-conscious subjects is not an addition to their self-consciousness. A formally represented order that sustains first person thought and its way of knowing as such sustains second person thought and its way of knowing. An order that is a source of self-consciousness as such is a source of mutual knowledge of its instances. Subjects united under an order of reason know each other through this order.

The Act of Thinking Expressed by "You . . ." and "I . . ."

Gottlob Frege held that I alone could think about me in the manner in which I do so when I think about myself in a way whose expression requires a first person pronoun.[16] He did not simply mean that only I could refer to me by means of a first person pronoun. Rather, he meant that

---

16. "Der Gedanke", p. 39.

there could be no linguistic expression by which someone else would express the thought I express by a first person pronoun, because no one but me can think that thought. Frege's thesis is often treated as routine. Compare, for example, Richard Heck:

> If I utter the sentence "I am a philosopher", then I thereby give voice to my self-conscious knowledge that I am a philosopher. [...] If someone else were to think that very same Thought, she would thereby think that I, Richard Heck, am a philosopher. But then that Thought could not be the content of my self-conscious knowledge that I am a philosopher; it could only be the content of a piece of third person knowledge that someone else (or, indeed, I) might have about me. [...] The self-conscious Thought that I am a philosopher is one that only I can entertain. ("Do Demonstratives Have Senses?", pp. 9–10)

Heck says that only he can think the thought he expresses by "I . . .", for, otherwise, this thought would not be self-conscious knowledge, but knowledge someone else might have about him, Richard Heck. This is no argument. It assumes that only first person sentences express self-conscious knowledge, which is the thesis in question. John McDowell writes on Frege's thesis:

> Frege's trouble about "I" cannot be blamed simply on the idea of special and primitive senses; they result, rather, from the assumption [...] that communication must involve sharing of thoughts between communicator and audience. That assumption is quite natural, and Frege seems to take it for granted. But there is no obvious reason why he could not have held, instead, that in linguistic interchange of the appropriate kind, mutual understanding—which is what successful communication achieves—requires not shared thoughts but different thoughts that, however, stand and are mutually known to stand in a suitable relation of correspondence. ("*De Re* Senses", p. 222)

In the text preceding this passage, which we quoted earlier, McDowell explains that I understand your "You . . ." by thinking something I would express by "I . . .". He now implies that I do not thereby think what you think. She who can think a thought expressed by "You . . ." is not its referent, and she who is not its referent cannot think a thought expressed by "I . . .". McDowell does not pause to contemplate why this should be so. He treats it as something anyone who reflects on the matter immediately recognizes.

However, his own text raises doubts. McDowell says there is no obvious reason not to hold that understanding requires not shared thoughts but different thoughts mutually known to stand in a suitable relation. But there is such a reason: the capacity to know that thoughts stand in a certain relation depends on the capacity to share them. Understanding you, who are addressing me with "You . . .", McDowell proposes, I know that your thought stands in a certain relation to a thought I think, and which I would express by "I . . .". But how do I represent your thought in knowing this? If I do not think your thought, how then does it figure in my thinking? Figuring there it must, if I am to know that you are thinking it. I can represent your thought as the thought you express by "You . . ."; but if that is the only way in which it figures in my thinking, then I do not understand you. Perhaps I represent it as a thought of the kind I express by "You . . .", differing from that one in being about me?[17] But if I do not understand your "You . . .", I have no notion of a thought that is expressed by "You . . ." and yet is about me. Since I acquire this notion by reflecting on acts of understanding you, we cannot appeal to my possessing it in an account of such acts. Or perhaps I represent your thought as the thought that bears a suitable relation of correspondence to the thought I express by "I . . ."? Now I am to reach your thought through a relation it bears, not to a thought I express by "You . . .", but to a thought I express by "I . . .". But this changes nothing: I possess the notion of a thought that bears the relevant relation to my thought only if I understand you; my understanding you is the source of my possessing that notion, not the other way around.

Neither Heck, nor McDowell says why only its referent can think a thought expressed by "I . . .". Indeed, the thesis is false. What we said in this section disproves it. In Chapter 3 we found that, in suitable cases, "Today . . ." said yesterday and "Yesterday . . ." said today express the same act of thinking. These cases are fundamental in that, without them, there would be no such thing as an act of thinking expressed by either phrase. And when ". . . today . . ." yesterday and ". . . yesterday . . ."

---

17. This is a version of the argument from analogy.

today express the same *act of thinking*, then they express the same *thought*. Therefore, it would be misleading to contrast "yesterday"-thoughts with "today"-thoughts; in the fundamental case, a "yesterday"-thought is a "today"-thought. What holds of "today" and "yesterday" holds of "I" and "you". We said that my thinking second personally about you and your receiving my second person thought, thinking back at me second personally, is one act of thinking, an act of thinking for two. But you receive my thought thinking an unmediated first person thought. Hence, my "You" addressed at you and your "I" that receives my address express the same act of thinking. This case is fundamental in that, without it, there would be no such thing as thoughts expressed by "You . . ." and, consequently, by "I . . .". As "You . . ." said by me to you and "I . . ." said by you in taking up my address, express the same *act of thinking*, they express the same *thought*. Therefore, it is wrong to oppose second person thought to first person thought. This is a difference in the means of expression, not in the thought expressed. Second person thought is first person thought. It is thought of the self-conscious.

Works Cited

Alston, William. "Level Confusions in Epistemology". *Midwest Studies in Philosophy* 5 (1980), pp. 135–150.

———. *The Reliability of Sense Perception*. Ithaca, N.Y.: Cornell University Press, 1993.

Anscombe, G. E. M. "Thought and Action in Aristotle". In *Collected Papers*, Vol. 1: *From Parmenides to Wittgenstein*. Minneapolis: University of Minnesota Press, 1981, pp. 66–77.

———. "The First Person". In *Collected Papers*, Vol. 2: *Metaphysics and the Philosophy of Mind*. Minneapolis: University of Minnesota Press, 1981, pp. 21–36.

———. "Authority in Morals". In *Collected Papers*, Vol. 3: *Ethics, Religion and Politics*. Oxford: Basil Blackwell, 1981, pp. 43–50.

———. "Practical Inference". In R. Hursthouse et al. (eds.), *Virtues and Reasons*. Oxford: Oxford University Press, 1995, pp. 1–34.

———. *Intention*. Cambridge, Mass.: Harvard University Press, 2000.

Aristotle. *Metaphysics*. W. D. Ross (ed.). Oxford: Clarendon Press, 1924.

———. *Nicomachean Ethics*. W. D. Ross (ed.). Oxford: Clarendon Press, 1925.

———. *On the Movement of Animals*. Martha Nussbaum (ed.). Princeton, N.J.: Princeton University Press, 1978.

Austin, J. L. "Other Minds". In *Philosophical Papers*. J. O. Urmson et al. (eds.). Oxford: Clarendon Press, 1978, pp. 76–116.

Ayer, Alfred J. *The Foundations of Empirical Knowledge*. London: Macmillan, 1964.

Baier, Annette. "Act and Intent". *The Journal of Philosophy* 67 (1970), pp. 648–658.

Bar-On, Dorit. *Speaking My Mind: Expression and Self-Knowledge*. Oxford: Clarendon Press, 2004.

Bieri, Peter. *Analytische Philosophie der Erkenntnis*. Frankfurt/Main: Athenäum, 1987.

———. "Evolution, Erkenntnis und Kognition". In W. Lütterfels (ed.), *Transzendentale oder evolutionäre Erkenntnistheorie?* Darmstadt: Wissenschaftliche Buchgesellschaft, 1987, pp. 117–147.

————. *Das Handwerk der Freiheit*. München: Hanser, 2001.

Boyle, Matthew (with Doug Lavin). "Goodness and Desire". Unpublished manuscript.

Brandom, Robert. *Making It Explicit*. Cambridge, Mass.: Harvard University Press, 1994.

————. "Facts, Norms, and Normative Facts". *European Journal of Philosophy* 8 (2000), pp. 356–374.

————. "Some Pragmatist Themes in Hegel's Idealism". In *Tales of the Mighty Dead*. Cambridge, Mass.: Harvard University Press, 2002, pp. 210–234.

Bratman, Michael. *Intention, Plans, and Practical Reason*, Cambridge, Mass.: Harvard University Press, 1987.

Burge, Tyler. "Reason and the First Person". In C. Wright et al. (eds.), *Knowing Our Own Minds*. Oxford: Oxford University Press, 1998, pp. 243–270.

Castañeda, Hector-Neri. "'He': A Study in the Logic of Self-Consciousness". *Ratio* 8 (1966), pp. 130–157.

Davidson, Donald, "Actions, Reasons, Causes". In *Essays on Actions and Events*. Oxford: Clarendon Press, 1980, pp. 3–19.

————. "Freedom to Act". In *Essays on Actions and Events*, pp. 63–82.

————. "Intending". In *Essays on Actions and Events*, pp. 83–102.

————. "Mental Events". In *Essays on Actions and Events*, pp. 207–225.

————. "Psychology as Philosophy". In *Essays on Actions and Events*, pp. 229–239.

————. "A Coherence Theory of Truth and Knowledge". In D. Henrich (ed.), *Kant oder Hegel*. Stuttgart: Klett, 1983, pp. 423–438.

————. "Thought and Talk". In *Inquiries into Truth and Interpretation*. Oxford: Clarendon Press, 1984, pp. 155–170.

————. "Replies to Essays". In B. Vermazen and M. B. Hintikka (eds.), *Essays on Davidson: Actions and Events*. Oxford: Clarendon Press, 1985, pp. 195–229 and 242–252.

————. "Laws and Cause". *Dialectica* 49 (1995), pp. 263–279.

————. "First Person Authority". In *Subjective, Intersubjective, Objective*. Oxford: Clarendon Press, 2001, pp. 3–14.

Dennett, Daniel. "Three Kinds of Intentional Psychology". In *The Intentional Stance*. Cambridge, Mass.: MIT Press, 1987, pp. 43–68.

Descartes, René. *Meditationes de prima philosophia*. In *Philosophische Schriften*. R. Specht (ed.). Hamburg: Meiner, 1996.

Engström, Stephen. "Understanding and Sensibility". *Inquiry* 49 (2006).

Evans, Gareth. *The Varieties of Reference*. Oxford: Oxford University Press, 1982.

————. "Identity and Predication". In *Collected Papers*. Oxford: Oxford University Press, 1983, pp. 25–48.

Finkelstein, David. *Expression and the Inner*. Cambridge, Mass.: Harvard University Press, 2003.

Fogelin, Robert J. *Pyrrhonian Reflections on Knowledge and Justification*. Oxford: Oxford University Press, 1994.

Foot, Philippa. *Natural Goodness*. Oxford: Clarendon Press, 2001.

Frege, Gottlob. "Über Sinn und Bedeutung". *Zeitschrift für Philosophie und philosophische Kritik NF* 100 (1892), pp. 25–50.

———. "Logik in der Mathematik". In H. Hermes and F. Kambartel (eds.), *Nachgelassene Schriften*. Hamburg: Meiner, 1969–76.

———. "Meine grundlegenden logischen Einsichten." In *Nachgelassene Schriften*.

———. "Der Gedanke". In *Logische Untersuchungen*. G. Patzig (ed.). Göttingen: Vandenhoeck, 1993, pp. 30–53.

———. "Gedankengefüge". In *Logische Untersuchungen*, pp. 72–91.

Gettier, Edmund. "Is Justified True Belief Knowledge?" *Analysis* 23 (1963), pp. 121–123.

Habermas, Jürgen. "Zur Kritik der Bedeutungstheorie". In *Nachmetaphysisches Denken. Philosophische Aufsätze*. Frankfurt/Main: Suhrkamp, 1992, pp. 105–135.

———. "Von Kant zu Hegel. Zu Robert Brandoms Sprachpragmatik". In *Wahrheit und Rechtfertigung. Philosophische Aufsätze*. Frankfurt/Main: Suhrkamp, 2004, pp. 138–185 (In English: *European Journal of Philosophy* 8 (2000), pp. 322–355).

Harcourt, Edward. "The First Person: Problems of Sense and Reference". In R. Teichmann (ed.), *Logic, Cause and Action: Essays in Honour of Elizabeth Anscombe*. Cambridge: Cambridge University Press, 2000, pp. 25–46.

Heck, Richard. "Do Demonstratives Have Senses?" *Philosopher's Imprint* 2 (2002), pp. 1–33.

Hegel, Georg Wilhelm Friedrich. *Wissenschaft der Logik*. Hamburg: Meiner, 1994.

Heidegger, Martin. "Der Ursprung des Kunstwerks". In *Holzwege*. Frankfurt/Main: Klostermann, 1950, pp. 1–72.

Henrich, Dieter. "Selbstbewußtsein und spekulatives Denken". In *Fluchtlinien*. Frankfurt/Main: Suhrkamp, 1982, pp. 125–181.

Hume, David. *A Treatise of Human Nature*. London: J. M. Dent & Sons, 1911.

Kant, Immanuel. *Grundlegung zur Metaphysik der Sitten*. Kants gesammelte Schriften, Vol. 4. Berlin: deGruyter, 1911.

———. *Kritik der reinen Vernunft*. Kants gesammelte Schriften, Vols. 3 and 4. Berlin: deGruyter, 1911.

———. *Kritik der praktischen Vernunft*. Kants gesammelte Schriften. Vol. 5. Berlin: deGruyter, 1913.

———. *Kritik der Urteilskraft*. Kants gesammelte Schriften, Vol. 5. Berlin: deGruyter, 1913.

———. *Logik*. Kants gesammelte Schriften, Vol. 9. Berlin: deGruyter, 1923.

Kern, Andrea. *Quellen des Wissens. Zum Begriff vernünftiger Erkenntnisfähigkeiten*. Frankfurt/Main: Suhrkamp, 2006.

———. "Does Knowledge Rest upon a Form of Life?" Unpublished manuscript.

Korsgaard, Christine. "The Normativity of Instrumental Reason". In G. Cullity et al. (eds.), *Ethical and Practical Reason*. Oxford: Oxford University Press, 1997, pp. 215–254.

Lavin, Doug (with Matthew Boyle). "Goodness and Desire". Unpublished manuscript.

Lewis, David. "Elusive Knowledge". *Australasian Journal of Philosophy* 74 (1996), pp. 549–567.

Marx, Karl. *Theses on Feuerbach*. In D. McLellan (ed.), *Karl Marx: Selected Writings*. Oxford: Oxford University Press, 2000, pp. 171–174.

McDowell, John. *Mind and World*. Cambridge, Mass.: Harvard University Press, 1994.

———. "On the Sense and Reference of a Proper Name". In *Meaning, Knowledge, and Reality*. Cambridge, Mass.: Harvard University Press, 1998, pp. 87–107.

———. "*De Re* Senses". In *Meaning, Knowledge, and Reality*, pp. 214–227.

———. "Anti-Realism and the Epistemology of Understanding". In *Meaning, Knowledge, and Reality*, pp. 314–343.

———. "Criteria, Defeasibility, and Knowledge". In *Meaning, Knowledge, and Reality*, pp. 369–394.

———. "Knowledge and the Internal". In *Meaning, Knowledge, and Reality*, pp. 395–413.

———. "The Role of *Eudaimonia* in Aristotle's Ethics". In *Mind, Value, and Reality*. Cambridge, Mass.: Harvard University Press, 1998, pp. 3–22.

———. "Virtue and Reason". In *Mind, Value, and Reality*, pp. 50–73.

———. "Functionalism and Anomalous Monism". In *Mind, Value, and Reality*, pp. 325–340.

———. "Reductionism and the First Person". In *Mind, Value, and Reality*, pp. 359–382.

———. "Hegel's Idealism as Radicalization of Kant". *International Yearbook of German Idealism* 5 (forthcoming).

Moline, Jon. "Provided Nothing External Interferes". *Mind* 84 (1975), pp. 244–254.

Moran, Richard. *Authority and Estrangement: An Essay on Self-Knowledge*. Princeton, N.J.: Princeton University Press, 2001.

Müller, Anselm Winfried. "How Theoretical Is Practical Reasoning?" In Cora Diamond et al. (eds.), *Intention and Intentionality: Essays in Honour of G. E. M. Anscombe*. Brighton: Harvester Press, 1979, pp. 91–100.

Nagel, Thomas. *The Possibility of Altruism*. Princeton, N.J.: Princeton University Press, 1978.

Owens, David. *Reason without Freedom*. London: Routledge, 2000.

Peacocke, Christopher. *A Study of Concepts*. Cambridge, Mass.: MIT Press, 1992.

Perry, John. "Frege on Demonstratives". *The Philosophical Review* 86 (1977), pp. 474–497.

———. "The Problem of the Essential Indexical". In Q. Cassam (ed.), *Self-Knowledge*. Oxford: Oxford University Press, 1994, pp. 167–183.

Pinkard, Terry. *German Philosophy, 1760–1860*. Cambridge: Cambridge University Press, 2002.

Pippin, Robert. "Hegel's Practical Philosophy". In K. Ameriks (ed.), *The Cambridge Companion to German Idealism*. Cambridge: Cambridge University Press, 2000, pp. 180–199.

Quine, W. V. O. *The Pursuit of Truth*. Cambridge, Mass.: Harvard University Press, 1992.

Reichenbach, Hans. *Elements of Symbolic Logic*. New York: Free Press, 1966.

Rödl, Sebastian. "Practice and the Unity of Action". In G. Meggle (ed.), *Social Facts and Collective Intentionality*. Frankfurt/Main: Hänsel-Hohenhausen, 2002, pp. 323–342.

———. *Kategorien des Zeitlichen*. Frankfurt/Main: Suhrkamp, 2005.

Rorty, Richard. *Truth and Progress*. Cambridge: Cambridge University Press, 1998.

———. "Universality and Truth". In R. Brandom (ed.), *Rorty and His Critics*. Oxford: Blackwell, 2000, pp. 1–30.

Ryle, Gilbert. *The Concept of Mind*. London: Hutchinson, 1949.

Searle, John. *The Rediscovery of the Mind*. Cambridge, Mass.: MIT Press, 1992.

Sellars, Wilfrid. *Empiricism and the Philosophy of Mind*. R. Brandom (ed.). Cambridge, Mass.: Harvard University Press, 2000.

Setiya, Kieran. *Reasons without Rationalism*. Forthcoming.

Strawson, Peter F. *Individuals*. London: Methuen, 1964.

———. *The Bounds of Sense: An Essay on Kant's Critique of Pure Reason*. London: Methuen, 1966.

———. "Singular Terms and Predication". In *Logico-Linguistic Papers*. London: Ashgate, 1971, pp. 41–56.

Thomas Aquinas. *Summa Theologica*.

Thompson, Michael. "The Representation of Life". In R. Hursthouse et al. (eds.), *Virtues and Reasons*. Oxford: Oxford University Press, 1995, pp. 247–296.

———. "What Is It to Wrong Someone? A Puzzle about Justice". In J. Wallace et al. (eds.), *Reason and Value: Essays on the Moral Philosophy of Joseph Raz*. Oxford: Oxford University Press, 2004, pp. 333–384.

———. "Naïve Action Theory". In *Life and Action*. Forthcoming.

———. "Apprehending Human Form". Unpublished manuscript.

Tugendhat, Ernst. "Überlegungen zur Methode der Philosophie aus analytischer Sicht". In *Philosophische Aufsätze*. Frankfurt/Main: Suhrkamp, 1992, pp. 261–272.

Velleman, David. *The Possibility of Practical Reason*. Oxford: Oxford University Press, 2000.

———. "The Guise of the Good". In *The Possibility of Practical Reason*, pp. 99–122.

Vogler, Candace. *Reasonably Vicious*. Cambridge, Mass.: Harvard University Press, 2002.

Wellmer, Albrecht. "Was ist eine pragmatische Bedeutungstheorie?" In *Zwischenbetrachtungen: Im Prozeß der Aufklärung*. A. Honneth et al. (eds.). Frankfurt/Main: Suhrkamp, 1989, pp. 318–370.

————. "Wahrheit, Kontingenz, Moderne". In *Endspiele. Die unversöhnliche Moderne*. Frankfurt/Main: Suhrkamp, 1993, pp. 157–177.

Williams, Michael. *Unnatural Doubts*. Princeton, N.J.: Princeton University Press, 1996.

————. *Problems of Knowledge*. Oxford: Oxford University Press, 2001.

Wittgenstein, Ludwig. *The Blue and the Brown Books*. New York: Harper and Row, 1958.

————. *Philosophische Untersuchungen*. Frankfurt/Main: Suhrkamp, 1984.

————. *Über Gewißheit*. Frankfurt/Main: Suhrkamp, 1984.

————. *Zettel*. Frankfurt/Main: Suhrkamp, 1984.

Index